ARDEN EARLY MODERN DRAMA

General Editors: Suzanne Gossett,
John Jowett and Gordon McMullan

A JOVIAL CREW,
OR
THE MERRY BEGGARS

D0556219

ARDEN EARLY MODERN DRAMA

A JOVIAL CREW,
OR
THE MERRY
BEGGARS

Richard Brome

for Beeston's Boys at the Phoenix

Edited by
TIFFANY STERN

BLOOMSBURY

LONDON • NEW DELHI • NEW YORK • SYDNEY

Bloomsbury Arden Shakespeare

An imprint of Bloomsbury Publishing Plc

50 Bedford Square	1385 Broadway
London	New York
WC1B 3DP	NY 10018
UK	USA

www.bloomsbury.com

Bloomsbury is a registered trade mark of Bloomsbury Publishing PLC

First published 2014

© Tiffany Stern 2014

Tiffany Stern has asserted her right under the Copyright, Designs and Patents Act, 1988, to be identified as Author of this work.

All rights reserved. No part of this publication may be reproduced or transmitted in any form or by any means, electronic or mechanical, including photocopying, recording, or any information storage or retrieval system, without prior permission in writing from the publishers.

No responsibility for loss caused to any individual or organization acting on or refraining from action as a result of the material in this publication can be accepted by Bloomsbury or the author.

British Library Cataloguing-in-Publication Data

A catalogue record for this book is available from the British Library.

ISBN:	HB:	978-1-4081-3001-8
	PB:	978-1-9042-7177-2
	ePDF:	978-1-4081-4012-3
	ePub:	978-1-4081-4013-0

Library of Congress Cataloging-in-Publication Data

A catalog record for this book is available from the Library of Congress.

Typeset by Graphicraft Limited, Hong Kong
Printed and bound in Great Britain

The Editor

Tiffany Stern is Professor of Early Modern Drama at Oxford University. Her publications include *Rehearsal from Shakespeare to Sheridan* (2000), *Making Shakespeare* (2004), *Shakespeare in Parts*, with Simon Palfrey (2007; winner of the 2009 David Bevington Award for Best New Book in Early Drama Studies) and *Documents of Early Modern Performance* (2009; winner of the 2010 David Bevington Award for Best New Book in Early Drama Studies). She has co-edited a collection of essays with Farah Karim-Cooper, *Shakespeare's Theatres and the Effects of Performance* (2013), and has edited the anonymous *King Leir* (2001), Sheridan's *The Rivals* (2004) and Farquhar's *Recruiting Officer* (2010). Tiffany Stern is a General Editor of the New Mermaids series and an Advisory General Editor for the Arden Shakespeare, and is on the editorial boards of the journals *SEDERI*, *Shakespeare Bulletin*, *The Hare* and *Shakespeare Quarterly*. She is the author of over forty chapters and articles on sixteenth- to eighteenth-century theatre and is currently writing a book about theatre and fairs.

To Daniel Grimley

CONTENTS

vii

LIST OF
ILLUSTRATIONS

GENERAL EDITORS' PREFACE

Arden Early Modern Drama (AEMD) is an expansion of the acclaimed Arden Shakespeare to include the plays of other dramatists of the early modern period. The series publishes dramatic texts from the early modern period in the established tradition of the Arden Shakespeare, using a similar style of presentation and offering the same depth of information and high standards of scholarship. We define 'early modern drama' broadly, to encompass plays written and performed at any time from the late fifteenth to the late seventeenth century. The attractive and accessible format and well-informed editorial content are designed with particular regard to the needs of students studying literature and drama in the final years of secondary school and in colleges and universities. Texts are presented in modern spelling and punctuation; stage directions are expanded to clarify theatrical requirements and possibilities; and speech prefixes (the markers of identity at the beginning of each new speech) are regularized. Each volume contains illustrations both from the period and from later performance history; a full discussion of the current state of criticism of the play; and information about the textual and performance contexts from which the play first emerged. The goal of the series is to make these wonderful but sometimes neglected plays as intelligible as those of Shakespeare to twenty-first-century readers.

AEMD editors bring a high level of critical engagement and textual sophistication to their work. They provide guidance in assessing critical approaches to their play, developing arguments from the best scholarly work to date and generating new perspectives. A particular focus of an AEMD edition is the play as it was first performed in the theatre. The title-page of each volume displays the name of the company for which the play was written and the theatre at which it was first staged: in the Introduction the play is discussed as part of a company repertory as well as of an authorial canon. Finally, each edition presents a full scholarly discussion of the base text and other relevant materials as physical and social documents, and the Introduction describes issues arising in the early history of the publication and reception of the text.

Commentary notes, printed immediately below the playtext, offer compact but detailed exposition of the language, historical context and theatrical significance of the play. They explain textual ambiguities and, when an action may be interpreted in different ways, they summarize the arguments. Where appropriate they point the reader to fuller discussions in the Introduction.

CONVENTIONS

AEMD editions always include illustrations of pages from the early texts on which they are based. Comparison between these illustrations and the edited text immediately enables the reader to see clearly what a critical edition is and does. In summary, the main changes to the base text – that is, the early text, most often a quarto, that serves as the copy from which the editor works – are these: certain and probable errors in the base text are corrected; typography and spelling are brought into line with current usage; and speech prefixes and stage directions are modified to assist the reader in imagining the play in performance.

Significant changes introduced by editors are recorded in the textual notes at the foot of the page. These are an important cache of information, presented in as compact a form as is possible without forfeiting intelligibility. The standard form can be seen in the following example:

31 doing of] *Coxeter;* of doing *Q;* doing *Rawl*

The line reference ('31') and the reading quoted from the present editor's text ('doing of') are printed before the closing square bracket. After the bracket, the source of the reading, often the name of the editor who first made the change to the base text ('*Coxeter*'), appears, and then other readings are given, followed by their source ('of doing *Q;* doing *Rawl*'). Where there is more than one alternative reading, they are listed in chronological order; hence in the example the base text Q (= Quarto) is given first. Abbreviations used to identify early texts and later editions are listed in the Abbreviations and References section towards the end of the volume. Editorial emendations to the text are discussed in the main commentary, where notes on emendations are highlighted with an asterisk.

Emendation necessarily takes account of early texts other than the base text, as well as of the editorial tradition. The amount of attention paid to other texts depends on the editor's assessment of their origin and importance. Emendation aims to correct errors while respecting the integrity of different versions as they might have emerged through revision and adaptation.

Modernization of spelling and punctuation in AEMD texts is thorough, avoiding the kind of partial modernization that produces language from no known period of English. Generally modernization is routine, involving thousands of alterations of letters. As original grammar is preserved in AEMD editions, most modernizations are as trivial as altering 'booke' to 'book', and are unworthy of record. But where the modernization is unexpected or ambiguous the change is noted in the textual notes, using the following format:

102 trolls] *(*trowles*)*

Speech prefixes are sometimes idiosyncratic and variable in the base texts, and almost always abbreviated. AEMD editions expand contractions, avoiding confusion of names that might be similarly abbreviated, such as Alonzo/Alsemero/Alibius from *The Changeling*. Preference is given to the verbal form that prevails in the base text, even if it identifies the role by type, such as 'Lady' or 'Clown', rather than by personal name. When an effect of standardization is to repress significant variations in the way that a role is conceptualized (in *Philaster*, for example, one text refers to a cross-dressed page as *Boy*, while another uses the character's assumed name), the issue is discussed in the Introduction.

Stage directions in early modern texts are often inconsistent, incomplete or unclear. They are preserved in the edition as far as is possible, but are expanded where necessary to ensure that the dramatic action is coherent and self-consistent. Square brackets are used to indicate editorial additions to stage directions. Directions that lend themselves to multiple staging possibilities, as well as the performance tradition of particular moments, may be discussed in the commentary.

Verse lineation sometimes goes astray in early modern play-texts, as does the distinction between verse and prose, especially where a wide manuscript layout has been transferred to the narrower measure of a printed page. AEMD editions correct such mistakes. Where a verse line is shared between more than one speaker, this series follows the usual modern practice of indenting the second and subsequent part-lines to make it clear that they belong to the same verse line.

The textual notes allow the reader to keep track of all these interventions. The notes use variations on the basic format described above to reflect the changes. In notes, '31 SD' indicates a stage direction in or immediately after line 31. Where there is more than one stage direction, they are identified as, for example, '31 SD1', '31 SD2'. The second line of a stage direction will be identified as, for instance, '31.2'. A forward slash / indicates a line-break in verse.

We hope that these conventions make as clear as possible the editor's engagement with and interventions in the text: our aim is to keep the reader fully informed of the editor's role without intruding unnecessarily on the flow of reading. Equally, we hope – since one of our aims is to encourage the performance of more plays from the early modern period beyond the Shakespeare canon – to provide texts which materially assist performers, as well as readers, of these plays.

PREFACE

This work would not have been possible without Ann Haaker's edition of the play for the venerable Regents Renaissance Drama series (1968) and R. G. Lawrence's good (if hasty) text for his collection of *Jacobean and Caroline Comedies* (1973). It has also benefited a great deal from the excellent *Richard Brome Online* site, which includes an edition of *A Jovial Crew* by Eleanor Lowe (Original Text), Helen Ostovich (Modern Text) and Richard Cave (General). Insights from all three editions have informed this text.

Having the opportunity to edit for Arden Early Modern Drama's wonderful general editors, Suzanne Gossett, John Jowett and Gordon McMullan, has been a delight. Warm friends and great editors, they were unstinting in their advice, and, as I worked on *A Jovial Crew*, revealed layers that helped me to look again at what I thought I knew. They also let me choose which play to edit in the first place. I am grateful to have been allowed to work on the poignant end-point of AEMD: the last play to be put on before the closure of the theatres for the interregnum.

My particular thanks go to my general editor, Suzanne Gossett, whose support and guidance were invaluable. Her encouragement, and her close scrutiny of the text and notes, improved the text; her friendship and good advice – about jovial crews in life as well as in literature – made the process of editing a real pleasure. To Jane Armstrong, I am profoundly grateful. A formidable and wonderful copy editor, her thoroughness and critical eye have made this a better book. Emily Hockley, Arden's editorial assistant, was extremely helpful with images. Margaret Bartley, Arden's publisher, has been a dear friend as well as a supportive publisher, and I owe her a debt of thanks for her wise and seasoned guidance throughout the preparation of this book.

I could not have completed my work without the assistance of librarians across the country. My grateful thanks to the staff of the following libraries: the British Library, the Bodleian Library, the Cambridge University Library, the Leeds University Library, the National Library of Scotland, the Royal Shakespeare Company Archives, the Shakespeare Institute Library and the Victoria and Albert Museum Library.

Being part of a real jovial crew, 'Team English' at Univ, has been an inspiration. Thank you, Nicholas Halmi, Laura Varnam and, latterly, Christopher Salamone, for your collegiality and friendship.

Daniel Grimley inspired the musical appendix to this book, and helped me write it. *A Jovial Crew* is, with love, dedicated to him.

Tiffany Stern
University College, Oxford

INTRODUCTION

Richard Brome, as he dedicates *A Jovial Crew, or The Merry Beggars* (hereafter *A Jovial Crew*) to Thomas Stanley, claims that his play had what he calls 'the luck' to 'tumble last of all in the epidemical ruin of the scene': it was the last play staged before the theatres closed in 1642 as the English Civil War began. Brome's mixed metaphors conflate the problems faced by his play and his country: it 'tumble[s]' (loses footing) into the 'epidemical' (loses health) 'ruin' (loses building) of the 'scene' (the back wall of the stage, but also the story of England conceived of as a play). But this dedication, written not when *A Jovial Crew* was performed at the Cockpit/Phoenix in 1641 or 1642, but when it was printed in 1652, gives the text a 'certain poignancy which it would not originally have possessed' (Butler, *Theatre*, 269; see pp. 49–50).

Tension between the text of around 1640 and the preliminary matter of 1652 explains not just the conflict within the play itself, but also the conflicting attitudes with which it has been judged. So the play has been said to be using escapism to counter the troubles of the times (Andrews; Haaker; Kaufmann) and, alternatively, to be a parody of the theme of escapism (Butler, *Theatre*). It has been seen as a nostalgia piece about the Elizabethan period (Lawrence) and the reverse: a frankly realistic appraisal of contemporary Caroline troubles (Butler, *Theatre*; Gaby). The 'begging progress' made by the gentrified protagonists has been described as an escape from society's rules (Sullivan), or, conversely, as a reflection of the King's northern progress in 1641–2 to rally troops (Steggle, 'Redating'). The 'beggars' commonwealth' has thus been seen as an acknowledgement that beggars too create hierarchies (Carroll) or, alternatively, as a recognition that society can structure itself without enforced leadership (Gaby). As a result, the play has been judged to be radical (Butler, *Theatre*; Sanders, *Caroline*)

1

or Cavalier (Farley-Hills), and the happy ending is thus said to be genuinely happy (Ingram; Haaker), ironically happy (Farley-Hills; Clark) or disturbingly troubled (Sanders, *Caroline*; Steggle, *Brome*). This introduction will try to mediate between these attitudes while illustrating how carefully, both in 1641/2 and in 1652, Brome steers his drama between opposites. *A Jovial Crew*, with its aim of cheering up a troubled country, also maintains that that can only be achieved – if at all – in the world of fiction.

Put on at the conventional terminus of early modern drama, *A Jovial Crew* is a work whose theatrical position is as fascinating as its political one. Brome used his play to attack contemporary romantic drama, while upholding the themes and concerns of Jacobean and Elizabethan writers – he was in some ways an old-fashioned playwright, and his style was connected to that of his mentor, Ben Jonson. Nevertheless, *A Jovial Crew's* simple humour and accessible style were also forward-looking. The play would become one of the first dramas mounted after the interregnum, perhaps even shaping what Restoration comedies were to become. Popular thereafter too, *A Jovial Crew* would later, in the eighteenth century, be adapted into an opera. It only ceased to be performed when John Gay's *Beggar's Opera*, designed to rival or complement it, took over. *A Jovial Crew*, then, says as much about the history of theatre as it does about the history of England.

THE PLAY

Mood and title

For many years *A Jovial Crew* was famous simply for its good humour. Its story is, after all, a happy one. Though Oldrents has been given a terrible prophecy – that his children will become beggars – he responds with kindness, giving shelter and money to visiting vagrants. When his daughters, Rachel and Meriel, do end up as beggars, it is through choice: they join the beggar community in search of adventure. Their faithful lovers, Vincent and Hilliard, follow them, as does the charismatic and mysterious Springlove, steward to Oldrents, but also, it emerges, king of the beggars. The play is, then, in structure, a genial pastoral comedy about a crisis averted. Immediately accepted into the beggar community, the young gentry find themselves in a life of drink, song and, surprisingly, hardship. Oldrents, meanwhile, learning that his children are indeed beggars, seeks happiness through drink and song of his own, encouraged by his friend Hearty. As a result, the middle of *A Jovial Crew* consists of drunken singing. At the play's conclusion, children and father are reunited. The gentry, chastened by their beggar experiences, agree to return to their noble life, and marry their lovers. Springlove, too, arranges to marry – during the beggars' sojourn he has met and fallen in love with Amy as she attempted to escape from two other less desirable fiancés. The play thus has a typical 'comedy' ending with multiple prospective weddings. It also concludes with some telling disclosures. The beggars have a 'priest', called 'the Patrico' in cant, who reveals that Oldrents had, in his youth, dallied with a beggar-woman who bore him a son: that son, explains the Patrico, is Springlove. The Patrico also reveals that he is himself from a noble family brought to ruin by Oldrents' ancestors. Patrico, then, is all noble blood and also all beggar, while Springlove's blood unites beggars and gentry. 'Here are no beggars', concludes Oldrents, raising questions about what 'beggar' even means, '. . . but a select company to fill this house with mirth' (5.1.529–31). Through the temporary beggardom of Oldrents' children, the events of the past have been revealed and assuaged. Oldrents and his children, including his newfound son Springlove, prepare to return to their old lives with new knowledge: the remaining beggars are given a 'free pass' to go on their way unpunished.

The play, wrote A. C. Swinburne, is a composition of 'quaint, extravagant, and consistent characters' who collectively produce 'harmony of dramatic evolution and vivacity of theatrical event' (507). A century later G. E. Bentley thought the play a 'gay and captivating comedy' (3.71), and Thomas Marc Parrott and Robert Hamilton Ball maintained that 'a fresh breath of country air blows through the playhouse while the story of good squire Oldrents and his merry daughters is unrolled' (Parrott and Ball, 178). As recently as 1992, John Peter, commenting on the Royal Shakespeare Company production of the play, concluded, 'Brome is a shrewd observer . . . determined not to give offence to anyone. The beggars are good-natured and colourful; the gentry mostly jovial and generous; the two girls tease and simper pleasantly, with a touch of the naughties' (*Sunday Times*, 26 April 1992).

Detractors have likewise focused on the play's mood. In the eighteenth century, *A Jovial Crew*, in its revised form, was said by one newspaper to be an 'incongruous . . . mixture of mirth, absurdity, and low humour' (*Morning Chronicle and London Advertiser*, 10 February 1777); the play's popularity was traced to its ability to amuse the unthinking. 'I cannot', wrote David Erskine Baker, 'help looking on the great Approbation it met with as a Kind of Reflection on the public Taste' (*Companion*, 1, sig. K6ʳ); later he repeated Theophilus Cibber's sentiment that 'Brome's applauses' conferred 'no great honour' on his admirers (Baker, *Biographia*, 1.119). A. W. Ward based his opprobrium on the play's merriment: 'The scenes illustrating the title of the play contain little that to a modern reader will be otherwise than repulsive' (3.127).

Both sets of critics are responding to the fact that *A Jovial Crew* is a 'feel-good' play. It is filled with puns, jokes and songs. Its characters are happy from name onwards: Meriel has 'merry' in her name and believes 'We cannot live but by laughing' (2.1.74); Springlove loves spring, springs out of love, and falls in love in springtime; Hearty's name speaks for itself – with his hearty singing and drinking he is a locus for the play's good humour. As well as happy in its characterization,

4

the play is positive about humanity generally. Many of its characters are decent at root – the servant Randall seeks help in order to resist the temptation to steal the money that has been left in his care, for instance. Others are benevolent – Oldrents responds to the sins of his past by giving plentifully to the beggars, and reacts to the disappearance of his children by absolving his tenants of all rent and doubling his servants' wages. Even the broad plot structure of the play is positive, forever hinting at a happy solution to come: Oldrents first mentions his children together with Springlove (1.1.103–4); Oldrents' friend Hearty, later, feels Springlove and Oldrents are connected (2.2.53–4); Oldrents sees in the beggar-priest Patrico 'more soul than a born beggar' (2.2.316–17). At the conclusion there is no retribution, and the villains turn out to have been less bad than feared. Justice Clack, to whom the beggars have been sent for punishment, gives the beggars a free pass instead of a whipping; Oliver, Clack's son, hitherto a ne'er-do-well without an emotional core, apologizes to the women he attempted to purchase and rape – 'I hope we all are friends' (5.1.559). Oliver's depiction, in particular, reminds us how even great sins can be amended, for he is now what Oldrents once was. Oldrents, we learn, had, as the text puts it, 'assaulted' a beggar-woman 'With amorous, though loose, desires' (5.1.474–5). He had then left his lover when she had had his son, tossing her some money and, by mistake, a relic. That is why, in the play, he is struck with guilt by beggars in general, and why he is sickened when offered a doxy: 'A sudden qualm overchills my stomach' (2.2.297). Oldrents, however, has subsequently lived his life making amends for his past wrongs; in the play, he is finally forgiven them. He is the good man that Oliver can become: even the most serious suffering detailed in the play is utterly reformable.

Yet looked at closely, the play is ambiguous. Its mood and tone are not quite the same as its content. Though Brome once boasted that he never 'spilt Ink' outside comedies 'Which in the thronged Theatres did appear / All Mirth and Laughter' ('To . . . Hastings, Deceased', 74), not all comedies are light-hearted. *A Jovial Crew*, which is insistently happy in feel, wrestles with some dark issues.

'Jovial', the first word of the title, and a theme of the play throughout, is a loaded adjective. It derives from Jove, or Jupiter, king of the classical gods and god of joy – and thunder. 'Jovial', then, might equally signify 'happy' or 'turbulent and ungovernable'. The early modern phrase 'jovial crew', reflecting this dichotomy, teetered between pleasure and threat: it was regularly used, ironically, to describe a beggar community. Brome was highly conscious of the nuances of the phrase. He compared his earlier play *The Northern Lass* to a beggar '*Jovially* begot' because, he explained, it 'came out of the cold North, thinly clad' (sig. A2ʳ). *A Jovial Crew*, with its ragged beggars, is about both the wild happiness and the suffering of the beggar community. For Brome, joviality and distress were closely allied.

Furthering this ambiguity was the fact that the phrase 'jovial crew' was also used to describe a group of abandoned drinkers (Steggle, *Brome*, 171–3). So in a drinking song in John Ford's *Lady's Trial*, it is 'a Joviall crew' who can 'drinke till all looke blew' (sig. H1ᵛ) – an idea ironically rephrased for *A Jovial Crew*'s 'round' or catch, 'Old sack, and old songs' (see p. 269). Yet the drinkers in *A Jovial Crew* are not presented as actually happy. The beggars 'bowse [drink] in defiance o'th' harman-beck [constable]' (2.2.180); Oldrents drinks because, as he instructs Tallboy, 'sack' will help 'drown . . . suspirations [sighs]' (4.1.280); the grey-beards drink in order that 'sorrow be drowned' (4.1.258); Hearty's instructive song about the 'old fellow at Waltham Cross' concerns a man who opted for 'sack' because he had lost everything else: 'He cheered up his heart when his goods went to wrack, / With a "hem boy, hem" and a cup of old sack' (2.2.100–1). Even Justice Clack, one of the few drinkers who is not depressed, drinks for bad reasons, wolfing down his own alcohol in order to prevent his guests getting too much of it. The fact that the play is 'jovial' may not, perversely, mean that it is happy.

Brome was, moreover, pointedly choosing 'jovial' to replace his more usual term, 'mirth'. In his *City Wit*, 'nothing but mirth's intended' (sig. G4^r); *The Court Beggar* is 'But a slight piece of mirth' (sig. N4^v); *The Damoiselle* offers 'familiar mirth' (sig. A2^r); *The English Moor* presents 'wit and harmless mirth' (sig. A2^r); *Mad Couple* asks, 'had you Mirth enough?' (sig. H2^r); *A Novella* says 'all we pretend to is but Mirth and Sence' (sig. H4^r). But *A Jovial Crew*, performed in a troubled age and printed in a yet more troubled one, maintains in its prologue that 'mirth' is a 'forced thing in these . . . days' (Prol.2–3). Haunted by the very sorrow it is intended to dispel, the prologue acknowledges that mirth has gone out of fashion, and ends on the concept of grief: it wishes of the play that 'the dullness may make no man sleep, / Nor sadness of it any woman weep' (21–2). True, the play ultimately claims to have been 'intended for your mirth' (Epil.8) – but it begins after the word 'weep'.

Looked at more closely, many of the seemingly merry characters in *A Jovial Crew* are sad. Oldrents, obsessed with 'jovial mirth' (2.2.114), is in a highly anxious state. He opens the play so doom-laden about calamities that may befall his children that he drives them away: 'our father . . . makes us even sick of his sadness' (2.1.27–9). His daughters join the beggar community, unwittingly fulfilling Oldrents' greatest fears; on learning of their departure, Oldrents opts for 'Forced mirth', hoping that it can be 'by strife and custom . . . made good' (2.2.33–6). After that, he laughs for the same reason that he drinks – in order not to cry: 'jovial mirth . . . I will force out of my spleen so freely / That grief shall lose her name where I have being' (2.2.114–16). His grey-beard friends are the same: though they constitute, as their song has it, a 'merry old crew' (4.1.259), their ditty is an instruction to find happiness in alcohol when feeling sad or 'blue'. This, of course, raises questions about the beggars, the most determinedly happy group in the play. Are they as delighted with life as they seem? There, too, the play offers alternative and contradictory answers.

Character development and genre

The play's ambiguous characterization, one of its salient features, is nowhere more obvious than in the depiction of the beggars. They seem recklessly happy; their songs, though, hint at sadnesses not mentioned in the dialogue (see p. 256). More troublingly, they have unfixed natures, altering in attitude, language and class during the progress of the drama. First courtly and symbolic, later poverty-stricken and realistic, the beggars may constantly sing and dance, but their dispositions, and hence the meaning of their actions, change over time.

At the start of the play, the beggars are like other early modern theatrical beggars. First described, then heard offstage and only afterwards revealed, they are given a protracted, highly theatrical entrance, recalling the introduction of dancing beggars and gypsies in masques. This connection is furthered by the fact that a curtain has to be drawn in order to 'discover' the beggars in their '*postures*' (1.1.375.3). When they then ask, 'Shall we dance, shall we sing, to welcome our king?', and demand, 'Strike up, piper, a merry, merry dance, / That we on our stampers may foot it and prance' (378–80), they emerge as joyous fictions, whose performances will bring pleasure alike to the stage gentry and to us, the actual spectators. They do, however, offer a commentary upon the gentry. Their barn abuts so closely onto Oldrents' house that the two spaces are separated by a door: Springlove '*opens the scene*' (375.1) from inside Oldrents' house to reveal the beggars' dwelling. Perhaps the two groups are more similar than might have been anticipated.

Key beggars are introduced in a way that continues to highlight their fictional nature. Called 'Soldier', 'Lawyer',

'Scribble' (a poet) and 'Courtier', they are conventional rather than realistic, recalling in name and character the play's older gentry, Oldrents and Hearty. They are also presented as the well-born professionals they once were, reflecting other dramas in which beggars are actually upper class (*King Lear* has as its sole beggar Poor Tom, a disguised member of the gentry, despite its stated concern with 'unaccommodated man' and the plight of the poor – see Haynes, 22). Each beggar is, moreover, in theatrical fashion, 'narrated' into being as his background is supplied by a fellow beggar:

> LAWYER   Sir . . . He is a decayed poet, newly fallen in
> among us, and begs as well as the best of us. He
> learned it pretty well in his own profession before
> and can the better practise it in ours now.
> SPRINGLOVE   Thou art a wit too, it seems.
> SOLDIER   He should have wit and knavery too, sir, for
> he was an attorney till he was pitched over the bar.
>
> (1.1.390–7)

Though happy and carefree, then, these beggars are 'not on the same representational level' as the younger gentry (Womack, 257). They do, however, share with the gentry the fact that they have given over regular lives for the thrill of vagabondage. Once again, the beggars and the nobility are shown as quintessentially similar.

Over the course of the play, however, who the beggars are, and what they represent, is altered. The social reality of beggar life in early modern England becomes a topic as the courtly lovers find themselves living an authentic rather than a literary beggar life. After a fiercely uncomfortable night sleeping in lice-filled straw, Meriel and Rachel, taken to be real beggar-wenches, are almost raped by Oliver; later, a choice of vagabond women is offered as 'coarse fare' to Oldrents and Hearty (2.2.289–94). As 'real life' beggar events become part of the drama, lower-class and more 'realistic' beggars are introduced: one is a doxy who is heard '*crying out*' in labour (129.2); a further two are drunken octogenarian beggars who undergo a crude marriage. Both the birth and the marriage involve singing and dancing – but the noise created is a way of hiding the cries of labour and the sexual fumbling of the elderly couple. Thus the music that at the start of the play highlighted and celebrated artifice now serves the purpose of drowning out reality.

The remaining 'real' beggars at the end of the play are given a free pass to wander off again. But since they have moved from performing a dramatic function to performing a documentary one, it is unclear whether this freedom is a good or bad thing. In 'fictional' terms, they can now continue their merry wandering. In 'realistic' terms, however, they are being sent back to their lives of begging, dirt and sexual exploitation. More than that, the play shows that the beggars will now be poorer than ever: without access to the sums of money Oldrents gave them in his grief, and bereft of their 'king' Springlove, the beggars will lack money and a protector. *A Jovial Crew, or The Merry Beggars*, a play named after the beggars it features, seems to drop its focus as easily as the gentry do. This may, of course, be because *A Jovial Crew* itself is really about landed gentry, not beggars; the beggar crew, important for as long as they are a repository for the Oldrents family's secrets, cease to be relevant at the play's conclusion. But this may also be a way of, bleakly, completing the beggars' story.

Other protagonists, too, change their natures over the course of the play – in particular, Oldrents' daughters and their lovers, who at first seem to come from a different form of fiction altogether. Their story initially suggests the popular 1630s 'romances / Of lovers' (Prol.8–9) that the prologue bemoaned were in fashion, in which 'afflicted wanderers' (11) go through a series of trials ending in 'some impossibility' (13). In romance fashion, the young gentry have elegant and somewhat contrived names – Meriel, Rachel, Vincent and Hilliard (see List of Roles,

2, 3, 11, 12nn.); in romance fashion, too, the men follow the women into the beggar community to prove their love; and in romance fashion, all expect the beggars to provide a pastoral idyll – Meriel rejects communal celebrations like horse races or Dover's Olympics (see 2.1.94–7) for the greater joy of playing at poverty. Yet the gentry's unthinking belief that their own lives are full of care and responsibility, while beggars are free, is challenged by the 'reality' they confront. When the lovers all confess to being disillusioned by actual beggar life, they query their own romantic natures: beggar life is meaner and tougher than literature had suggested.

The older generation also changes character, though not in quite the same way. Both Hearty and Oldrents are ambiguous throughout. Hearty, for all his merriment, displays a strangely knowing attitude to the world: the analogies he draws at the beginning of the play are with thieving lawyers, religious hypocrites and medical quacks. A man with no apparent obligations, financial or moral, Hearty can be seen as a comforter, curing Oldrents' unhappiness with his joy, or as a corrupter, battening on Oldrents' unhappiness to finance his own merriment – or does he flit between the two? Even Hearty's 'meaningful' name, which indicates that he is 'great hearted', may equally mean 'full of heart', or 'unrestrained'. The same ambiguities haunt Oldrents, whose character is sometimes at the extreme of sadness and sometimes happy. His name, too, bears a number of readings (see List of Roles, 1n.). At first, 'Oldrents' seems to suggest a reliance, as a member of the landed gentry, on rent for income; but when the man's generosity is revealed, 'Oldrents' comes to seem a description of the reasonable rents (rents charged at the 'old' rather than new price) that he offers his tenants. But then again, when it becomes clear that his current household has been 'rent' or torn by a promise that his children will end up as beggars – or, rather, as Hearty suggests in a joke, with 'old rents' (1.1.96) in their clothes – his name comes to point towards his fears. His actions and his worries are competing aspects of his personality, as his changeable mood makes clear.

Linking the two groups, beggars and gentry, are Springlove and the Patrico. They, like the beggars, change class – only theirs is an upward trajectory. Springlove starts as, seemingly, another character from a 1630s dramatic romance: he is a servant and a king of beggars – but he has an innate nobility that shines through; by the play's conclusion, he has accepted a life amongst the gentry. Confusingly, he then returns to the trade of beggar in the epilogue, making the 'moral' with respect to him hard to draw. He compares tellingly with the Patrico, who also seems at first a romance-style character. The Patrico appears, Prospero-like, to shape the events of the drama: he 'predicts' to Oldrents the disaster that causes his melancholy; and he reveals the 'Agnus Dei' that brings about the play's solution. It is he who halts the play within the play, moreover, when the time comes to disclose Oldrents' history. Yet at the conclusion of *A Jovial Crew*, the Patrico, the only beggar (apart from his wife) whose name even comes from the beggars' language, cant, is shown to be a man of noble blood as well. Unlike Springlove, however, he is not assumed into the gentry, and does not even receive back the money of which his family was defrauded. Instead, he accepts a 'competent annuity' (5.1.546), and promises to pray forever for the man whose family ruined his own (547–8). His final actions question the relative worth of the beggar and the noble life. The Patrico may have planned the events that the play relates, but he oddly neglected to reinstate himself as part of the resolution.

In reversing the characterization of Springlove and the Patrico at the end of the play, making Hearty and Oldrents ambiguous and thrusting the courtly lovers, Rachel, Meriel, Hillier and Vincent, into an idealistic, romantic pastoral world only to show that it is not ideal at all, Brome seems to be self-consciously reinterpreting saccharine 1630s romantic dramas. When he stages scenic tableaux, singing and dancing

– everything that might be desired in court romance dramas – but puts it all in the mouths and bodies of increasingly unsanitary and suffering beggars, Brome appears to be creating a non-romance out of the very romance features he is apparently adopting. His characters' instability seems to be an extension of this fact; he is superficially writing one kind of drama, but actually writing its reverse.

Politics

A major question disputed by critics is whether the play is focused on politics, is incidentally political or is avoiding politics altogether. When *A Jovial Crew* was written, around 1640, and first performed, in 1641 or 1642, England was in a very particular state of political turmoil. The King, Charles I, was wildly unpopular, and a faction had formed intent on removing him, by force if necessary, and transforming the country into a republic – the result was to be the English Civil War, the beheading of the King and the establishment of the Commonwealth of England, Scotland and Ireland under the Lord Protector, Oliver Cromwell. In 1639, when the play will have been planned or penned, the prelude to the Civil War was taking place. Charles had attempted to impose an Episcopalian system of church government (with bishops) in Scotland; the Scottish, who favoured the Presbyterian Church, had mustered their own army, creating a conflict that became known as the First Bishops' War (1639). *A Jovial Crew*, then, was written as small wars started to break out over Britain, heralding the huge crisis to come. With its conflicts and resolutions, its gentry and its beggars, its kingships and its commonwealths, *A Jovial Crew* is clearly exploring issues of its time. But is it *about* those issues?

Recent critics have maintained that Brome's drama engages politically with the events of the early 1640s through reflecting upon what happens if a group leaves their aristocratic certainty for a beggar 'commonwealth'. The play, which comments upon, warns and rebukes English society, is thus seen to be a hard-hitting political allegory: its 'alternative kingdom' in the beggar community is analogous to Caroline England (Butler, *Theatre*, 274); its affectionate picture of English landscape and culture shows what is being put under threat by contemporary politics (272, 275). Alternatively, as Charles had dissolved Parliament in 1629 and only summoned another in 1640, the play might be about the eleven-year 'tyranny', which had redistributed bureaucratic responsibility to the provinces and given power and potential to rural communities (Sanders, *Caroline*, 60). If so, Brome adopts 'the pastoral genre' not so much for parodic reasons as for its 'nuanced inflections of the vocabulary and discourse of the countryside and the country's community' (67).

In fact, however, there is only one moment in the play when contemporary politics are obviously addressed – and that may be a 1652 addition to the text (see pp. 49–50). Late in the story, the beggars suggest performing a drama on the subject of 'Utopia' (see 4.2.199). Their title is pointed. Ever since Thomas More's *Utopia* (1516), a book about a mythical island somewhat resembling England, the term 'Utopia' had been used for discussing what was good and bad about a country ('utopia' signifies equally 'good place' and 'no place'). The beggars say their 'Utopia' playlet will concern a land in crisis where law and divinity fail to 'appease' or 'reconcile' anything, where 'the country, the city and the court' vie for superiority, and where the soldiers ultimately 'cudgel them all together' so that everyone is reduced to 'Beggars' Hall' (4.2.228–39). They seem to be indicating that England is destroying itself through war. But their play is not, ultimately, performed. Is that because it is not of a piece with the rest of the text? Or because the real play about England is *A Jovial Crew* itself? For the true politics of the play may reside not in large allegories but in the play's very characterization. The depiction of the beggars may be a rebuke to contemporary society, now so corrupt that a beggar alternative is preferable (Bevan, 456). Alternatively, the beggars show how respected professionals are being reduced to beggary in Caroline England (Goodman, 239).

On the other hand, there are those who say that *A Jovial Crew* is not about politics, but is – like its avoidance of mounting 'Utopia' – side-stepping them. William C. Carroll thinks that the play dictates what government attitude ought to be not through story, but through its illustration of goodwill (211). David Farley-Hills sees the play as an escapist romantic drama. After all, actual, literal escape is a serious possibility in *A Jovial Crew*: Springlove escapes from the servitude of being a steward; Rachel and Meriel join him and escape from their unhappy household; Amy escapes from a marriage she does not want (Farley-Hills, 155). If so, then the joy of the play can be located in the promise that every trial can likewise be overcome. Maybe Brome is trying to cheer up a nation at an unhappy point in its history, or even revealing his political affiliations – the Royalist community, the Cavaliers, were laughing to keep up morale and in defiance of the government; possibly Cavalier values, if not political ideas, are reflected by this drama (153).

The problem is that Brome's actual political affiliations are hard to guage, and can only be guessed from the play itself, as his views are otherwise unknown. It is possible to argue that the play is not an escapist drama but a despairing, ironic parody of the very idea of escapism. Brome's *Lovesick Court* parodies tragicomedies, and his *Antipodes* parodies satire; *A Jovial Crew*, which declares its intention to tell unlikely stories (Prol.13–15), could likewise be seen as thoroughly parodic: it would be odd for Brome, who had spent his life writing plays that satirized escapist drama, to turn to such fantasy without simultaneously critiquing it (Shaw, 118, 129). Possibly, then, the play is about the impossibility of escapism, in which case it still addresses contemporary events through mood – but through a sad mood rather than a happy one.

Yet some aspects of the play seem not to be about politics but about social reality. The breaking up of bands of feudal retainers and the dissolution of the monasteries had led to an influx of beggars in rural England, and perhaps these issues are as germane to *A Jovial Crew*'s story as the events of the late 1630s (Chiang, 120). Indeed, sometimes the play has been said to be simply literal. For instance, beggars plagued the barns of Hertfordshire in 1641, and one landlord, Richard Haynes, got into legal trouble for sheltering them. Though Haynes's legal troubles date from 1641, when the play was probably already in performance, he had committed a similar offence in 1636 (Cressy, *England*, 354). If this is Brome's source, then he is finding value in a lightly fictionalized 'true' story about kindness in times of despair. Alternatively, his 'real' interests may be related to a potential source of much-needed money from patronage. It has been suggested that a 'real' location for Oldrents' house exists in Maplebeck, Nottinghamshire (Sanders, 'Commonwealths', 5), in which case *A Jovial Crew* might additionally be a homage from Brome to a famous Nottinghamshire family, the Cavendishes (Steggle, *Brome*, 166).

Michel Bitot, however, suggests that Brome responds to current affairs theatrically rather than politically; he describes Brome's interest in freedom as descending from a desire for freedom of the stage rather than – or before – the freedom of the nation.

Themes

In his dedicatory poem to *A Jovial Crew* (pp. 76–7), John Hall called the play one of a series of 'instructive recreations' (1), yet, as has been discussed, quite what it instructs or teaches is unclear, because Brome's politics are less obvious than his concerns and values. Just as the play's characters are inconsistent, so the play itself seems to promote simultaneous contradictory beliefs – perhaps because it finds it hard to commit to anything in an unstable world.

Marriage, for instance, is promoted by the drama, yet undercut by it too. Oldrents enjoins the lovers, 'Be one another's, and you all are mine', and Vincent and Hilliard consent: 'We are agreed on that' (5.1.497–8); a few lines later, Oldrents, perhaps assuming that *de praesenti* marriage contracts (mutual promises of immediate matrimony) have been made, calls his daughters' suitors 'husbands' (532). Yet the play, showing a studied indifference to its own romance, never even reveals which man, Vincent or Hilliard, is dating which woman, Rachel or Meriel. Oldrents himself, meanwhile, is discovered to have avoided at least one marriage by sleeping with a beggar-woman he later abandoned, while Martin, having eloped with Amy in order to advance in social rank, is so unwilling to see the marriage through that he reveals the beggars' whereabouts to get out of the arrangement. At the core of the play is a freak-show beggar wedding in which a lame old man and a blind old woman marry; they are drunk and farting, more desperate for sex than love, and more interested in inheritance than in one another. Marriage itself, here, seems to be being parodied. This is partly, of course, because Brome wants to promote marriage only when it is for the right reasons and stems from love. Amy's happy match with Springlove saves her from the man she is supposed to marry, Tallboy, as well as the man with whom she elopes, Martin, neither of whom she desires. Yet when, in a lengthy analogy in the dedication (p. 75, 34–5), Brome depicts himself as a limping bridegroom – analogous to the lame old beggar Lothario of the text we are about to read – the meaning of marriage to the author himself is raised. Brome, whose marital state is unknown, has a cynical attitude that questions the worth of the play's weddings.

The linked theme of birth, like that of marriage, is treated ambivalently. Positive images of birth and rebirth attach to Springlove. As Springlove puts it when he introduces the lovers to the beggars, 'this is your birthnight into a new world' (3.1.36–7); the story of his own birth is part of the play's conclusion. Yet the theme of fathers abandoning children also haunts the play, from Oldrents' actions in the past to Oliver's in the present: Oliver justifies his attempt to rape 'beggar-braches' (293) with the excuse that children move compassion, so that 'He feeds a beggar-wench well that fills her belly with young bones' (311–12). Though Brome is undoubtedly suggesting that the parental role should be taken seriously, he nevertheless creates an ironic situation in which Oldrents, on learning of the disappearance of his children – about whose future he had been so worried – can declare, 'I am happy; all my cares are flown' (2.2.111).

Likewise, the religious affiliations of the play can be seen in a number of ways. On one hand, religion in the play is parodied, when a curate, perhaps the Patrico himself, is sought who is 'so scrupulous' (3.1.619) that he will only marry a couple if they have already slept together, and when a baptism for the beggar-baby is instantly rejected ('They'll not endure / A ceremony that is not their own', 2.2.157–8). Though God is heard of in sighs such as 'God forgive him' (2.1.37) and begging phrases like 'the good Lord . . . bless you and restore it you in heaven' (336–7), God has not obviously redressed any of the play's problems, and references to His design and purpose are always, as Farley-Hills puts it, 'hedged with uncertainty' (154). The word 'God' is strangely missing from the Butler's repeated phrase '(—— make us/me thankful for it)' (4.1.190–1, 193–4, 206, 209), and is avoided by Vincent, who titles Him 'the maker of those happy creatures' (i.e. the beggars) in 2.1.258. Yet Catholicism is, in some ways, promoted: the young gentry project a voyage to a site of Catholic pilgrimage, Saint Winifred's Well (2.1.107–8); the Patrico is jokingly called, in priest-like fashion, 'ghostly father' (4.2.218); at the drama's denouement Oldrents receives back a Catholic 'Agnus Dei' he once gave to a beggar-woman. Brome may daringly be suggesting that a Catholic revelation is the solution that England needs (while Protestantism is leading the country into civil war). Yet when the Patrico promises to end his days as a 'beadsman' (5.1.547), or praying pilgrim – a further Catholic reference – to Oldrents, the play's attitude to Catholicism too comes into question. Has the Patrico's magic been reduced to this? Does Catholicism simply reconcile people to their humble places?

As it seems, Brome flirts with 'solutions', but then shows them to be inadequate, or even gives up on them. That, certainly, is what happens in his depiction of the law. As Justice Clack's approach to the law, with his ideas of punishing first and examining afterwards shows (see 5.1.34–6), he is a 'bad' Justice – a caricature met with in many other plays of the period. His ironic concern about the way justice will be presented in the beggars' playlet also highlights the way justice is presented, through him, in *A Jovial Crew*: in the person of Clack, Brome is perhaps staging the lack of justice he sees at the heart of Caroline England. If so, he once again does not see this point through. In a drunken good humour, Justice Clack releases the beggars at the end of the play, and agrees to the marriages. Law is neither fully criticized nor corrected; it is, ultimately, simply not important.

Even liberty and freedom, main themes of the drama, are surprisingly hard to locate: who in the play is free? The idea that 'true liberty' – the liberty of thought and action – is to be found in vagabondage, and that beggars are the 'only people can boast the benefit of a free state' (2.1.3–4) is maintained by Vincent and Hilliard, but that is in order to follow their lovers into the beggar community. Their sentiments are roundly contradicted by the play, which repeatedly shows how beggars are constrained by the need for money, as is everyone else. Randall, servant to Oldrents, is given twenty-five pounds for the beggars, though he himself has devoted his entire lifetime to saving a mere forty. His questions on the morality of this imbalance invite the audience to think of the problems behind generosity, governance, escapism and liberty. The same issues are underlined when the Butler is introduced: he too has devoted his life to saving a 'brace of hundred pounds' (4.1.205), which is only double the sum that Springlove and Oldrents spend on the beggars every year (Steggle, *Brome*, 170). Even the needy beggars are oddly knowing about cash. They humble themselves to anyone who gives them money, yet they also, by telling fortunes, 'cozen our poor country people of their single money' (5.1.100–1), living equally at the expense of the rich and the gullible poor. They are even shown making shrewd financial calculations: the old couple will not marry until they have arranged 'portion and jointure' (4.2.55), ironizing the notion that the beggars are free of financial and property cares. The beggars, then, show the corrupting power of money even, or perhaps especially, in those who barely have any of it (Steggle, *Brome*, 169). In other ways, also, the beggars are not free. They live in a society as hierarchically structured and ordered as the one from which the gentry are escaping.

On the other hand, the gentry are not free either; they, too, are imprisoned in their societal rank. The gentlewomen, in particular, are constrained. Amy has no choice over whom she shall marry; Meriel and Rachel are confined by 'our father's rule and government, or . . . his allowance' (2.1.19–20). Yet they all run back from the perceived freedom of the beggar community to their old lives. If they had intended to learn that poverty leads to contentment, that is what they are abandoning; if they had intended to learn that rebellion is empowering, that is what they have given over.

With the freedom of beggar and gentry life alike questioned, the analogy with caged or wild birds becomes complex: it is uncertain which group, if either, is at liberty (1.1.183; 2.1.231–4). Hence the play's ambiguous conclusion. The beggars remain putatively free at the end of the play, while the gentlefolks are 'enslaved' by society again – but what does that mean? Perhaps both groups are free, but perhaps neither is or ever was.

With a play so fascinated by giving equal weight to opposite views, it is no surprise that the actual level of happiness in the play's superficially 'happy' ending is particularly hard to gauge. When, in the conclusion, Springlove acquires Oldrents' wealthy family and an heiress to marry, the play's topics of marriage and money – and perhaps religion and liberty, too – seem to join together in a harmonious resolution. Yet they are confused by contradiction. Amy had thought she had chosen to marry the king of beggars; she has in fact chosen to marry a wealthy heir. The epilogue introduces yet more uncertainty. When Springlove, returned to beggardom, asks the audience to provide for the beggar-actors, he conflates the world of the audience, the players and the play's story. The beggars, reports Springlove, are 'under censure, till we do obtain / Your suffrages that we may beg again' (Epil.5–6) – yet the result of the audience's 'suffrage' will be merely to allow the story to return to its unhappy start on some future day. An end, rather than a solution, this passage will have been heart-breaking if spoken on the play's, and theatre's, final performance. Unable to assent to any further productions, the audience will not have been able to relieve the beggar-actors from censure at all. Perhaps the epilogue was written to make just that point. Either way, the play concludes by highlighting the issues that have filled the drama, rather than actually resolving them.

Naturally, critics are continually confused as to what Brome's conclusions are; hence their problem in evaluating the play. Brome's targets are more obvious than his views, a point Ira Clark makes forcefully (158). *Brome Online* suggests, using a cinematic analogy of 'montage', that Brome chose to explore varied points of view rather than fix on one particular point, because a contradictory spectrum expressed best what he felt, and allowed for a fuller range of understanding in the reader/ watcher (Cave *et al.*). This may be because Brome is offering a play in which absolutes are not the goal. It certainly seems to have been extremes that bothered him. The hospitality of Clack is a form of selfishness; the Fate or Providence governing the twists of the play turns out to be the Patrico; civilization is as corrupt as its opposite. Instead of projecting an impossible new society, or even criticizing an old one, Brome may be showing the good and bad in established society.

Then too, Brome had long been interested in the idea of 'reversal', where an upside-down world provided a way of revealing issues about its opposite. His play *The Antipodes* had depicted a world in which servants rule masters, women court men and gallants beg from beggars. *A Jovial Crew* may be another version of *Antipodes*: flouting convention, the play's bastard, Springlove, is a hero rather than a villain; flouting convention again, the daughters leave home not when they are poorly treated or hunting for lovers, but when they are content and have already found their love-matches. 'Reversal', in which the audience can see their priorities laughed at and can rethink as a result, might explain why the play is so taken with ambiguity and duality. And, as a play within the play is put on to cure the Joyless family in *Antipodes*, and another play within the play is put on to cure Oldrents of his grief as in *A Jovial Crew*, perhaps, in larger terms, *A Jovial Crew* is intended to 'cure' its audience of unhappiness through its depiction of a topsy-turvy world, rather than solve anything. Disenchanted with contemporary despair, Brome may simply have shrugged his shoulders and attempted to laugh his country into a better mood. If so, then his focus on reconciliation and forgiveness is delightful but poignant: Brome cannot offer suggestions as to how, outside the world of fiction, they can be brought about.

Language

A Jovial Crew seems to reflect a world where themes and values had become unclear, even at the level of language. Brome's adoption, in the play, of 'whim', a term coined by him for puns, homonyms and other forms of double-speak – as when a man is predicted a future as a thief, and ends up a lawyer (1.1.35–9) – shows how alert he was to tension between language and meaning. In this, Brome is probably reflecting the way larger linguistic 'truths' had, at that difficult time, become open to question – what 'king', 'beggar', 'gentleman' and 'common-wealth' actually mean in a time of crisis are issues the play sets out to explore; 'whim', where a phrase may imply its opposite, seems to relate to this.

Tellingly, in *A Jovial Crew*, the noise of happiness is a 'whim' of its own: it is almost interchangeable with the noise of sadness. The closeness between a shout of joy, 'a-hey' (used regularly by Clack), an invitation to dance, 'hey toss' (used by Springlove), a merry way of singing, 'hey down' or 'hey trolly lo' (both used by Hearty) and a sorrowful sigh, 'hey ho' (also used by Hearty), is continually observable; likewise, Rachel and Meriel's regular 'ha, ha, ha', is counterbalanced by Tallboy's 'ah', used to indicate crying, and Springlove's 'ah' shout of pain when he is beaten with the switch.

Yet Brome seems to have found solace in language too. Ambiguous about other issues, he appears to have been excited by English as a shared language uniting rich and poor. His focus, then, was not elevated and class-bound vocabulary, but the language of the common people – slang and, more specifically, cant.

Cant, the secret language of vagabonds, said to have come into being around 1530, had long been a strange source of national pride. As Richard Head wrote of the beggar, 'His language is always one and the same; the Northern speech differs from . . . South, Welch from the Cornish, but Canting is general, nor ever could be altered by Conquest of the Saxon, Dane, or Norman' (140). This special, created tongue was unpretentious, communal and joyful; Brome obviously relished it. Made up of onomatopoeia ('bleater' and 'grunter' for 'lamb' and 'pork'), slang ('stampers' for 'shoes'), popular argot ('to couch a hogshead' for 'to lie down and sleep') and Latinisms ('bene' for 'good'), cant was not really a language but a vocabulary battened onto English sentence structure; it could be taught in a single play. 'Here, safe in our skipper, let's cly off our peck / And bowse in defiance o'th'harman-beck' (2.2.179–80), for instance, means, 'Here, safe in our barn, let's seize our food / And drink in defiance of the constable': learn the nouns and a few verbs, and you have learned the 'language'. Part of cant's positive quality, indeed, comes from the fact that it is so easily acquired. Another part comes from the fact that, confined largely to words concerning food, drink and sex, cant is incapable of being over-political.

When the Victorian teacher T. C. Clough of Carlisle was given the task of reading volume three of Brome's collected works for the original *Oxford English Dictionary*, he turned to *A Jovial Crew* for its expansive and explanatory use of cant (PG). *OED* words he chose to illustrate from *A Jovial Crew* include a large quantity of known cant – 'bien', 'bing', 'bouse', 'bousing ken', 'canting', 'cassan', 'cly', 'couch a hogshead', 'cuffin', 'gan', etc. But he also found the play full of cant-like terms that were apparently coined by Brome – 'riddlemy riddle-mies', 'remore', 'stockant', 'whippant', 'bratling', 'catcher', 'crib', 'cribbing'. The play likewise promotes slang – in *OED* it illustrates words to do with games, sports and dances ('capering', 'clutterdepouch', 'fling', 'gambol'), and varieties of happiness ('crouse', 'lustick', 'merry', 'hey', 'hoigh', 'hoy'). Compound nouns, made from common words, a form Brome also favoured, make their way from *A Jovial Crew* into *OED*; they too are chatty and slangy – 'ape-leader', 'beer-bombard', 'beggar-sport', 'bride-barn', 'crupper-cramped', 'sheet-leaf', 'trencher-fee'. In all, *A Jovial Crew*, in *OED*[2] – the revised *OED* – is now used to illustrate 183 words, justifying Swinburne's sense that 'The text of Brome's plays . . . might supply the English dictionary with several rare and noticeable words' (507). It does so; but almost all the words it supplies are popular slang or cant.

This need to bolster language at its lower end differentiates Brome's writing from that of other playwrights. Jonson, too, had expanded language, but he had added to it 'literary' words, often coined from Latin. When Brome coins new cant words, he may be suggesting that society can profitably expand along its lower end: as perhaps can literature. Brome in *A Jovial Crew* seems to be locating Englishness and worth outside the pretentious or upper class, and back in the colloquial, unlearned English of the travelling vagrant.

Brome's cant, however, appears to be learned from books as much as – or rather than – from actual beggars. His language is, for instance, out of date in relation to the language of real vagabonds. 'Couch a hogshead' and even 'beggar-nigglers' are described by Samuel Rid in his *Martin Markall, Beadle of Bridewell* as outdated terms as early as 1610, though Thomas Dekker, probably Brome's source, is ignorant of this: he published them without comment in *The Bellman of London* (1608) and *Lantern and Candlelight* (1609). Brome's cant, then, pays homage to the kinds of texts he appreciated, and adds to them. 'Beggar', 'gypsy' or 'thief' plays (tellingly, the terms were used almost indistinguishably) were further sources. As Jonson and John Fletcher were mentors to Brome, and as the first wrote *Gypsies Metamorphosed*, and the second co-wrote *Beggars' Bush*, both featuring cant, these works in particular seem to have inspired Brome – he may have acquired from them, too, the sense that cant worked well as a poetic medium. Much of the cant in *A Jovial Crew* is in rhyme, though the beggars are talented enough to 'translate' with ease from one linguistic form into another – 'Now, bounteous sir, before you go, / Hear me, the beggar "patrico", / Or "priest", if you do rather choose / That we no word of canting use' (2.2.220–3).

A Jovial Crew champions the easy linguistic facility of the beggars against the linguistic limitations of the gentry. This is most apparent earlier on in the play, when the gentry are beholden to 1630s 'romance' themes and attendant language. After a night of sleeping rough with the beggars, the gentry greet one another in overblown and artificial fashion:

25

RACHEL

    ... Now you appear the glories of the spring,
    Darlings of Phoebus and the summer's heirs.

HILLIARD

    How fairer than fair Flora's self appear,
    To deck the spring, Diana's darlings dear!
    Oh, let us not, Actaeon-like, be strook –
    With greedy eyes while we presume to look
    On your half-nakedness, since courteous rags
    Cover the rest – into the shape of stags.

(3.1.100–7)

As the play has already illustrated, these sentiments are far from the real feelings of the lovers (Hilliard describes the women's actual appearances when he privately renames them 'Madam Fewclothes and my Lady Bonnyrag', 94–5).

Later, the young lovers show themselves incapable of embracing the lively language of beggars' cant, just as they are unable to fit in with the beggar lifestyle: 'I am a stranger in these parts', says Vincent in his attempt to beg, 'and destitute of means and apparel . . . Will you therefore be pleased, as you are worthy gentlemen and blessed with plenty . . . out of your abundant store, towards my relief in extreme necessity, to furnish me with a small parcel of money' (3.1.215–23). He then ridiculously begs to be given ten or twenty pounds for some fine clothes (when, as the play has already explained, the life savings of the servant Randall had been a mere forty pounds). Ultimately, the young gentry are reduced to repeating endlessly the one 'begging' phrase they have been able to learn, the cant-free 'duly and truly pray for you'. Their inability to speak outside a courtly register, let alone learn cant, reveals that they cannot understand those who do: out of their own contexts, they are naive and foolish. Through the gentlefolk, in particular, Brome is able to mock two things – plays in which young people talk in courtly fashion (a literary point) and courtiers and their way of speaking and acting (a social point). As courtiers wrote romance plays, however, the one critique easily gave way to the other; indeed, that was one of Brome's points.

Brome had long despised a particular kind of theatrical writing, which he described as 'Flourishes of Art' ('To . . . Hastings, Deceased', 75). He regularly poked fun at plays that used Latinate or intentionally obscure words, aimed at showing the brilliance of the writer rather than being explicable. Thus Pate, in *Northern Lass*, exclaims 'what big words and terrible action he has!' (sig. B4ᵛ). Taking up this battle, Alexander Brome, Richard Brome's first editor, draws attention to the way Brome eschewed words that were Latinate and long, and opted instead for explicability:

> No stradling Tetrasyllables are brought
> To fill up room, and little spell, or nought.
> No Bumbast Raptures, and no lines immense,
> That's call'd (by th' curtesie of *England*) sence.
> But all's so plaine, that one may see, he made it
> T' inform the understanding, not invade it.

> (*Five New*, 1653, sig. A3ʳ)

The kinds of plays that adopted syllable-rich, Latinate language tended to be written not by professional playwrights but by courtiers or courtly hangers-on. Their productions, generally self-financed, or even financed with help from the King, were as lavish with scenery as they were with words. Worryingly, they sometimes transferred from court to the professional theatre, where they threatened the simpler productions of professional playwrights (see pp. 283–6). Financially threatened, Brome, in *Court Beggar* ironically suggests to the professional theatre, only too ready to accept free amateur plays,

> that no Playes may be admitted to the Stage, but of their making who Professe or indeavour to live by the quality: That no Courtiers, Divines, Students at Law,

27

Lawyers-clearks, Tradesmen or Prentises be allow'd to
write 'em, nor the Works of any lay-Poet whatsoever
. . . be receav'd to the Stage, though freely given unto
the Actors, nay though any such Poet should give a
summe of money with his Play

(sig. P4ʳ)

Two courtier poets were particularly responsible for the
spectacular and wordy plays Brome loathed. One was a 'son of
Ben' (one of Jonson's adopted literary heirs), metaphorically,
and claimed to be literally the son of Shakespeare: William
Davenant. The other was in the 'tribe of Ben' – a group that
followed Jonson's lead, but had not been formally taken on by
him – Sir John Suckling (see Steggle, *Wars*, 114–17).

Davenant, in 1639, had had a petition granted to raise a
theatre 'to exercise action, musical presentments, Scenes,
Dancing and the like' – in other words, a theatre dedicated to
the performance of the romance dramas, descendants of the
masque, that Brome so disliked (Rymer, 378). Though it was
never actually built, the projected new theatre would have
further threatened the livelihood of Brome and his fellow
professionals. But Brome disliked Davenant for another reason
too: in 1638, Davenant had acquired the title 'poet laureate',
formerly held by Jonson. Brome was outraged at the suggestion
that the two might be equivalent, as well as somewhat jealous:
when, in *Damoiselle*, he declares that he 'won't be calld /
Author, or Poet), nor beg to be installd / Sir *Lawreat*)' (sig.
A2ʳ), he is making a pointed dig at Davenant; when, in *A Jovial
Crew*, he has Scribble, the beggar-poet and author of the
beggars' 'revels', described as 'poet laureate' (4.2.150), he
indicates that Davenant is a beggar equivalent, reducing his
grand masques to beggar displays (Freehafer, 381).

Suckling annoyed Brome for similar reasons. He wrote a
romance drama, *Aglaura*, which was performed first at court
and then, in 1638, transferred to the Blackfriars playhouse

replete with costumes fringed with genuine gold and silver lace. Suckling, who did not need money from playwriting, had mounted *Aglaura* at his own expense. He compounded his sins by then subsidizing the publication of *Aglaura* so that it could be printed in folio size, incensing Brome with his grandiose pretensions on page as well as stage. 'Never did I see', wrote Brome of the folio text, 'So little in so much' ('Upon *Aglaura*').

As a final straw, while *A Jovial Crew* was being written, Davenant was offering the King help in the First Bishops' War, while Suckling was gathering an army to help with the fighting. Brome, sometime between around 1637 and 1640, penned *The English Moor*, which argues that playwrights who aim at political advancement are bad writers. Seemingly directing his criticism at Davenant and Suckling, he places himself above those who:

> in this latter age
> Have sown such pleasing errors on the stage,
> Which he no more will chuse to imitate
> Then they to fly from truth, and run the State.

> (F5^v)

Hardly surprisingly, the language and style that is most parodied in *A Jovial Crew* is also that of the romance plays mounted by Davenant and Suckling. *A Jovial Crew*'s prologue harps upon romances, describing them as obsessed with lovers who decide to wander but are finally rescued by 'stout chivalry' (Prol.11). Ending as foolishly as they began, 'some impossibility / Concludes all strife and makes a comedy' (13–14). Here Brome seems to point an accusing finger at Davenant's *Distresses* (1639) in particular, which describes itself as being full of 'romance humor' and as illustrating the 'romance way' (*Works*, sig. 4h3^{r-v}).

In a surprising volte-face, Brome then asserts that he has been obliged to capitulate to popular taste and that *A Jovial*

Crew will give the audience precisely what it wants: a standard court-style romance drama filled with those very wanderers, lovers and chivalric episodes he despised. But Brome's actual play, though it superficially resembles a romance, subtly moves into romantic parody: its dances are beggar dances; its clothes are rags. With its use of courtly language for ridicule, it undoes what it putatively does, denigrating everything that smacks of the 'courtier' and his writing: 'I . . . cannot cringe nor court with the powdered and ribboned wits of our days', writes Brome pointedly in his dedication (p. 74; 26–7). The play is his attempt to situate himself, linguistically, socially and in literary terms, firmly on the side of the beggar – while seeming to be on the side of the courtier.

SOURCES

Jonson

A Jovial Crew often does not appear to be quite of its time – and that is not only because it is reacting against the prevailing romantic form of drama. It also harks strongly back to plays by Ben Jonson, though written some time after his death. The reason for the close connection between the men's styles is that Brome had been Jonson's servant and playwriting apprentice in his youth (see pp. 280–1). So *A Jovial Crew*'s Jonsonian echoes are acts of homage that proudly maintain the connection between the two men.

The content of *A Jovial Crew* recalls, in particular, Jonson's masque *The Gypsies Metamorphosed*, which had been performed in 1621. Featuring a band of gypsies who sing in cant and offer an alternative community to England's monarchical one, the masque glorified and exoticized vagabond life. But as a production paid for by George Villiers, Duke of Buckingham, and performed three times – including once at Windsor Castle – *Gypsies Metamorphosed* had been played by a mixture of noblemen and professional actors; Buckingham even had a speaking part in which he was able to address the King directly. Thus *Gypsies Metamorphosed* had also been a reflection of Jonson's ironic view of court life, since it represented the lowest members of society as literally identical with the highest. Brome seems to have picked up on both the content and mood of *Gypsies Metamorphosed*. Much of his play is angled towards illustrating the lack of distinction between gentlemen and beggars. In *A Jovial Crew* the beggars are courtly enough to have a beggar king and to prepare a play using their own master of the revels and poet laureate; 'a courtier', conversely, is described as 'a great court beggar' (1.1.426–7), and gibes are made about courtiers who beg '*by covetise, not need*' (429). *A Jovial Crew* is, on one level, a reprisal of or homage to Jonson's *Gypsies Metamorphosed*.

Brome also used other Jonson texts to provide plot moments for *A Jovial Crew*. He had internalized many of his master's plays, as his repeated references show. *The Staple of News* (performed 1625) contains a moment in which Pennyboy Senior, while disguised, 'predicts' to his son that a beggar's future awaits, just as the Patrico/fortune-teller's predictions of beggary set in motion the plot of *A Jovial Crew*. Jonson's play, too, features well-born people who dress as beggars, and may further have fed Brome's obsession with the relationship between courtiers and their opposites. Jonson's *A Tale of a Tub* (performed 1633) meanwhile, seems to have suggested the ending of *A Jovial Crew*. Both plays conclude with an entertainment, the title of which reflects the title of the larger play: *A Tale of a Tub*'s masque is called *A Tale of a Tub*; *A Jovial Crew*'s internal play is named after the play's subtitle, *The Merry Beggars*. In both, the play within the play retells and explains aspects of the larger play itself while, of course, metatheatrically raising questions about performance and reality.

Other plot moments in *A Jovial Crew* seem to relate to Jonson's *Every Man In his Humour* (performed 1598). In both

31

plays, one man is a single catalyst for the plot – Brainworm in *Every Man In*, Springlove in *A Jovial Crew*; in both, the conclusion involves a revelation of a complicated back story, a reconciliation and a moment where reasons and solutions are offered for the events that have been staged (Crowther, 133).

Plot aside, Brome also echoed Jonson in his characterization. Jonson had created characters who were victims of their 'humours' and had quirks that expressed which of the four elements, blood, black bile, yellow bile and phlegm, was driving them. Brome did the same: 'In imitation of his Master Mr. *Johnson*, he studied Men and Humor, more than Books', wrote Langbaine (35). As names in *A Jovial Crew* illustrate, Hearty is sanguine, as is Springlove (spring was traditionally associated with sanguinity). Other characters display their humours in their actions: Tallboy, who weeps all the time, is melancholic; Clack, an irritable bully and monomaniac, is choleric; Oldrents' real melancholy breaks through his phoney sanguinity. Some of these characters seem to have direct parallels in Jonsonian plays. For example, Hearty is, on one level, a parasite, as it were a genial version of Fly in *The New Inn*; Clack is an 'unjust justice' in the mould of Justice Overdo in *Bartholomew Fair*.

A Jovial Crew even adopts Jonsonian linguistic quirks. Brome attaches fixed phrases to certain characters. Clack is obsessed by 'as I said before' and 'that is to say', and Tallboy by 'd'ye see', as shorthand for their repetitive natures and habits of speaking over their interlocutors. Tallboy's phrase, in particular, shows him to be inarticulate either on a romance or cant level – he is as linguistically challenged as he is intellectually and emotionally. Clack's phrases show that he is otiose and unable to form arguments and so lacks all the essential skills to be a good justice – he is even named after his irritatingly clacking or 'chattering' tongue. Both men are, then, reminiscent of Touchstone, who, in *Eastward Ho*, by Jonson and others, repeatedly says, 'work upon that now', though

32

Clack's refusal to listen to anyone else also recalls Morose in Jonson's *Epicoene, or the Silent Woman* (1609), whose servants have to convey information to him through gesture. Jokes such as these serve as shorthand for characterization, and suggest that people are manifestations of definable humours.

Since Jonson's plays had all been (re)published in his *Works* of 1640–1, they were enjoying a new wave of popularity at the time when Brome was writing *A Jovial Crew*. As well as remembering the techniques Jonson had taught him in the past, Brome may have had a Jonson folio to hand as he wrote.

Elizabethan literature

In view of his training under Jonson, it was natural for Brome to have inherited a nostalgia for earlier, pre-Caroline literature. Indeed, he went to some effort to identify his style with that of the stars of the Elizabethan period, and repeatedly asked to be viewed in their light, rather than judged against the writers of his time. In the prologue to *Court Beggar*, he identified his drama with the plays of yesteryear 'writ / By our great Masters of the Stage and Wit' (sig. N4^v); in the epilogue to *English Moor* he asked the audience to 'judge' his work 'by the antient Comick Lawes' (F5^v). In the prologue to *Antipodes* he recalled that 'The *Poets* late sublimed from our Age ... Did well approve, and lead ... this humble way' in which he was now writing (sig. A3^v).

It is his Elizabethan interests that have sometimes made Brome seem a conservative writer, obsessed with preserving and reproducing Tudor literature and, through it, Tudor values (Kaufmann, 3). Parrott and Ball write that 'Brome's success ... was due to his diligence in following an established and acceptable formula ... and his ingenuity in varying the pattern' (174). And indeed, when Hilliard and Vincent determine, in *A Jovial Crew*, to become 'beggar-errants' – comic reworkings of romantic 'knight-errants' – they seem to be gesturing towards chivalric tales such as Edmund Spenser's *Faerie Queene*

(1590–6), an idea highlighted when Oldrents' house is described as being 'as fortunate a house for servants as ever was built upon fairy-ground' (4.1.194–5). But of course the parallels are there, too, to point the differences between Elizabethan and Caroline writing and times. Spenser had written in an age when England felt secure politically and when literature was expanding and developing. Brome was writing in an age when England felt insecure and when contemporary dramatic romances were trivializing all that pastoral had stood for.

Jacobean and Caroline literature

Brome had great respect for his professional playwriting forebears. That, too, is reflected in *A Jovial Crew*. Francis Beaumont and John Fletcher's *Beggars' Bush* of 1622 concerns a beggar community that lives in a commonwealth of its own, has its own respected overlord or king, keeps its own laws, speaks cant and expresses 'freedom' through song. It also contains disguised nobles who temporarily become part of the 'crew', a complicated father and son relationship, a heroine who runs away and is pursued by a search party, a merry friend and a benevolent aristocracy. So similar, indeed, are *Beggars' Bush* and *A Jovial Crew* in design that when *Beggars' Bush* was revived in the nineteenth century it was viewed as an imitation of *A Jovial Crew* (rather than the other way round): 'The resemblance which part of the plot bears to that of *The Jovial Crew* . . . [has] not the effect of novelty, as the frequent representations of [*A Jovial Crew*] put that out of the power of ingenuity' (*Morning Post*, 15 December 1815).

The Spanish Gypsy, a collaboration of 1623 by Thomas Middleton, William Rowley, Thomas Dekker and John Ford, also resembles *Beggars' Bush*, which resembles *Gypsies Metamorphosed*. *A Jovial Crew* also borrows from this play. *Spanish Gypsy* features a lost child whose parentage is revealed after a play is put on, and a religious relic (a crucifix) which provides final identification. Even some characters in *Spanish Gypsy* have counterparts in *A Jovial Crew*. Sancho, the unlucky and foolish lover, is like Tallboy; Roderigo, the licentious young man, is like Oliver; Fernando de Azevedo, who, in the play mounted in *Spanish Gypsy*, recognizes his son Roderigo as one of the gypsy players, resembles Oldrents, who recognizes his own children in the play *The Merry Beggars*.

As it is a late contribution to the school of rogue plays, *A Jovial Crew* calls, too, upon other early modern plays that explored alternative commonwealths – though it may relate to them at one remove, as all such plays borrowed heavily from one another. For example, Middleton's *More Dissemblers Besides Women* (performed *c.* 1619), which contains a woman who joins the gypsies in order to escape a marriage, may have inspired *A Jovial Crew*'s Amy subplot. Certainly Brome's preoccupation with beggars, freedom and cant belonged not so much to the 1640s, when *A Jovial Crew* was staged, but to the 1620s and earlier – though revisiting ideas about alternative commonwealths in the atmosphere of the politically troubled 1640s gave them a very different aspect.

Professional contemporaries

The contemporaries who influenced Brome positively were his fellow professionals and friends. In Beaumont's *Knight of the Burning Pestle* (performed in 1607, but revived in the 1630s by Beeston's Boys), the cheerful spendthrift Merrythought exhibits constant merriment expressed through singing. He seems to be the model for Hearty, who does much the same thing, while Humphrey, the wealthy idiot in Beaumont's play who loses Luce to Jasper, may have contributed to the characterization of Tallboy.

James Shirley, writing for the King's Men, shared Brome's nostalgia for a better past, and likewise despised the direction playwriting was taking. Depending on dating, Shirley's *Sisters* (performed in 1642) may have influenced *A Jovial Crew* or vice versa: both plays present an alternative commonwealth and a

series of aristocrats and vagabonds (Steggle, 'Redating', 368).
Another play, hard to date, either picks up on *A Jovial Crew* or,
again, influences it: *The Humorous Magistrate*, an anonymous
manuscript play that may even be by Brome, has a prologue
and epilogue expressing concerns much like those of *A Jovial
Crew*; the play also stages a corrupt judge, Thrifty, who, like
Justice Clack with his incessant 'as I said before', constantly
repeats the words 'as I told you before' (Polito and Windle).

The most pervasive contemporary influence on Brome is
certainly himself – his own plays and, behind them, his own
life, are crucial to the development of *A Jovial Crew*. As has
long been recognized, ultimately 'His Plots were his own, and
he forg'd all his various Characters from the Mint of his own
Experience, and Judgment' (Langbaine, 35). Distrusting many
modern playwrights, it was to his bank of previous plays that
Brome seems to have turned for inspiration. So like the heroes
of his *City Wit* (*c.* 1629–32), those in *A Jovial Crew* take on
pretended roles in an attempt to change their situations; like
Dryground and Brookall in Brome's *Damoiselle* (*c.* 1638),
Oldrents considers the way seduction has brought about a curse
and attendant poverty; like Justice Squelch in *Northern Lass*
(1629), Oldrents is absent and the servants have to promise his
speedy return; like Torchwood in *Sparagus Garden* (1635),
Oldrents had an illegitimate son in his youth. *Court Beggar*
(*c.* 1640) is recalled throughout *A Jovial Crew*, from its title,
which maintains that courtiers are beggars (and vice versa)
onwards. Perhaps that is little more than to say that Brome
plays sound like Brome plays – except that at the time of
writing *A Jovial Crew* Brome will have been conscious that
this play was likely to be his last, because the political situation
was so ominous. *A Jovial Crew* can be seen as a summation
of everything Brome most admired in earlier literature, a
rejection of everything he most hated in contemporary
literature and perhaps, too, a summative farewell to his own
playwriting.

PERFORMANCE

The company and theatre

In 1635 Brome had become house dramatist for the Salisbury Court theatre, penning plays for both the King's Revels Company and Queen Henrietta's Men as they sojourned there. His Salisbury Court contract demanded that he write three plays a year exclusively for that theatre, a task he never quite managed. In April 1639, according to a 1640 Requests Proceedings Document filed on 12 February 1640, he left Salisbury Court in favour of its rivals, Beeston's Boys, or 'the King and Queen's Young Company' as they were formally known (see Haaker, 'Plague'; Collins). This was a company that had been set up by Christopher Beeston and was in the process of being taken over by his son, William Beeston. It was the company for which Brome wrote *A Jovial Crew*.

While writing for his new company, Beeston's Boys, Brome was beleaguered by Salisbury Court. His financial future was in jeopardy as he fought his old employers against a charge of breach of contract. So in the early 1640s, while completing *A Jovial Crew*, Brome was fending off attack from erstwhile colleagues.

His new company affiliation was equally problematic, however. Soon after his arrival, Beeston's Boys performed a new, unlicensed play that touched upon 'passages of the K[ing']s journey into the Northe'; it infuriated Charles I and, consequently, Henry Herbert, Master of the Revels. Brome's friend and new employer, William Beeston, was imprisoned on 5 May 1640 as a result of this unfortunate violation of Charles's sensibilities and the licensing rules. Though legal documents do not name the offending play, it is often thought to have been Brome's *Court Beggar*, which specifically refers to the King's northern journey while alluding negatively to the political and theatrical ambitions of Suckling and Davenant, writers and

37

politicians the King respected (Freehafer; Steggle, *Brome*, 156). Whether or not Beeston's imprisonment was directly Brome's fault, its result was devastating. The new temporary manager imposed on the company was, of all people, Davenant, the man whose dramas and ambitions had so long been the focus of Brome's anger.

By 1640, then, Brome had abandoned a previous employer, may have caused his new employer and friend to be imprisoned, and was attached to a company in the hands of a man he despised. When he started writing *A Jovial Crew*, he was probably as concerned about his personal situation as he was about the country's.

Though Davenant's exposure in an army plot in 1641 ultimately led to his house arrest, allowing William Beeston to be reappointed as manager of the company, Brome would not have known, while penning *A Jovial Crew*, under whose governance the play would be performed. *A Jovial Crew*'s appearance of being written in the romantic mould of Davenant's plays makes it seem on one level to be an apology for the troublesome *Court Beggar*. Yet, as has been discussed, it is really an anti-romance and thus a continued attack on the plays Davenant valued. Indeed, a moment of self-justification even breaks out at the play's conclusion when Oldrents reprises *Court Beggar*'s point, agreeing that Springlove should beg no more 'Except it be at court' (5.1.562). The company's situation may have shaped this drama more profoundly than has been recognized.

The theatre for which the play was destined will have had an effect too. Beeston's company performed at a playhouse initially called the Cockpit and built, in 1616, out of a venue for cockfighting whose semi-circular shape it may have kept. That theatre, however, had been damaged by rioting and fire shortly after its construction; it had been rebuilt in 1617, possibly to fit the old footprint of the Cockpit, and had been renamed the Phoenix. It was regularly known thereafter by both names:

repeated bird references in a Cockpit/Phoenix play, such as to the nightingale, cuckoo and other birds that herald spring in *A Jovial Crew*, are therefore, metatheatrical; when they are praised in the play, so is the theatre that houses them. Yet Brome's preference for calling his theatre by its older name, the Cockpit – the play's title-page declares, 'Presented in a COMEDIE, AT The Cock-pit' – may suggest that he particularly enjoyed the *frisson* of the fighting overtones that survived in the earlier designation.

The Cockpit/Phoenix had been built as the indoor substitute for the popular outdoor theatre, the Red Bull, where the company had previously performed; it was, like the Blackfriars playhouse (the King's Men's indoor substitute for the outdoor Globe), more expensive than its outdoor counterpart. It likewise anticipated a grander audience than that at its previous theatre, and proudly used the possibilities to which indoor theatre gave rise, including complex stage-effects and regular musical scenes and interludes. Thought to have been of the 'same shape and size as Blackfriars (which was a rectangle 66′ × 46′) and Salisbury Court Playhouse' (Berry, 629) or even smaller (Gurr, 164), it will have been made of brick and tiled, as recent Jacobean building proclamations had demanded (Orrell, *Human*, 43). Perhaps something of its décor can be guessed at. John Orrell suggested that pictures and plans for a theatre found in Worcester College Library, Oxford, were Inigo Jones's designs for the Cockpit itself ('Inigo'). These architectural drawings have since been reattributed to Jones's pupil John Webb, but they may nevertheless hint at what indoor theatres looked like from the late Jacobean period onward (Teague, 244). Jones had gone to Italy in 1613–14 and the 'English Palladianism' he developed as a result of what he had seen there was imitated by other architects, Webb in particular. The rebuilt Cockpit/Phoenix, whether designed by Jones, Webb or someone else, is likely to have been in Jones's late, pseudo-Palladian style. The play's suggestion that the stage of the Cockpit/Phoenix was spacious, though its dimensions seem to have been the same as those of other theatres, perhaps relate to this – Palladian-style structures, with their reduced ornamentation and light-coloured walls, gave the impression of greater space and, with their reduced clutter, could house more dramatic activity.

The staging required by *A Jovial Crew* is a spacious area for acting. 'Revelation' of entire tableaux scenes is used twice, suggesting that the stage had a prominent central discovery place or offered a grandiose means of hiding and revealing large groups through moving scenery. Either alternative would have enabled first Randall and then Springlove to show a host of beggars in fixed postures, creating a scene poised and posed like a work of art. As the beggars relax into a sizeable band of singer/dancers who then perform on the open stage, the staging makes one art form give way to another, so that *A Jovial Crew* becomes as visual and kinetic as it is verbal and musical.

The stage also had a sizeable area 'within' from which the many actors could emanate and from which sounds were easily audible: in the play the beggars are heard singing before they are seen, and 'birdsong' several times disrupts the speaking, refocusing attention onto what is out of sight and suggesting a drama haunted by the uncontrolled/uncontrollable whims of nature or fate. However, the play lacks directions for activity to take place 'above'. That, too, may be telling, given when *A Jovial Crew* was first performed. This is a play in which supernatural possibilities are repeatedly denied.

Composition and production

A Jovial Crew opened, according to G. E. Bentley, on 25 April 1641 'or thereabouts' (3.71). This mixture of precision and vagueness relates to external and internal evidence. Though the title-page maintains that the 'comedie' was put on 'at The Cock-pit in Drury-Lane, in the yeer 1641', it is unclear whether or not the playbook is using the civic calendar, in which the 'new year' began on Lady Day, 25 March, or the calendar year.

Thus the first performance could have taken place at any time between (new style) 1 January 1641 and 24 March 1642. Moreover, though the play itself refers to events taking place on what is in fact 24 April – Springlove's accounts are presented, he says, thirty days after Lady Day – there is no obvious reason to take the day and month when the play was set as a guide to first performance. Rather, as the theatres closed for plague from 5 August to 26/27 November 1641, the play is likely to have been first put on in the last five months before the banning of theatre (perhaps around the time that Shirley's *Sisters* was licensed by Henry Herbert – April 1642), which would explain its political topicality (Steggle, 'Redating', 367–8).

Probably before *A Jovial Crew* was fully written, it was obvious that theatres were going to be suppressed by Parliament. *A Jovial Crew* was the play selected for Beeston's Boys' final performance, heralding what was to become an eighteen-year closure of the theatres. Hence Brome's boast, in the dedication written for the play's publication in 1652, that his play was the 'last . . . in the epidemical ruin of the scene' (see p. 74; 31–2). Its final performance, on 2 September 1642, was, then, also the Cockpit/Phoenix's farewell to the stage, the audience, peace and the undivided country. That this affected the production itself is evident: the play showcases all the men and boys of the company, probably as Beeston's Boys' grand final gesture. *A Jovial Crew* has thirty speaking roles, introduces new major characters towards the end and fills the stage with aural and visual delights – dances, songs, music and tableaux. In Acts 1, 2 and 5, characters have overlapping entrances and exits, uniting the play 'into one panoramic picture', ensuring that the stage is continually occupied and making doubling almost impossible – especially as the conclusion requires almost all the characters to be onstage at once (Allen, 50). The players can therefore, to a man (and boy), show their range of skills before leaving the stage for a farewell that, as it turned out, lasted until 1660.

41

The company being so promoted, Beeston's Boys, consisted largely of teenage players, but also contained some adult men: the purpose of the company had been to train players from minority to adulthood. Brome will have been familiar with the prodigious talents of the boys Ezekiel Fenn, Nicholas Burt, Robert Cox, Edward Davenport, John Lacy, Samuel Mannery, Michael Mohun, Robert Shatterell, William Trigg and John Wright amongst others (Bentley, 1.324–36). *A Jovial Crew*, however, makes a point of highlighting the number of beguiling boy players in the company, demanding, amongst its leads, three separate young couples, all at a sexual threshold. It also requires additional groups of talented boys who, as beggars, can hold postures, sing and dance, illustrating the visual and oral talents of the company.

The play makes equally large requests of its adult players. The mature actors, who when Brome joined the company will have included William Beeston himself, as well as Robert Axen, Theophilus Bird, Edward Gibbes, John Page and George Stutville, were needed to play the older roles, including Oldrents, Hearty, Clack and the Patrico (Bentley, 1.324–36). Most, too, are asked to sing; they also have constantly to veer between the two extremes, happiness and sorrow, as company and country were also doing.

As a means of exhibiting both junior and adult talents, the play employs telling boy/adult exchanges; boy players at the end of *A Jovial Crew* even have to imitate the adult players who opened the play; in *The Merry Beggars* an alternative Oldrents (the beggar-lawyer) reprises the start of the play with an alternative Hearty (the beggar-soldier). Towards the end, in a dialogue between Clack, presumably performed by an adult, and Martin, presumably performed by a youth, Brome exploits cueing possibilities, suggesting actors well versed in the complex techniques demanded by actors' parts. At one point, the player of Martin will, when conversing with Justice Clack, have been listening for the phrase Clack repeats so often, 'as I said before'. His part, on which, as was usual, only lines and cues were provided, will probably have looked something like this at 5.1.14–15, assuming a cue of four words or fewer:

———————————— [as] [I] [said] before

Mine intent, sir, and my only way –

But Clack actually speaks the words 'as I said before' more than once:

> CLACK . . . You have it. Provided, I say, **as I said before**, that she be safe, that is to say, uncorrupted, undefiled, that is to say – **as I said before**.
>
> MARTIN Mine intent, sir, and my only way –
>
> CLACK Nay, if we both speak together, how shall we hear one another? **As I said before**. Your intent, and your only way, you would ha' said, was to run away with her

(5.1.11–19)

Brome appears to be making use of a well-worn theatrical device, the 'premature cue' (Palfrey and Stern, ch. 6). If Martin starts to respond each time he hears the cue, that makes sense both of Clack's 'Nay, if we both speak together, how shall we hear one another?' and his 'Your intent, and your only way, you would ha' said'. Likewise Sentwell's part at 5.1.52–3 will have looked something like this:

———————————— [That] [is] [to] say –

True, Sir Oliver, I found her –

But, again, this is a 'premature cue':

> CLACK **That is to say**, you have found my niece among the beggars. **That is to say** –
>
> SENTWELL True, Sir Oliver, I found her –
>
> CLACK Now if we both speak together, who shall hear one another?

(5.1.51–5)

If Sentwell responds each time he hears the cue, he too will bring about the riposte, 'if we both speak together, who shall hear one another?' As it seems, whenever Clack accuses other characters of speaking on top of him, the text makes sure that that happens. This display of part techniques shows that Brome was writing for a company knowledgeable about and trusting of one another's acting; by so doing, he is also mourning their cessation.

The play's conflicts are laid open in the performance of the inner play, for that piece of metatheatre questions the purpose of this play, and theatre, altogether. As the many names the beggars propose for the plays they could put on – *The Two Lost Daughters, The Vagrant Steward, The Old Squire and the Fortune-Teller, The Beggar's Prophecy* – indicate only one story under its many titles, Oldrents' life emerges as the subject both of the play within the play and of the actual play. Oldrents rejects titles that he perceives as reflecting on his own life, failing to realize that they all do. At this moment, we realize that even the full title of Brome's play, *A Jovial Crew, or The Merry Beggars*, is metatheatrical, merging inner and outer play: unlike us, however, Oldrents does not know that *The Merry Beggars* is the subtitle of *A Jovial Crew*. So the inner play is both an encapsulation or miniature of *A Jovial Crew* and a reading of it. Just as the gentry in the play are play-acting at being beggars, so the beggars put on a play in which they play-act at being gentry; indeed, they play-act at being the very people who are present with them. By the end of *A Jovial Crew* the audience has seen actors who are playing at being gentry who are playing at being beggars who are playing at being actors – putting on a play very like the one we are watching. As actors were always in danger of being labelled 'Rogues, Vagabonds, and Sturdy Beggars' (see 1.1.191n.), Brome had probably long felt a particular association with the beggar community – but at this moment in the drama he extends that association to everyone. Gentry and beggars, actors and audience, may be one and the same thing – an important point for a play that was introducing the end of theatre.

PUBLICATION

Publication and allusions

One of the most important publication facts about *A Jovial Crew* is that it was printed in 1652, ten years after its first performance and three years after the King had been beheaded. When the play was performed, and when its surrounding paratext, created for publication, was written, are quite different matters.

In 1651, a year before *A Jovial Crew* was published, Samuel Sheppard, the writer of the Royalist pamphlets *Mercurius Pragmaticus*, had put out a short tract in play form: *The Jovial Crew, or, the Devil turned Ranter*. The pamphlet provides a 1650s take on Brome's play: its title may reflect knowledge that *A Jovial Crew* was about to be published, or may have helped bring that about. It is a tale of two wives who, like Brome's young gentlefolk, are tempted by a merry, musical, alternative society, in this case, the Ranters. 'Come away,' sing the Ranters, 'make no delay, of mirth we are no scanters, / Dance and sing all in a Ring, for we are Joviall Ranters' (sig. A3^r). The frontispiece of Sheppard's tract, however, is a picture of a devil riding his chariot through a map of the British isles; the Ranters are scions of the devil (see Fig. 1). Yet Sheppard's Ranters, like Brome's beggars, consist of people from different walks of life – a Scholar, a Painter, an Apothecary, a Tailor, a Soldier and a Gentleman – all of whom have chosen to join an alternative society; like the beggars, they are constantly merry, share their property and enjoy regular bouts of drink and sex:

The *Prologue*.

Bedlam broke loofe? yes, *Hell* is open'd too:
Mad-men, & *Fiends*, & *Harpies* to your view
VV'e do prefent: but who fhall cure the *Tumor?*
All the world now is in the *Ranting Humor.*

1 Frontispiece to S. Sheppard, *The Jovial Crew, or, The Devil turned Ranter*
(1651)

> our women are all in common.
> We drink quite drunk together, share our Oaths,
> If one man's cloak be rent, all tear their Cloaths.

(sigs B4ᵛ–C1ʳ)

The difference is that Sheppard condemns what Brome admired;
in the text itself, the devil, who has a speaking part, goes on
to explain how he has 'blinded [the Ranters] with pleasures of
this world, by putting on a mask of Religion to make't no

sin' (sig. A2ᵛ). In Sheppard's tract, then, the Ranters have lost their moral core as much as have the women who run away with them. But parallels between the two plays are striking. If the tract's Ranters are spendthrift and morally bankrupt, so, by implication, are Brome's beggars. Despite the fact that the pamphlet critiques its alternative society, its point that England was filled with 'other' commonwealths, and that the general populace was disaffected enough to want to run away from home, not only lifts themes from Brome: it suggests, by the 1650s, their likelihood in a disintegrating country.

Brome's own *A Jovial Crew*, finally published after this tract, may, then, have come into print bolstered or questioned by its connection to Sheppard's demonic take on alternative societies. It certainly confronts head on the theme of the 'other' communities in contemporary England. In his 1652 dedication to '*To the right noble . . . Thomas Stanley*' (see pp. 73–5), Brome observes that 'the times conspire to make us all beggars' (34–5), addressing the way what had seemed a fiction when the play was first performed had actually happened by the 1650s: a real alternative society, with its poverty and depression, had taken over the country. Conflating his own case not just with that of beggars in general, whom he calls his 'brethren', but with the very beggars he had fictionalized, whom he titles 'harmless', and with whom he desires to share lodging in the barns and sheds of his dedicatee's thoughts, Brome differentiates his play from Sheppard's pamphlet (17–18, 37–8): Sheppard had picked up a structure from Brome's decade-old drama and used it as a threat; in his dedication Brome picked up that same structure and turned it into a statement.

As these comments show, *A Jovial Crew*'s dedication reflects Brome's new, 1650s view on publication, historical events and himself. For though Brome somewhat disappears from record after the performance of *A Jovial Crew* – what he did and where he went during the Civil War is unclear – he kept on writing. He may have written the play *Time's Distractions*; he certainly

47

wrote some poetry. His last surviving piece of writing, however, is his dedication to *A Jovial Crew* (see pp. 73–5). As it was penned shortly before he died in Charterhouse hospital, also in 1652 (Evans), the dedication conflates his age, his farewell, his fiction and his beggarly status; in it, Brome reminds readers both that he is, as he put it, 'proud', and that he is ending his life as he started it, humbly (15). Opening on what is effectively Brome's farewell, it is a retrospective of life, theatre and the country, from the hospital bed of a dying man.

Various elements of the play's paratext – dedication, dedicatory poems, etc., by him and his supporters (see pp. 73–85) – also touch upon general 1650s concerns. They bemoan the fact that the theatres have long been closed, and that plays consequently all belong to the page. Brome's dedication refers to 'the . . . ruin of the scene' (31–2), and is an extension of a regretful statement he had made in 1647: that 'the Stage; /. . . nothing now presents unto the Eye, / But in Dumb-shews her own sad Tragedy' ('To the memory', sig. g1ʳ). Alexander Brome's commendatory poem headed '*To Master Richard Brome, upon his Comedy*' equally mourns the fact that 'we've lost [the stage's] dress', and suggests that the publication of this play allows us 'To see and think on th'happiness we had' (41–2). So *A Jovial Crew*, in paratext, as well as in the very fact of its existence, provides a wistful reminder of pre-war entertainments.

The paratext also fights Brome's literary battles. Brome had long had strong views about the nature of commendatory poems, how many there should be and what relationship they should bear to the work they herald. In the past he had attacked the publication of Coryate's *Works* because its had garnered enough commendatory poems to be sold as a separate book ('the Witty Coppies tooke / Of his Encomiums made themselves a Booke'), and he had declared himself door-keeper to the 1647 Beaumont and Fletcher *Comedies and Tragedies*, with the job of keeping out vain authors of commendations, writing just for self-promotion ('To the memory', sig. g1ʳ). Thus his friends' inveighing, in their affectionate commendations to *A Jovial Crew*, against unnecessary commendatory poems, is at his suggestion, or on his behalf. They repeatedly attack Cartwright's *Comedies*, just published in 1651, because it was flanked with, in some editions, fifty-two commendatory verses, in others, fifty-three: 'I do know there comes / A shoal, with regiments of encomiums / . . . whose astronomy / Can calculate a praise to fifty-three', writes 'J. B.' (7–10); Shirley is sure *A Jovial Crew* will last 'although / Not elevated unto fifty-two' (7–8); Hall berates a 'stupid stationer's care' who only 'gathered verses . . . To make a shout before the idle show' (9, 11–12). This, too, may relate to one of Brome's other battles: Cartwright was one of the writers whose 'free' productions had threatened the plays of professional playwrights.

Yet it is possible that the new material of 1652 is not confined simply to the paratext. In *Antipodes*, published in 1638, Brome wrote to the reader, 'You shal find in this Booke more then was presented upon the *Stage*' (sig. L4ᵛ); he was delighted to offer William, Earl of Hertford, to whom the edition is dedicated, 'the perusall' of his play in its ideal version. Brome cared about plays in page form, and saw printing as a way of showing what could have been staged, rather than what was. *A Jovial Crew* may well have been reworked for publication – not least because Jonson, Brome's mentor, was famous for rethinking his plays for the page. The negative prologue, concerned about 'these sad and tragic days' (Prol.3), for instance, strongly resembles the 1652 paratexts amongst which it nestles. As some of Brome's other prologues were rewritten specifically for the page (see PROLOGUE.n.), this one too may have been revised or written afresh in the 1650s. The same possibility may even affect some of the play's internal passages. In particular, the beggars' proposed play, 'Utopia', which critiques the state of the commonwealth and outlines a hypothetical civil war, may be a 1652 retrospective rather than a 1641/2 prediction. The fact that the description of 'Utopia' is not germane to the story and bears no relationship to the play within the play that is actually mounted – it is not performed within *A Jovial Crew*, just as no professional plays were legally performed in the 1650s – suggests revision. Moreover, 'Utopia' ends on war and beggary: and the country had not quite reached that stage by 1641/2, though arguably it had by the 1650s. Revision for the page would, too, explain the mixture in *A Jovial Crew* of possible happiness and actual sadness: the play may have moments within it reflective of two different periods and two different attitudes, in Brome and in the country. It is certainly the 1652 paratext, perhaps in tandem with other 1652 aspects of the play, that has stilted critical readings of *A Jovial Crew*: scholars have tended to read the play through its framing melancholia.

Text

There is no entry for *A Jovial Crew* in the Stationers' Register. It was, however, according to the title-page, printed 'by J[ames]. Y[oung]. for E[dward]. D[od]. and N[athaniel]. E[kins].'. As Dod and Ekins usually published serious works – they were known for having published most of Thomas Browne's writings – and Young had never set up a play before, all were unused to play publication. This may be the reason why, though the play is neat throughout, some individual words, not more important thematically than other words, are repeatedly printed in italic, in particular 'beggars', 'whim' and 'nature': the habit may have been adopted to preserve roman type.

A Jovial Crew seems to have been set by two compositors: spelling differentiates the first five gatherings from the last five, suggesting that on the first recto of signature I a new compositor, who favoured 'than' for 'then', 'oh' for 'o', 'ess' for 'esse' and 'Randall' for 'Randal', was now setting type. There are, however, no substantial changes to printing method, spelling aside, though the second compositor also favoured entrances on the same line as dialogue, while the first compositor had tended to centre them on lines of their own.

The text is a clean one. Characters are almost always consistently designated in speech prefixes, with only a few minor confusions: the speech prefix '2 Beg.' (i.e. Second Beggar) initially stands for the beggar-lawyer but later comes to be used for the beggar-soldier; in 4.1.283, 'Old.', for 'Oldrents', is used as a speech prefix instead of 'Ol.', for 'Oliver'. All entrances and most exits are supplied, and care is taken to make sure that the Latin is correct in the differentiation between, for instance, '*exit*' and '*exeunt*'. Asides are generally indicated by brackets; and speeches to be said in a beggar's whining tone are usually printed in italics. Some of the stage directions are descriptive and seem readerly rather than theatrical – they explicate the text, rather than stage action, for instance when the stage direction has '*Enter* HEARTY *singing*', to explain Hearty's 'Hey down, hey down a down, *etc.*' (2.2.19 SD2, 20). All of these bolster the idea that Brome himself had prepared the text for printing.

It thus becomes relevant to consider what the layout may say about Brome – for the design of a text on the page mattered to him. When criticizing the publication of Suckling's *Aglaura*, for instance, he had attacked its oversized margins: 'By this large Margent did the Poet mean / To have a Comment writ upon his Scene?' ('Upon *Aglaura*'). Brome is relatively likely to have been involved with the printers in the page-design of *A Jovial Crew*. Certainly the text's running title – 'A Jovial Crew, or:' on the verso of every page and 'The Merry Beggars' on the recto – means that 'Jovial' and 'Merry' are counterbalanced throughout, as are 'Crew' and 'Beggars'; the first title is eternally redefined and undercut by the second.

The title-page, which will have been hung up as an advertisement for the book, seems, too, to have been designed by Brome, for it links *A Jovial Crew* with other of Brome's published works. It bears a motto taken from Martial, '*Hic totus volo rideat Libellus*' ('I want all of this little book to laugh'; *Epigrams*, 11.15.3), which had also been employed on the title-pages of Brome's *Northern Lass* (published 1632), *Antipodes* (published 1640) and *Sparagus Garden* (published 1640); the motto was later used on Brome's behalf (or perhaps it was on the manuscripts behind the printed texts) for *Court Beggar* and *Novella*, both published in 1653 after Brome's death. *A Jovial Crew*, then, joins Brome's other printed plays as one of a series of comedic 'little books'; like them, it is surprisingly self-conscious in providing Martial's phrase in Latin, untranslated. Perhaps this phrase is designed to highlight the link between Brome's plays and those of Jonson, which are often introduced with Latin tags; Brome may even have hoped that his work as a whole amounted to a new 'genre' – if Jonson was known for 'humorous' writing, Brome may have wanted to be known for 'laughing' literature.

A Jovial Crew's printing also appears to have been intended to introduce a new publishing venture. When Alexander Brome promises in his commendation to *A Jovial Crew* that if the text 'please' readers 'more / May be made public' (p. 84; 39–40), he both reveals that he has access to the plays in manuscript and prompts the reader to lobby for them in print. As Alexander Brome then published five of the plays in 1653, after Brome's death – followed, in 1659, by another five – he seems, with Richard Brome's assent, to have become executor of the plays. In the 1659 edition, the plays are said to have been printed as the stationers 'had them from the author; not suffering any false or busy hand to adde or make the least mutilation' ('To the Readers', in *Five New*, 1659, sig. A5ᵛ), suggesting that Richard Brome had given his plays in fair form directly to Alexander Brome. Indeed, he seems to have transcribed or corrected them for print, for most of these plays have a high degree of accuracy, which furthers the likelihood that *A Jovial Crew*, too, was prepared and perhaps revised for the page.

Seventeen copies of Q1 are recorded in Wing; of these, eight were collated by Ann Haaker in her 1968 edition. She notes only one press variant: the mis-signed sig. L5 in one of the

Bodleian quartos is corrected to L3 in all other copies (Haaker, xxi). W. W. Greg had observed an additional press variant, again in a signature: K3 is misprinted Kk3 in the British Library copy (*Bibliography*, 2.825). Using Bodleian Q1 as my copy-text and collating other copies of Q1 in Britain not collated by Haaker (National Library of Scotland, Leeds University, Victoria and Albert Museum), I have found no other variants. Since Q2 (1661) was set from Q1, and Q3 (1684) was set from Q2 (with additions), later texts do not affect the copy-text.

AFTERLIFE

Later stage history

A Jovial Crew has often been said to anticipate the tone of the Restoration. Swinburne thinks the play provides a crucial link between the humour of Jonson and that of William Wycherley, for instance (505); Clifford Leech maintains that the play anticipates 'the Restoration mode' (97). Given the play's geniality and accessibility, it is no surprise that in 1660, when the theatres were reopened, *A Jovial Crew* was one of the first Caroline dramas performed. At that point, with no new plays instantly available and no trained playwrights to write them (performance having ceased for the last eighteen years), the new king, Charles II, divided existing Caroline and earlier plays between his two new theatre companies, the King's Men and the Duke's Men. He gave *A Jovial Crew* to his own favoured company, the King's Men, as is made clear on the title-page of the play's 1661 edition, which boasts that it is now acted 'by His Majesties servants at the New Theatre [Gibbon's Tennis Court] in Vere Street'. That same company also performed the play at the Red Bull (Bawcutt, 267), and when they moved to Lincoln's Inn performed it there: one audience member known only as 'Browne' recorded money paid to see *A Jovial Crew* 'at the new theatre in lincolnes inn fields' in 1662–3 (Greg,

'Theatrical'). The prompter John Downes summarizes the play's standing when he places *A Jovial Crew* on his list of 'Old Stock Plays' regularly performed at Lincoln's Inn Fields by the King's Men (8).

The play was extremely popular. Samuel Pepys was charmed by *A Jovial Crew*, seeing it three times in its first year of Restoration performance because it was 'the most innocent play that ever I saw' (25 July 1661) and 'full of mirth' (27 August 1661); he took Sir William Penn (father of William Penn the colonist) with him to watch the play on 1 November of that year. He continued to look out for the play throughout his lifetime, though a record he wrote on 11 January 1668/9 suggested either that the play had lost its allure, or that Pepys had lost his joy: he called the production 'ill acted', and lamented the fact that the actor John Lacy was now too old to dance in it (2.141, 164, 206; 9.411–12).

Updated with new prologues, *A Jovial Crew* was popular with companies outside London too: a prologue and epilogue survive for 'a Company of the Regimt. Of Guards whose Captain Treated them with the Play called The Jovial Crew' in the Smock Alley theatre, Dublin, *c.* 1683–8; and a prologue survives, written by Nahum Tate and addressed 'TO King WILLIAM & Queen MARY', for a court performance of the play on 15 November 1689 (Danchin, 2.654, 755). *A Jovial Crew* even had an extended life beyond the theatre: a ballad opera, *The Beggar's Wedding*, which had been 'made up from the Jovial Crew and other things', and 'Phoebe, the same piece cut into a farce' were regularly performed as 'drolls' at Southwark's annual fair by the Irish actor Charles Coffey in the 1720s and 1730s (Dibdin, 5.73).

From the 1660s onwards, however, the politics that had shadowed *A Jovial Crew* were no longer relevant. Reflecting that – or bringing it about – the play's dialogue was shortened, and the text started gathering ever more songs. The song 'There was a Jolly Beggar', printed as a separate broadside sheet in

2 'The Beggars Chorus, in the *Jovial Crew*. To a pleasant new Tune' (*c.* 1683)

1683 ('The Beggars Chorus, in the *Jovial Crew*. To a pleasant new Tune', see Fig. 2), may have joined the play as early as 1661, for the book *Wit and Drollery*, which dates from that year, already includes a parody of it: 'There was a Joviall Pedler / and he cried Cony skins' (Phillips, *Wit*, 83–5). The popularity of that ballad helped define and promote the play as a jubilant and uncritical celebration of beggars' life. The beggars of the story were no longer questioning society: gloriously carefree and unrestrained, they were a celebration of it, and as ever more upbeat songs were added to the play, so the text itself became increasingly rapturous.

A Jovial Crew was put on every year between 1704 and 1724, and frequently thereafter, bringing 'crowded audiences to the Theatre Royal in Covent Garden at all the frequent repetitions of its performance' (Baker, *Biographia*, 1.45). In 1708 the play was so popular that the two London theatrical companies, one at the Queen's Theatre and one at the Theatre

Royal, performed it at the same time and then, when united into one company, played it once more. This was a version of the text that was published with three cast lists representing the separate and conjoined companies: the play was treated as though contemporary, and readers wanted to compare modern performances in their minds. By that time the play had also been modernized, with offensive comments about 'Adamites' (2.1.83) and 'Lucifers' (3.1.254) removed and music replacing yet more text. *The Daily Courant* of 10 December 1705 advertised that the play would include 'a Two Part Song compos'd by the late Mr Henry Purcell'; and newspapers then and thereafter followed its title with lures such as 'With several Entertainments of Singing and Comic-Dancing proper to the Play' (*Daily Courant*, 14 June 1712). One undated music manuscript thought to be from about 1710 provides fifteen separate dances for *A Jovial Crew*, many more than any published text of the time dictates (Price, 320).

Because of its receptivity to music, the play in its revised, regularly altered form has sometimes been said to have inspired John Gay's *Beggar's Opera*, played and published to great acclaim in 1728 (Kephart, 266–71, 268). This seems possible, for though Gay's anti-heroes were actually thieves and high-waymen – the story is merely narrated by a beggar – he put 'beggar' in his title, seemingly asking for direct comparison with *A Jovial Crew, or The Merry Beggars*. At the time, Gay was trying to create an English form of 'opera' or text-with-music to counter the Italian operas that were currently taking over the English stage; *A Jovial Crew* in its increasingly musical, balladic, native and accessible form may have provided just the model he needed. The influence, however, redounded back onto *A Jovial Crew*, which was, in the light of *The Beggar's Opera*'s success, rewritten in opera form with fifty-three songs added to it and renamed '*The' Jovial Crew*; it was also performed as a reduced one-act musical afterpiece. Thomas Whincop recorded that 'This Comedy was . . . by the Addition of some

Songs, turn'd into a Ballad-Opera, in Imitation of the celebrated Beggar's Opera' (96); the play was described in 1760 as 'one out of the many musical entertainments, which the great success of the Beggar's Opera, during it's first run gave rise to' (*Public Ledger*, 22 February 1760).

From that time onwards *The Jovial Crew* and *The Beggar's Opera* had a shared trajectory and were often put on interchangeably. Both raised questions of relevance to the 1730s about liberty and property, money and poverty, low and high class; both could be seen as exposing the hypocrisy and corruption of upper-class rule embodied in the Walpole regime (Marriott, 53). *The Jovial Crew*, however, was less located in a stated time period, and thus easily inspired comparison with politics of all ages.

The Beggar's Opera came to have the edge onstage. Nevertheless, *The Jovial Crew* had a further burst of popularity in 1760 when yet further 'new Songs' were written for it (*London Evening Post*, 1 April 1760). These ditties, which consisted of songs from earlier versions of the play as well as additional ballads, were described in 1760 as adding 'infinite life' to a play that was thought, by this time and in this form, superficial, if vaguely pleasing: it provided 'an agreeable evening's amusement' and could 'bear repetition without cloying or giving disgust' (*Public Ledger*, 22 February 1760). The King and princes attended a 1760 performance (*Public Advertiser*, 26 April 1760), the King and Queen attended a 1761 performance (*St James's Chronicle*, 29 October 1761) and the King and princes saw it again in 1767 (*Lloyd's Evening Post*, 28 January 1767), by which time the play's language was said to be so improved as to be 'free from exceptions of every kind' (*Lloyd's Evening Post*, 2 February 1767); it was performed every year between 1760 and 1775 (Steggle, *Brome*, 192). Not, by this time, viewed as a very fixed text, *The Jovial Crew* did, over this period, gain yet further musical alterations: a 1765 Covent Garden performance for it included a new overture by 'Mr. Bates' and what was to become a popular 'Dance for the Beggars' by 'Mr. Bencraft' (*Lloyd's Evening Post*, 2 February 1767).

In 1770, James Dance, who published and performed under the name James Love, turned *The Jovial Crew* into a two-act farcical opera for Drury Lane, and retitled it *The Ladies Frolick* – suggesting that he viewed the women, rather than the beggars, as the piece's salient, or at least most sellable, characters. *The Ladies Frolick* was never published, but played regularly; its dances, including its assumption of the popular 'Crutch Dance', in which the beggars performed while halting and limping, became famous in their own right. Immediately, Covent Garden wanted to embrace *The Jovial Crew*'s new popularity; although the irascible George Colman called Love's shortened version 'inequitable' and said it 'ought not to be suffered' (*Morning Chronicle and London Advertiser*, 8 June 1773), he was hiding the fact that Covent Garden was preparing a shortened version of its own, also focused on actresses. This 1774 text, a showpiece for the sexy Miss Ann Catley, who was famous for her low humour, brought the play nearer to what would later be called music hall. Miss Catley 'missed no opportunity of marking a double entendre' in the play, and played up 'any warm passage that was likely to enflame the passions' (*Middlesex Journal and Evening Advertiser*, 1 November 1774): the innuendo so carefully excised from earlier versions of the text was back in force. Rachel, the character played by Miss Catley, was now a knowing, salty heroine: published versions of the play from the 1770s tend to include a picture of Miss Catley revealing her considerable *décolletage* (see Fig. 3). Given the play's lower tone, it is hardly surprising that a large number of 'common ballads' were added to the text, for, as advertisements explained, 'This opera has ever been reckoned one of the heaviest musical pieces upon the stage' – even though in terms of language, it contained the 'same sort of mirth' for three acts; reviewers professed themselves delighted that an 'insufferably dull and tedious' text had been so judiciously

3 'Miss [Ann] Catley in the Character of Rachel' (1781), frontispiece to *Bell's British Theatre*, vol. 21

cut (*General Evening Post*, 1 November 1774). This version was then itself further cut into an afterpiece in 1777, with the character of Randall removed and Rachel/Catley made even more prominent. Excusing and praising the alteration, one newspaper wrote of *The Jovial Crew* that

> In its original state it never was much admired, except for some of the excellent old airs and ballads that are to be found in it; and therefore it is not now injudiciously curtailed of a great many uninteresting scenes, and much insipid dialogue.

> (*London Chronicle*, 8 February 1777)

This version appears to have been the form of the play revived in 1819, after a successful run seven years earlier. It was admired by Charles Lamb, who was obviously as taken by Fanny Kelly's Rachel as earlier watchers had been by Miss Catley's. Lamb regarded the play as having proto-romantic features combined with feminist ones: 'Altogether, a brace of more romantic she-beggars it was never our fortune to meet in this supplicatory world' (6.209).

This was, however, the end of the professional performance life of *The* – and indeed *A* – *Jovial Crew* for two centuries: the play had been so bled of content that it had little further to go. Even by 1776, a performance of *The Jovial Crew* had been abandoned when *The Beggar's Opera* was 'particularly desired instead' (*Public Advertiser*, 28 October 1776); in the nineteenth century *The Beggar's Opera* alone possessed the stage.

In the late twentieth century, however, the two plays resumed their earlier habit of rivalry and mutual promotion. In light of the success of *Les Miserables*, the Royal Shakespeare Company in 1992 decided to mount both *The Beggar's Opera* and *A Jovial Crew*; the company was, remarked Michael Coveney ironically, now 'down and out in Paris and London and also the Warwickshire countryside' (*Observer*, 26 April 1992). As ever, *A Jovial Crew* and *The Beggar's Opera* were directly compared.

'Forget about the other show', wrote Carol Woddis; *A Jovial Crew*, she opined, 'is the real beggar's opera' (*What's On*, 28 April 1993).

Yet the RSC's version of *A Jovial Crew* was, as had so long been historically the case, a heftily adapted play. Stephen Jeffreys, the play's adaptor, and Max Stafford-Clark, its director, shared a sense that *A Jovial Crew* was a proto-Marxist manifesto that provided 'a fascinating social document of a precise historical period' (Jeffreys, 'Author's introduction', *A Jovial Crew*, unnumbered). Yet though Stafford-Clark maintained that the play was 'a coded message from a society on the brink of civil war' and was thus like 'many of the plays . . . written in Eastern Europe a few years ago' (Stafford-Clark), he also felt that Brome had been too politically repressed to see his points through. He asked Jeffreys to release the 'hidden play' from Brome's text ('Author's introduction', *A Jovial Crew*, unnumbered). Promoters of the result said that Jeffreys had brought out 'the concealed political theme of the Carolean comedy' (Soncini, 140); had 'pumped up the dark side, the political awareness and the pertinence of Brome's original' (Kate Bassett, *The Times*, 26 April 1993); and had 'hotted up the play's socio-political content' (Alastair Macaulay, *Financial Times*, 24 April 1993).

Yet Jeffreys had also 'created what is in effect a new text' written over an old one (White, 224). Over forty-five per cent of the redesigned play was written by Jeffreys himself; in the first scene, the ratio of Brome to Jeffreys is 10:90 (White, 226). Confusingly, passages that appear to be particularly early modern are often by Jeffreys. Topical references, including one to watching 'Beeston's Boys in "The Swaggering Damsel"' (Jeffreys, 24) are 'mock-antique' details that actually show how modern and ahistorical the piece now is (Steggle, *Brome*, 194). Jeffreys also added cant to the revamped play, including words tougher and more aggressive than those chosen by Brome: 'stow you' (hold your peace) and 'frummagem' (to strangle) emphasize the beggars' ill-treatment and distress. Brome's play, in rewritten form, was said to be prescient. It depicted strained relationships between poor and rich, class and money, employment and unemployment, set in a world that was disintegrating socially – but its prescience had partly been written into it. Stafford-Clark, conflating a country on the brink of civil war with a country dealing with the effects of Thatcherism, saw powerful links in the rewritten drama between Brome's society and his own. He sent his actors 'researching vagabondage and begging generally' by begging in London (Stafford-Clark), which doubled as a way of preparing the players and commenting on the state of the nation. In many ways, this production was actually about Margaret Thatcher's 'two nation' Britain, starkly divided between rich and poor (Cave *et al.*, White, 230).

Striking as the play was performatively, several reviewers said that they wished *A Jovial Crew* had been allowed to speak for itself, and complained that the insights of the original play had been hidden by this adaptation. Making Brome a proto-socialist, and using a 'pastiche seventeenth century voice to tackle the theme of arts politics in contemporary Britain' (Soncini, 140), gave Brome, wrote Michael Arditti, a political agenda that 'crudely intrudes' (*Evening Standard*, 26 April 1993); this 'tampering', wrote Nicholas De Jongh, 'betrays the original by disguising its qualities and gilding its limitations' (*Evening Standard*, 22 April 1992); 'Wouldn't it be nice if minor seventeenth century playwrights could have seen their own world through the eyes of twentieth century socialists who have read Marx and Christopher Hill?', wrote John Peter, questioning 'why . . . put on a play if you find its social stance so inadequate?' (*Sunday Times*, 26 April 1992).

Jeffreys, as well as individualizing the beggars to give them more humanity, rewrote the conclusion of *A Jovial Crew*. Believing that Brome had written a denouement too conven-tional and improbable to suit 'grown ups', Jeffreys gave the drama a bleaker and more evocative ending (Jeffreys, 'Author's introduction', *A Jovial Crew*, unnumbered). He made Meriel decide against returning to upper-class life in favour of staying with the beggars: 'There lies a world where people fight for / What I play'd but now: Utopia / In England . . . I must among them / Lest I shrink to nothing' (Jeffreys, 134).

As ever, the play's receptivity to new songs further enabled its contemporary application. Songwriters of The Blockheads, Ian Dury and Mickey Gallagher, set catchy and urgent gypsy-style music to new lyrics that emphasized social politics: 'beggar may live or beggar may die . . . hang him up and see him fly' (Jeffreys, 'Frummagen Rummagen [Reprise]', *A Jovial Crew*, unnumbered). Frenzied dances were added by Sue Lefton. This production was thus the culmination of the themes of music, dance, politics and textual fluidity that have typified the play from its inception. Stafford-Clark and Jeffreys, in adapting the play to contemporary circumstances, were continuing a process set in motion during the Restoration (see Figs 4 and 5).

4 Learning the beggars' dance, in Max Stafford-Clark's 1992 Royal Shakespeare Company production

5 Springlove (Ron Cook), Vincent (Pearce Quigley) and Hilliard (Stephen Casey), in Max Stafford-Clark's 1992 Royal Shakespeare Company production

Later print history

A Jovial Crew continued, over time, to be important as a book as well as a production. Its second edition (Q2), published in 1661, was advertised in *Mercurius Publicus* (31 October – 7 November 1661), thus becoming the first playbook promoted for sale in a newspaper. This edition was reprinted in 1684; in 1708 it was printed again with, for further ease of reference, 'a Key to the Beggars Cant' – oddly inaccurate – provided at the bottom of the relevant pages.

The play's songs had a separate popularity of their own aside from the play's dialogue. Parts of *A Jovial Crew* itself were extracted and made into ballads; 'The Beggars Wedding: or The Jovial crew' (1676) related in verse the marriage of the old couple described in 4.2; while 'The Beggars' Chorus in the Jovial Crew' (1683) seems to reflect a performance song – though the ballad itself only entered into the printed text a year later, in 1684. The play came to seem a continuation of a balladic concern with merry beggars – for a number of Restoration ballads, reflecting upon the play consciously or unconsciously, reinforce the idea that the story itself is an extended drinking ballad. They include C. H.'s 'A Merry New Song wherein You May View the Drinking Healths of a Jovial Crew' (1658–60); and 'The Jovial Crew, or, Beggars' Bush' (1660–5), 'In which a mad maunder doth vapour and swagger, with praising the trade of a bonny bold begger'. Other ballads highlight the relationship between 'jovial crews' and theft – 'The Jovial Beggars' Merry Crew' (1684) argued, '*When beggars that have coyn good store, yet still like vagrants live, they do but onely cheat the poor, 'tis pitty them to give.*' Ballads shaped perceptions of what *A Jovial Crew* was and hence the ways in which it was revised.

As *A Jovial Crew* gathered ever more music, it is no surprise that in 1731 it was printed as a ballad opera. The text named no new author, but the lawyer-cum-playwright Edward Roome – parodied in Alexander Pope's *Dunciad* – was responsible for this version. He had been aided by 'another gentleman', sometimes said to be the playwright George Colman, but more often said to be Matthew Concanen, with the additional help of William Younge (*Old Plays 2*, 10.327; Baker, *Biographia*, 1.95; Shiells, 31; *New and General*, 4.77). The new musical accompaniment for the whole was written by William Bates. *The* – rather than *A* – *Jovial Crew* was modern, collaborative and musical. Brome's primary authorship was all but forgotten: the new motto for its title-page in print, '*Novo splendore resurgit*' ('It rises up again with new splendour'), tells the reader that this version is the play's best so far. Abridged in story and bolstered in song, the dialogue had been cut down to three acts and rendered into prose throughout. Minor characters like Tallboy had been removed altogether. In published form, the text, now called an 'opera', explained how its fifty-three 'Songs, (except about half a Dozen) were written about three Years ago' – exactly when *The Beggar's Opera* had turned all attention to ballad opera. With the tunes 'prefix'd to each Song', this text was designed to mirror exactly the layout of *The Beggar's Opera* on the page. Yet advertisements of the time also explained, 'NB Books of the Play and Opera will be sold at the Theatre' (*Daily Post*, 23 March 1731), indicating that those who only wanted the songs to recreate at home could have them without the dialogue.

In its new comic opera form, *The Jovial Crew* was republished in 1732, and again in 1760 with further 'new Songs' written for it, the latter followed shortly after by publication of 'The Airs in the Jovial Crew, for the German Flute or Violin', at least some of which were by the famous composer Thomas Arne (*Lloyd's Evening Post*, 20 February 1761). People, in other words, continued to be anxious to own the new music to *The Jovial Crew* and perform it in their own homes. The play was printed together with the 'Airs' in 1761. Revised publications with new music continued to be written and published for as long as the play was performed – culminating in the RSC's heavily rewritten adaptation of the play in 1992, which contains seven totally new songs, with their melodies, written to replace Brome's.

As *The Jovial Crew* became ever more popular on stage and page, the original play, as written by Brome, became neglected. Brome's *A Jovial Crew* was nevertheless reproduced by Dodsley in his twelve-volume *Select Collection of Old Plays* of 1744, and was, in that form, republished in 1780 and regularly thereafter. Sir Walter Scott, in 1810, printed it in his three-volume *Ancient British Drama*; then, possibly drawn by the term 'scot-free', he used mildly altered lines from *A Jovial*

Crew as a motto for chapter 12 in volume 1 of his novel *The Antiquary*:

> Beggar? – the only freeman of your commonwealth;
> Free above Scot-free, that observes no laws,
> Obey no governor, use no religion
> But what they draw from their own ancient custom,
> Or constitute themselves, yet are no rebels.
>
> (256; see 2.1.198–202)

Presumably it was through Scott that other writers from Scotland learned about the play. Robert Burns, whose singing beggars in 'The Jolly Beggar' are thought to descend from or at least allude to *A Jovial Crew*, seems to have been inspired by Brome's presentation of rebels and rebellion (Pabisch, 8).

There has been no printed complete works of Brome since John Pearson's three-volume collection of 1873, *The Dramatic Works of Richard Brome: Containing Fifteen Comedies*, which merely reproduced the early modern printed texts. Since then, *A Jovial Crew* has been edited four times: by G. P. Baker in Charles Mills Gayley's *Representative English Comedies*, 3 vols (1914, reprinted 1969), vol. 3; by Ann Haaker (1968); by Robert G. Lawrence (1973) – though a substantial section of the play is missing in this edition; and by *Brome Online*, an important new searchable edition of all of Brome's works, with introductions, glosses and pop-up performances of particular sections, not currently available in book form. There are, at present, no editions of Brome's *A Jovial Crew* in print, though Jeffreys's adapted text of 1992 (published as *A Jovial Crew*, 'by Richard Brome adapted by Stephen Jeffreys') can still be purchased. Jeffreys writes of Brome's play that it is 'powered by a striking and original conceit', it contains 'brilliantly sustained comic scenes' and 'is a fascinating social document of a precise historical period' (Jeffreys, 'Author's introduction', *A Jovial Crew*, unnumbered). He uses these observations to explain why *A Jovial Crew* should be adapted; but they are strong reasons for making the genuine text, in original form, available in print once again.

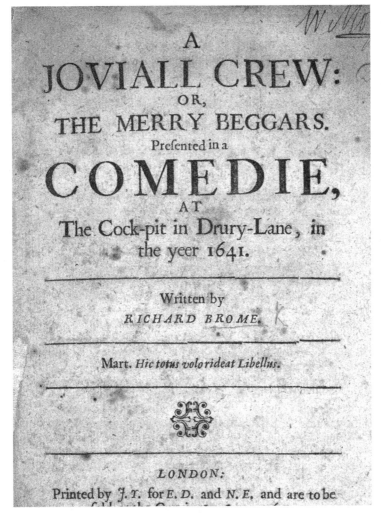

6 Title-page for Richard Brome's *A Jovial Crew* (1652)

A

JOVIAL CREW,

OR

THE MERRY BEGGARS,

Presented in a   5

COMEDY

AT

The Cockpit in Drury Lane, in

the year 1641.

Written by   10

RICHARD BROME.

Mart. *Hic totus volo rideat Libellus.*

LONDON:

Printed by J. Y. for E. D. and N. E. and are to be

sold at the Gun in Ivy Lane. 1652   15

1–2 A JOVIAL CREW any crew or group that exhibits *jovial* – Jove-like – characteristics: nobility, happiness, mirth and majesty. The phrase was most often used to indicate (1) a happy group (as in, 'You are a jovial crew; the only people / Whose happiness I admire', 1.1.488–9); (2) beggars (a 1660 ballad is named 'The Jovial Crew, or the Merry Beggars'); (3) inveterate drinkers (in a drinking song in *Lady's Trial*, 'a Joviall crew' can 'drinke till all looke blew', sig. H1ᵛ).

8 **Cockpit . . . Lane** First built as an actual cockpit in 1606, the Cockpit was redeveloped as a theatre by Christopher Beeston in 1616. After being burnt in riots of 1617, it was rebuilt, probably to the old footprint, and named the Phoenix in recognition of the fact that it had risen from the flames. It continued to be referred to as both Phoenix and Cockpit, though Brome's choice of name on this title-page may reflect an interest in the past or a wish to present his plays as sparring birds – throughout his time at the Cockpit he was fighting battles with his previous employers at the Salisbury Court theatre, and with the amateur poets he disliked, in particular, William Davenant and John Suckling. See pp. 28–9 and 284.

9 **1641** This may be a reference to the calendar year or to the civic year; in the latter the 'new year' occurred on Lady Day, 25 March. The first performance, then,

could have taken place at any time between 1 January 1641 and 24 March 1642.

12 **Mart. . . . *Libellus*** a quotation from Martial, epigram 11.15: 'I want all of this little book to laugh' (vol. 3). Martial used the phrase to declare his light-hearted intent and to position his 'little book' against more serious writing like epic poetry. Brome's motto likewise proclaims a light-hearted and deprecatory approach to writing, but also situates the play as a book (rather than a staged performance). The same motto was also employed by Brome on the title-pages of his plays *Northern Lass* (published 1632), *Antipodes* (published 1640) and *Sparagus Garden* (published 1640); it was later used on his behalf (or perhaps it was inscribed on his manuscripts) for *Court Beggar* and *Novella* (both published 1653). Brome's use of Latin may be a gesture towards his master and 'father', Ben Jonson. See p. 283.

14 **J. Y. . . . E. D. . . . N. E.** identified by W. W. Greg as James Young, Edward Dod and Nathaniel Ekins (*Bibliography*, 2.825). This is the only play known to have been printed by James Young, and the only play published by Dod and Ekins, who tended to produce more serious books. Dod and Ekins worked together from about 1650, when they published Thomas Browne's *Pseudodoxia Epidemica*; they had separated by 1658 when they published rival editions of that same book.

The Persons of the Play

Oldrents, an ancient esquire

Hearty, his friend, and merry companion, but a decayed
    gentleman

Springlove, steward to Master Oldrents

Vincent,
Hilliard, } two young gentlemen   5

Randal, a groom, servant to Oldrents

Master Sentwell
and two other gentlemen } friends to Justice Clack

Oliver, the Justice's son   10

Master *Clack*, the Justice himself

Master *Tallboy*, lover to the Justice's niece

Chaplain,
Usher,
Butler, } to Oldrents   15
Cook,

Rachel,
Meriel, } Oldrents' daughters

Amy, Justice Clack's niece

Autem Mort, an old beggar-woman   20

Patrico,
Soldier,
Lawyer, } four especial beggars
Courtier,

Scribble, their poet   25

Divers other *Beggars*, *Fiddlers* and *Mutes*

---

18 Oldrents'] *this edn;* Oldrent's *Q1*

To the right noble, ingenious and judicious gentleman,
Thomas Stanley, Esq.

SIR,

I have long since studied, in these anti-ingenious times,
to find out a man that might, at once, be both a judge and   5
patron to this issue of my old age, which needs both.
And my blessed stars have flung me upon you, in whom
both those attributes concentre and flourish; nor can I yet
find a reason why I should present it to you (it being
below your acceptance or censure) but only my own   10
confidence, which had not grown to this forwardness,
had it not been encouraged by your goodness. Yet we all
know beggars use to flock to great men's gates. And,
though my fortune has cast me in that mould, I am poor
and proud, and preserve the humour of him who could   15

1–41 This dedication, written in the year of Brome's death, appears to have been the last piece of writing that he produced.

2 **_Thomas Stanley_** (1625–78), poet, philosopher, translator and classical scholar, who gathered and promoted a literary coterie of Royalist writers including his cousin, the poet Richard Lovelace (1617–57); his kinsman, the poet and scholar Sir Edward Sherburne (1616–1702); and his friends, the poet Robert Herrick (1591–1674), the poet and translator John Hall (1627–56), the playwright James Shirley (1596–1666), the playwright and editor Alexander Brome (1620–60) and Richard Brome. Stanley may have facilitated Brome's admittance into Charterhouse Hospital on 25 March 1650, in which case this dedication is a 'thank you' for Stanley's practical as well as intellectual help (Steggle, *Brome*, 187). Stanley went on to write a long commendatory poem congratulating Alexander Brome for editing Brome's works, 'To my most ingenious friend, Mr. *ALEX. BROME* Upon his setting forth *Mr. RICH. BROMES*

PLAYES', in *Five New* (1659), sigs A7^r–A9^r; Alexander Brome recalled the relationship between Stanley and Brome when he suggested, '*Dick Bromes* plays . . . good must be, / Because they were approv'd by thee' (*Songs*, 167–70).

4 **studied** searched; cast about
   anti-ingenious undiscerning. The word refers both to the time's lack of discernment of poetic talent and its lack of discernment in making political decisions.

5 **at once** simultaneously

6 **issue** (1) product; (2) offspring
   old age Brome was born *c.* 1590 and so was about sixty-two years old when the play was published; he died on 24 September 1652.

8 **concentre** agree; coincide

13 **use to** are accustomed to

14 **cast . . . mould** i.e. cast me as a beggar

15 **humour** mental disposition (as determined by the proportion of the bodily 'humours'); see also 3.1.282n.

15–16 **could . . . boons** Ann Haaker (3), traces this from Martial's epigram 11.68: '*Parva*

not beg for anything but great boons, such as are your
kind acceptance and protection. I dare not say (as my
brethren use) that I present this as a testimonial of my
gratitude or recompense for your favours, for, I protest, I
conceive it so far from quitting old engagements that it   20
creates new. So that all that this play can do is but to
make more work, and involves me in debts beyond a
possibility of satisfaction. Sir, it were a folly in me to tell
you of your worth. The world knows it enough, and are
bold to say fortune and nature scarce ever clubbed so   25
well. You know, sir, I am old and cannot cringe nor court
with the powdered and ribboned wits of our days; but
though I cannot speak so much, I can think as well, and
as honourably, as the best. All the arguments I can use to
induce you to take notice of this thing of nothing is that   30
it had the luck to tumble last of all in the epidemical ruin

*rogas magnos; sed non dant haec quoque
magni. / Ut pudeat levius, tu, Matho, magna
roga*' (vol. 3), translated by Thomas May
as, 'Thou begg'st small gifts of great ones,
which they yet Deny. To be lesse sham'd,
begge gifts more great' (May, sig. G5ᵛ),

18 **brethren use** fellow writers tend to do
19 **protest** declare
20 **quitting** repaying
23 **satisfaction** reparation; compensation
25 **clubbed** combined together (*OED* club, *v.*
7, citing this entry)
26 **cringe** bow obsequiously or sycophantically
27 **powdered ... wits** The foppish court *wits*
are trivialized here by being defined as an
extension of the fashionable clothes they
wear. Cf. the 'Praeludium', thought to be
by Brome, to *Careless Shepherdess*: 'Sir,
by your powdred hair, and gawdy cloaths /
I do presume you are a Courtier' (2). This

is probably a reference to the courtly playwrights whose dramas were threatening the
finances of professional writers. See Prol.8n.
and pp. 284–6.

30 **thing of nothing** trivial thing; an adaptation of Psalms, 144.5: 'Man is like a thing
of nought'
31–2 **luck ... scene** 'the chance/bad luck to
be the last play precipitated into the
universal ruin of the playhouses'. Brome
claims that *A Jovial Crew* was the last play
performed, either at all, or at the Cockpit,
before the closing of the theatres by parliamentary order on 2 September 1642.
31 **epidemical** general, universal; but retaining
its sense of 'illness' as the country is perceived to be sick. The term may also literally
recall the bout of plague – an *epidemical
ruin* – that had closed the theatres from
5 August to 26 November 1641.

27 ribboned] (Ribbanded)

of the scene, and now limps hither with a wooden leg to beg an alms at your hands. I will wind up all with a use of exhortation: that since the times conspire to make us all beggars, let us make ourselves merry, which, if I am not mistaken, this drives at. Be pleased, therefore, sir, to lodge these harmless beggars in the outhouses of your thoughts, and among the rest, him, that in this cuckoo-time, puts in for a membership, and will fill the choir of those that 'duly and truly pray for you', and is,

35

40

SIR, your humble servant RICHARD BROME.

32–3 **limps . . . hands** Brome presents the play as a limping beggar – like the lame bridegroom of the play's wedding – asking for alms from Stanley. By extension, Stanley is a parallel to the generous Oldrents. If Brome was housed at Charterhouse because of Stanley's patronage, then Stanley was indeed 'Oldrents' to Brome's beggar.

33 **wind up all** conclude everything

34 **exhortation** homily or sermon of admonishment
conspire 'concur' or possibly 'plot'. The Civil War, which had only ended in 1651, had reduced England to a state of poverty, unhappiness and, consequently, non-stop conspiracies and plots – to reinstate the monarchy, overthrow Parliament or oppose (or impose) religious dissent.

34–5 **make . . . beggars** This may be a general reference to the fact that some people had lost their livelihoods and been reduced to begging; or a specific reference to playwrights and actors, now without a trade.

36 **this** i.e. this play

37 **lodge . . . outhouses** Continuing the analogy between Stanley and Oldrents, the request is that the beggars of the play – and so the play itself – be given accommodation in the barn of Stanley's good wishes.

38 **him** i.e. Brome

38–9 **cuckoo-time** i.e. spring – the time in which, heralded by the sound of cuckoos in the play, Springlove needs to go on a pilgrimage to join the beggars (see 1.1.223 SD, 5.1.417). Brome here casts himself as Springlove, who is associated with cuckoos in the play. In addition, however, *cuckoo-time* suggests the period during which cuckoos lay eggs in other birds' nests; this might be a reference to the Puritans, who were trying to get one of their own into power.

39 **puts . . . membership** bids or applies for a place in the society (of beggars)
choir organized company; chorus

40 **duly . . . you** foreshadowing 'duly and truly pray for you', the refrain that the disguised gentry will regularly use when they attempt to beg

41 RICHARD] *Haaker;* RIC: *Q1*

To Master Richard Brome on his play called A Jovial Crew:
or the Merry BEGGARS

Plays are instructive recreations
Which, who would write, may not expect – at once,
No, nor with every breeding – to write well.   5
And though some itching academics fell
Lately upon this task, their products were
Lame and imperfect, and did grate the ear,
So that they mocked the stupid stationer's care,
That both with gelt and cringes did prepare   10
Fine copper-cuts, and gathered verses, too,
To make a shout before the idle show.

Your fate is other: you do not invade,
But by great Jonson were made free o'th' trade,

3   **instructive recreations** pastimes that also
teach; *recreations* is pronounced with five
syllables to rhyme with *once* (4).
4   **who would write** those people who wish
to write
5   **every breeding** i.e. each time a play is
written
6   **itching academics** academics who had
the 'itch' to write drama, such as William
Cartwright (1611–43), Peter Hausted
(1605–44), Shackerley Marmion (1603–
39), Jasper Mayne (1604–72) and Thomas
Randolph (1605–35). Professional playwrights despised them for writing for glory,
not money. James Shirley, in *Witty Fair One*,
relates how the 'Schollers . . . come from
Oxford and *Cambridge* . . . full of lamentable Tragedies, and ridiculous Comedies
which they might . . . vent to the Players, but
they will take no money for 'em' (sig. G2ʳ);
Court Beggar refers to academics who sell
plays to courtiers who pretend to have written
them, and 'boast to have made those enter-
ludes, when . . . they bought 'em of Univer-
sitie Scholars . . . and onely shew their own
wits in owning other mens' (sig. S8ʳ).
6–7 **fell / Lately upon** recently took up

8   **grate** harass; irritate
9   **stupid** slow-witted; dull
10 **gelt and cringes** money and sycophantic
bows
11 **Fine copper-cuts** engravings made from
designs cut upon copper. This criticism is
probably a reference to Cartwright's recently
published *Comedies* (1651), which were
fronted with an engraved portrait of the
author.
12 'to make a clamorous welcome before the
vain display'. This reference to prefatory
poems is, like J. B.'s poem (p. 77, 7–10),
and James Shirley's poem (p. 79, 4–8),
an attack on the large number of poems
printed as prefatory material to Cartwright's
Comedies.
13 **invade** i.e. take over the stage by force as
the academic dramatists do
14 **Jonson . . . trade** a continuation of Jonson's
claim that Brome served 'A Prentiseship'
under him, 'which few doe now a dayes'
(Jonson, 'To my . . . Servant'). Brome will
have learned from Jonson, but describing
the process as an apprenticeship is ironic:
there was no guild of playwrights. See
p. 281.

So that we must in this your labour find   15
Some image and fair relic of his mind.

JOHN HALL

To master Richard Brome, on his comedy of A Jovial Crew:
or The Merry Beggars

Not to commend or censure thee or thine,
Nor like a bush to signify good wine,
Nor yet to publish to the world, or thee,   5
Thou merit'st bays by wit and poetry,
Do I stand here. Though I do know there comes
A shoal, with regiments of encomiums
On all occasions, whose astronomy
Can calculate a praise to fifty-three,   10

---

15 **this your labour** i.e. this play
16 **image ... relic** i.e. a trace of Jonson –
but the Catholic analogy perhaps hints
at Jonson's own Catholicism. As the play
to come will revolve around a Catholic
'Agnus Dei', it is possible that Brome was,
or was perceived to be, Catholic too. By
making Brome the echo of Jonson, Hall
both promotes the play and demotes the
originality of the writer.
17 **JOHN HALL** (1627–56), poet and pamphleteer; a member of Stanley's literary
coterie
4 **bush ... wine** An ivy bush hung outside a
building indicated that a tavern or alehouse
was within; hence the proverb 'Good wine
needs no bush' (Tilley, W462).
5 **publish** announce; disseminate
6 **bays** laurel wreaths – the classical award
for triumphant poets
7 **I stand here** The dedicatory poem, or
perhaps its author, 'J. B.', is personified; it
'stands' before the play.
8 **shoal** troop; crowd
  regiments i.e. a number large enough to
resemble a battalion

8–9 **encomiums / On** formal expressions of
praise for
9–12 **astronomy ... altitude** A complicated
analogy is made here between the way
astronomers calculate the altitude of the air
'under' the sun and the writing of encomiums
to Cartwright's *Comedies*. In the final poem
preceding Cartwright's *Comedies*, 'The
Stationer', by Humphrey Moseley, the
number of commendatory verses is said to
be both fifty-two and fifty-three: as many
'as there are *Shires* in England, *Weeks*
i'th'*Yeare*, but actually fifty-three' – in fact
the number varied between fifty-two and
fifty according to issue (sig. 3*11^r). Using
astronomy to calculate 52 is explicated in
John Wilkins's *Discourse*, which explains
how 'there are divers wayes used by
Astronomers, to take the altitude of this
vaporous aire', including 'observing ...
how high that aire must be above us, which
the Sun could shine upon, when hee was 18
degrees below us. And from this observation, it was concluded to bee about 52 miles
high' (228–9). See also James Shirley's
commendatory poem (p. 79, 7–8).

And write blank copies, such as, being viewed,
May serve indifferently each altitude,
And make books, like petitions, whose commands
Are not from worth, but multitude of hands –
Those will prove wit by power, and make a trade   15
To force by number when they can't persuade.
Here's no such need, for books, like children, be
Well christened when their sureties are but three,
And those which to twelve godfathers do come,
Signify former guilt, or speedy doom.   20

Nor need the stationer, when all th'wits are past,
Bring his own periwig-poetry at last.
All this won't do, for when their labour's done,
The reader's ruled not by their tastes but's own,
And he, that for encomiastics looks,   25

11 **blank copies** i.e. encomiums in which no name is inserted, so that they can be used as praise for anyone. Cf. *MW*, 2.1.66–7: 'I warrant he hath a thousand of these letters, writ with blank space for different names.'

13–14 **books ... hands** books that gain their worth, as petitions do, not by what they say, but by the number of people who have signed them

15 **Those** i.e. people who write such commendatory poems
trade practice

18 **sureties** 'Sureties' and 'sponsors' are alternative titles for godparents.
but three Charles Wheatly writes, 'How long the Church has fix'd the Number of these Sureties, I cannot tell; but by a Constitution of *Edmond* Archbishop of *Canterbury* . . . I find the same Provision made as is now requir'd by our Rubrick, viz. *That there shall be for every Male-Child that is to be baptiz'd two Godfathers and one Godmother, and for every Female one Godfather, and two Godmothers*' (324).

19 **twelve godfathers** a reference to the twelve men who make up a jury, who

were jocularly and commonly known as 'godfathers'. In *MV*, 4.1.394–6, Gratiano says, 'In christening thou shalt have two godfathers. / Had I been judge, thou shouldst have had ten more, / To bring thee to the gallows, not to the font.'

20 **Signify** indicate
guilt perhaps a pun on 'guilt' (in terms of the child who needs twelve, rather than the usual three, godparents) and 'gelt' (*OED* gelt *n.²* 1), ready money or gold (in terms of the playwright). See John Hall's commendatory poem (p. 76, 10).

21–2 **stationer ... last** a further reference to the final encomium before Cartwright's *Comedies*

22 **periwig-poetry** bad poetry; *periwig*, a wig, is here used figuratively to signify a covering used to hide a defect.

23 **their** 'they' = the poets who write encomiums

25–6 **he ... books** i.e. he who buys a book for its commendatory poems will find a text that is fat rather than good.

25 **encomiastics** from 'encomiums' – commendatory pieces

18 christened] *(Christ'ned)*

May find the bigger, not the better books.
So that the most our leavers serve for, shows
Only that we're his friends, and do suppose
'Tis good: and that is all that I shall say.
In truth I love him well, and like his play.   30
And if there's any that don't think so too,
Let them let it alone for them that do.

J. B.

*To his worthy friend Master Richard Brome, upon his comedy
called A Jovial Crew: or the Merry Beggars*

This comedy, ingenious friend, will raise
Itself a monument, without a praise
Begged by the stationer who, with strength of purse   5
And pens, takes care to make his book sell worse.
And I dare calculate thy play, although

---

27 **leavers** A leaver is, according to *OED* leaver *n.*, citing this line, 'one who leaves'. It is more likely to mean 'leavings', the poems that are left (with a pun on 'leaf', as the poems cover leaves of paper).

33 **J. B.** Though Keith Whitlock (561) suggests that J. B. was John Benson, the printer of Jonson's 1640 *Poems*, there is no evidence that Benson was in the habit of writing commendatory verses, nor is it clear that he knew Brome or the other writers gathered together here. Given that all these encomiums share themes, J. B. is much more likely to have been Sir John Berkenhead (1617–79), journalist and poet, friend of Stanley and Shirley, who often signed his published verses and prefaces only with initials, and who had previously appeared alongside Richard Brome, Alexander Brome, Herrick and Sir John Denham in the commendatory poems to Francis Beaumont and John Fletcher's *Comedies and Tragedies* of 1647.

4 **monument ... praise** The phraseology probably intentionally recalls Jonson's epitaph on Shakespeare, 'Thou art a monument, without a tomb' ('To the Memory of my Belovèd', 22).

4–6 **a praise ... sell worse** i.e. the poems, designed to increase the sale of the book rather than to attest to Cartwright's worth, put the thoughtful purchaser off.

4–5 **praise ... stationer** either a reference to the way the stationer Humphrey Moseley begged poets to write commendations for Cartwright's *Comedies*, or a reference to the poem that Moseley himself included in the *Comedies*, which begged praise for that edition.

5–6 **strength ... pens** quantity of money and number of pens

7–8 **calculate ... fifty-two** another allusion both to astronomy and to Cartwright's *Comedies* (see J. B.'s commendatory poem, p. 77, 9–12n.)

Not elevated unto fifty-two,
It may grow old as time or wit; and he,
That dares despise, may after envy thee.   10

Learning, the file of poesy, may be
Fetched from the arts and university,
But he that writes a play, and good, must know
Beyond his books, men and their actions too.
Copies of verse, that make the new men sweat,   15
Reach not a poem, nor the muse's heat;
Small bavin wits and wood may burn awhile,
And make more noise than forests on a pile,
Whose fibres shrunk, may invite a piteous stream,
Not to lament, but to extinguish them.   20
Thy fancy's metal, and thy strain's much higher
Proof 'gainst their wit and what that dreads, the fire.

James Shirley

---

11 **Learning . . . poesy** learning, the shaper and polisher of poetry; in Caesar Ripa's *Iconologia*, Fig. 2, Academia is represented by 'a Lady . . . having . . . a File in her right Hand, and a Garland in her left'. The file is described as denoting 'the *polishing* of pieces, and freeing them from *Superfluities*'.

12 another dig at academic playwrights either in their own right or as providers of commendations (see John Hall's poem, p. 76, 6 and n.).

15 **Copies of verse** The accusation is that the people who wrote praise for Cartwright's *Comedies* are versifiers rather than writers of proper poems.
   new men sweat i.e. newcomers to the job of writing commendations sweat with excitement

16 **Reach not** do not amount to

17 **bavin wits** A bavin is a bundle of brushwood or light underwood; *bavin wits* are inferior, bavin-like, literary men

who only make a short-lived blaze. Cf. *1H4*, 3.2.61–2: 'shallow jesters and rash bavin wits, / Soon kindled and soon burnt'. The reference is probably to the poets who wrote the encomiums to Cartwright's *Comedies*, but may also be to contemporary playwrights.

18 **forests . . . pile** a heap or stack for burning made up of forest trees

21 **fancy's metal** i.e. Brome's imagination is permanent (unlike wood)

21–2 **higher / Proof** (1) greater evidence; (2) of greater strength or quality

23 **James Shirley** English dramatist, whose career of playwriting extended from 1625 to 1642, when the theatres were closed. He and Brome were in Stanley's coterie; both were professional playwrights and at different points wrote plays for Christopher and William Beeston at the Cockpit/Phoenix in Drury Lane.

19 fibres] *Haaker;* fivres *Q1*   may] *(ma')*   23 James] *Haaker;* Ja: *Q1*

*To my worthy friend Master Richard Brome, on his excellent
play called A Jovial Crew: or The Merry Beggars*

There is a faction, friend, in town, that cries,
'Down with the dagon-poet! Jonson dies!
His works were too elaborate, not fit   5
To come within the verge, or face, of wit.
Beaumont and Fletcher', they say, 'perhaps, might
Pass well for current coin, in a dark night;
But Shakespeare, the plebeian driller, was
Foundered in's *Pericles*, and must not pass' –   10
And so at all men fly, that have but been
Thought worthy of applause; therefore, their spleen.
Ingrateful negro-kind, dart you your rage
Against the beams that warmed you, and the stage?
This malice shows it is unhallowed heat   15

4   **dagon-poet** Dagon was the national deity of the ancient Philistines; *dagon-poet* was a term of reproach for a poet held up as an idol by the unknowing.
   Jonson dies! i.e. Jonson's works ought to 'die'.

6   **within . . . face** within the area or within the sight of

8   **Pass . . . coin** easily be taken for contemporary currency

9   **driller** (1) one who entices or allures (*OED n.*[1], in which this line is sole recorded usage of the term); i.e. Shakespeare entices or allures plebeians; (2) one who 'protracts' or 'lengthens out' (*OED* drill *v.*[1] 2); i.e. Shakespeare protracts plebeian tales like *Pericles* (10). Alternatively, a misprint for 'droller'. In that case, the claim is that Shakespeare wrote drolls (farces, skits or puppet shows) for plebeians, or was himself a plebeian droll-writer.

10   **Foundered in's *Pericles*** undermined in his *Pericles*. Tatham here writes of those who belittle *Pericles* for being popular or populist; its appeal to common people was much attested: *Pimlico* depicts a crowd in a park and wonders whether 'all *These* / Came to see [Jane] *Shore*, or *Pericles*' (sig. C1[r]).
   must not pass cannot be approved or allowed

11   **at . . . fly** i.e. fly at or attack all playwrights

12   **worthy . . . spleen** i.e. those thought worthy of applause are consequently thought worthy of attack (by the outspoken *faction*, 3).

13–14 Those who dislike the great writers of the past who had *warmed* (roused) the stage are said to resemble Africans who rage at the sun that warms them. In making earlier playwrights, by analogy, the sun, Tatham suggests that writers of the past are a source for what is good on the stage now; their detractors, who resemble *negro-kind*, are both wrong and unEnglish.

15   **unhallowed heat** profane, impious heat (i.e. not the good heat of the sun referred to in 14)

That boils your raw brains, and your temples beat.
Adulterate pieces may retain the mould
Or stamp, but want the pureness of the gold.
But the world's mad; those jewels that were worn
In high esteem, by some laid by in scorn –   20
Like Indians, who their native wealth despise
And dote on stranger's trash and trumperies.
Yet, if it be not too far spent, there is
Some hopes left us, that this, thy well-wrought piece,
May bring it cure, reduce it to its sight,   25
To judge th' difference 'twixt the day and night;
Draw th' curtain of their errors, that their sense
May be conformable to Ben's influence,
And finding here nature and art agree,
May swear, thou livest in him, and he in thee.   30

John Tatham

16 **raw** uncivilized; coarse; brutal
beat beats
17 **Adulterate pieces** Plays written by, or liked by, the *faction* are here compared to false currency that has the correct image on it but, unlike the old coins/plays it superficially resembles, lacks the full gold content.
19 **jewels** i.e. plays by the older writers mentioned above: Jonson, Beaumont, Fletcher and Shakespeare
21–2 i.e. audiences nowadays despise their old native plays in favour of the superficial and gaudy, here presented as, also, less English. That native Americans (*Indians*) would 'sell pure Gold for basest merchandize', was a commonplace (Hagthorpe, 21).
23 **it . . . spent** i.e. the play isn't too exhausted of power (with a pun on money and spending)

24 **well-wrought piece** a return to the analogy in 8 and 17; this play is a proper, well-wrought, coin.
25 'may cure it (the *faction*) and bring it (the *faction*) to its (the play's) viewpoint'
26 metaphorically, 'so that they can analyse the difference between good and bad plays'
27 **Draw . . . errors** pull back the curtain from the *faction*'s errors
28 **conformable to** in conformity (agreement) with
Ben's Ben Jonson's
29 **here** in this play
30 **thou . . . him** Brome . . . Jonson
31 **John Tatham** (fl. 1632–64), dramatist, and also city poet. Brome wrote commendatory verses for his poetry collection *Fancies Theatre* (1640).

31 John] *Haaker;* Jo: *Q1*

To Master Richard Brome, upon his Comedy called
A Jovial Crew: or The Merry Beggars

Something I'd say, but not to praise thee, friend,
For thou thyself dost best thyself commend,
And he that with an eulogy doth come   5
May to's own wit raise an encomium,
But not to thine. Yet I'll before thee go,
Though whiffler-like, to usher in the show,
And like a quarter-clock, foretell the time
Is come about for greater bells to chime.   10

I must not praise thy poetry nor wit,
Though both are very good; yet that's not it.
The reader in his progress will find more
Wit in a line, than I praise in a score.
I shall be read with prejudice, for each line   15
I write of thee, or anything that's thine,
Be't name, or muse, will all be read of me,
As if I clawed myself by praising thee.

But though I may not praise, I hope I may
Be bold to love thee, and the world shall say   20
I've reason for't. I love thee for thy name;
I love thee for thy merit and thy fame;
I love thee for thy neat and harmless wit,
Thy mirth that does so clean and closely hit;

8 **whiffler-like** like one armed with a javelin and employed to keep the way clear before a public spectacle, from 'wifle' = javelin
9 **quarter-clock** clock that strikes the quarter-hours
13 **progress** advancement through the text – but with a hint at the *progress* that the courtiers will make in the play to join the beggars. See 2.1.79, 167, 216.
14 **a score** twenty

17 **of** as though it is about
18 **clawed** flattered
20 **Be bold** dare
21 **thy name** 'Brome' was a named shared by Alexander Brome, author of this poem, and Richard Brome, though they are not thought to have been related.
23 **neat** cleverly contrived
24 **clean** innocently
   hit succeed

Thy luck to please so well: who could go faster, 25
At first, to be the envy of thy master?
I love thee for thyself, for who can choose
But like the fountain of so brisk a muse?
I love this comedy, and every line,
Because 'tis good, as well's because 'tis thine. 30

Thou tell'st the world the life that beggars lead;
'Tis seasonable, 'twill become our trade.
'T must be our study too, for, in this time,
Who'll not be innocent, since wealth's a crime?
Thou'rt th'age's doctor now, for, since all go 35
To make us poor, thou mak'st us merry too.

Go on, and thrive; may all thy sportings be
Delightful unto all as th'are to me.
May this so please t'encourage thee that more
May be made public which thou keep'st in store; 40

25–6 **faster . . . master** Jonson was upset by the instant success of Brome's now lost *Lovesick Maid* at Blackfriars, which followed closely upon the failure of Jonson's *New Inn* in 1629 at the same theatre. Edmond Malone, looking at Herbert's office book, now lost, records: 'after the ill success of Jonson's piece The New Inn, the King's Company brought out at the same theatre a new play called The Love-Sick Maid, which was . . . acted with extraordinary applause. This play, which was written by Jonson's own servant, Richard Brome, was so popular that the managers of the King's Company . . . presented the Master of the Revels with the sum of two pounds, "on the good success of the Honour of Ladies"' (Bawcutt, 177). Jonson expressed his envy by bemoaning that '*Broomes sweepings*

doe as well . . . as his Masters Meale' (Jonson, 'Ode to himself').

28 **fountain . . . muse** The Muses were associated with fountains, being thought to be, in origin, water nymphs; they were said to live on Mount Helicon, where there were two sacred fountains dedicated to them, Aganippe and Hippocrene.

32 **seasonable** opportune
   'twill . . . trade (1) it (telling the world) will befit our trade; (2) it (being a beggar) will become our profession

33 **study** pursuit

34 **innocent** i.e. like the beggars

37 **sportings** amusements

39 **May . . . thee** may this please enough to encourage you

40 **keep'st in store** The suggestion is that Brome has other unpublished plays; he is encouraged to release them to the press.

That, though we've lost their dress, we may be glad
To see and think on th'happiness we had,
And thou thereby mayst make our name to shine:
'Twas royal once, but now 'twill be divine.

Alexander Brome   45

41 **their dress** i.e. their theatrical performance

43 **our name** the two men's shared name of 'Brome'; see 21n.

44 **royal once** Alexander Brome is associating 'Brome' with the yellow broom sprig or *planta genesta* taken up by Geoffrey IV, Duke of Anjou, and worn on his helmet in battle. Geoffrey's royal heirs – his son was Henry II – assumed the name 'Plantagenet' as a consequence. The association between the plant and Brome was also made by Aston Cokain in his preliminary poem to Brome's *Five New* (1653): '(with a justly attributed praise) / Wee change our faded Broom, to deathlesse Baies' (sig. A2ᵛ).

44 **divine** immortal
Alexander Brome (1620–60), poet and dramatist, edited Brome's *Five New Plays* in 1653 and a further *Five New Plays* in 1659.

45 Alexander] *Haaker;* Alex. *Q1*

A
JOVIAL CREW,
OR
THE MERRY
BEGGARS

LIST OF ROLES

OLDRENTS	*a landowner*
RACHEL	*his older daughter; lover to Vincent or Hilliard*
MERIEL	*his younger daughter; lover to Vincent or Hilliard*
SPRINGLOVE	*steward to Oldrents*
HEARTY	*his friend; Martin's uncle* 5
RANDALL, *a groom*	
USHER	
BUTLER	*servants to Oldrents*
COOK	
CHAPLAIN	10
VINCENT	*suitor to Rachel or Meriel*
HILLIARD	*suitor to Rachel or Meriel*
Justice CLACK	*a judge*
OLIVER	*his son*
AMY	*his niece; affianced to Tallboy* 15
MARTIN	*his clerk; nephew to Hearty and suitor to Amy*
SENTWELL	
1 GENTLEMAN	*friends to Clack*
2 GENTLEMAN	
TALLBOY	*affianced to Amy* 20
CONSTABLE	
PATRICO, *a beggar-priest*	
AUTEM MORT, *his wife*	
SOLDIER	
LAWYER	25
COURTIER	*beggars*
SCRIBBLE, *a beggar-poet*	
BRIDE	
GROOM	
1 BEGGAR	30

Beggar-dancers; Beggar-fiddlers; Beggar-piper; Servants; Watch

1 OLDRENTS a name combining (1) one who has, from ancient times, lived on the rents he garners from his property; (2) one who offers reasonable ('old price') rents to his tenants; (3) one whose house is divided by old 'rents' or fractures

2 RACHEL a (parody) 'romance' name; see p. 10.

3 MERIEL a (parody) 'romance' name that may also, with its suggestions of 'merry', hint at Meriel's good humour; see p. 10.

4 SPRINGLOVE a name combining (1) a lover of the spring; (2) one who energetically falls ('springs') into love; (3) one whose nature 'springs' from the sexual passion that brought him about

5 HEARTY a name combining (1) full of heart, trustworthy; (2) genial, obsessed with merriment

6 RANDALL Randall, when angry, rands (tears apart – thus also recalling the 'rents' of Oldrents) or rants at all things. His name may also have been chosen for its association with servants; the servant to Thomas More in the play of that name is called Randall.

7–10 All four servants are described as having the same grey 'livery-beards'; references to 'grey-beards' in the play are to these servants together with Oldrents and Hearty (see 4.1.256.3n.).

11 VINCENT a (parody) 'romance' name that may also hint at the character's naivety. Robert Greene, in *2 Coney-catching*, defines 'The vincent' as 'the simple man that stands by, & [is] not acquainted with . . . cosenage' (sig. A4ʳ).

12 HILLIARD a (parody) 'romance' name

13 CLACK named after his 'clacking' tongue – to 'clack' meaning to chatter, prate or talk loquaciously

14 OLIVER a (parody) romance name that may also reflect Oliver's aggressive character. A famous phrase of the time was 'A Roland for an Oliver', Roland and Oliver having been heroes of romance, and friends who were equally good at fighting.

15 AMY The name means 'beloved', but was also chosen because of its links to sighing, as the words of Tallboy's song, *Amy . . . Ay me* (4.1.2–3) make clear.

17 SENTWELL The name either suggests that Sentwell is 'well sent' on errands, or that it is 'well' that he is 'sent'.

20 TALLBOY Jokes about Tallboy throughout the play concern his height, as lines such as 'thou art a tall fellow' (4.1.365) make clear. They also concern his youthful appearance ('art not ashamed to cry at this growth?', 10–11; 'young . . . by the beard you wear', 90–1); he is called a *lamb* and offered a *suckbottle* (baby's feeding bottle) to cheer him up (5.1.542, 541). Depending on the nature of the joke, he will have been played by a particularly tall or a particularly short boy.

22 PATRICO A description, rather than a name, 'Patrico' was the title given a beggar-priest whose job was to marry young couples.

23 AUTEM MORT A description, rather than a name, 'Autem Mort' was beggars' cant for a married woman.

24–5 SOLDIER, LAWYER beggars whose characters are defined by the social position they once had

26 COURTIER a beggar whose character is defined by the social position he once had. He is lame or pretends to be; in 1.1.422 he is described as wanting a leg.

27 SCRIBBLE a beggar whose character is defined by the social position he once had. He may be a parody of the playwright William Davenant; see p. 28.

31 **Beggar-fiddlers; Beggar-piper** The fiddlers are only mentioned in 'The Persons of the Play'; in the text the specific music asked for (at 1.1.382 SD and 4.2.171 SD) requires a beggar-piper.

A JOVIAL CREW

PROLOGUE.

The title of our play, *A Jovial Crew*,
May seem to promise mirth, which were a new
And forced thing, in these sad and tragic days,
For you to find, or we express, in plays.
We wish you, then, would change that expectation,   5
Since jovial mirth is now grown out of fashion,
Or much not to expect. For now it chances,
Our comic writer, finding that romances
Of lovers, through much travel and distress –
Till it be thought no power can redress   10

PROLOGUE. It is unclear whether this text was written in the 1640s or 1652, so it is impossible to say who its speaker may have been, if anyone. The prologue's regret about current times is of a piece with the dedication and preliminary poems for *A Jovial Crew*; it is situated with those paratexts in Q. Given that Brome's *City Wit*, in *Five New* (1653), appears to have been published with a prologue written for the page rather than the stage – it asks 'that you will not looke, / To find more in the Title then the Booke' and names its pedantic speaker 'a Page, compar'd to the whole volume' (sigs A2ᵛ–A3ʳ) – the prologue to *A Jovial Crew* may be a publication statement from 1652, and hence a prologue for readers. It was not unusual for Brome to add new, later, prologues to plays he had written earlier. His *Weeding*, in *Five New* (1659), includes 'Another Prologue' written 'some ten years' after the play itself (sig. A2ᵛ). See p. 49.

3   **sad . . . days** The days are *tragic* either because the English Civil War and closure

of the theatres are approaching (if the prologue dates to 1640 or 1641 when the play was staged), or because the Civil War has taken place and the theatres are now closed (if it was written in 1651 or 1652 when the play was published)

7   **much . . . expect** not much to be expected
    chances happens

8   **romances** decadent, ornate, spectacular plays about impossible knightly adventures for love, written by Cavalier playwrights including Aston Cokain (1608–94), Lodowick Carlell (1601/2–75), William Cartwright (1611–43), William Habington (1605–54), Henry Glapthorne (1610–c. 43), Thomas Killigrew (1612–83), Richard Lovelace (1617–57), Jasper Mayne (1604–72) and Sir John Suckling (*c.* 1609–41). William Davenant, who had planned to set up a theatre that would perform court-style romances, had written some prototype plays including, in 1639, *The Distresses*, which claimed to be full of 'romance humor' and to show the 'romance way' (*Works*, sig. 4h3ʳ ᵛ); see p. 29.

PROLOGUE.] *Q1*

90

Th'afflicted wanderers, though stout chivalry
Lend all his aid for their delivery,
Till, lastly, some impossibility
Concludes all strife and makes a comedy –
Finding, he says, such stories bear the sway,   15
Near as he could, he has composed a play
Of fortune-tellers, damsels and their squires,
Exposed to strange adventures through the briers
Of love and fate. But why need I forestall
What shall so soon be obvious to you all,   20
But wish the dullness may make no man sleep,
Nor sadness of it any woman weep.

1.1   [*Enter*] OLDRENTS [*and*] HEARTY.

OLDRENTS

It has indeed, friend, much afflicted me.

HEARTY

And very justly, let me tell you, sir,
That could so impiously be curious

---

11 **chivalry** bravery or prowess in war;
warlike distinction or glory (*OED n.* 3b
cites this line)
15 **bear the sway** domineer; rule
17–19 **fortune-tellers . . . fate** The prologue
is a critique of public taste, as well as a
capitulation to it; though *A Jovial Crew*
includes these features, it is a satire on
what constitutes a romance as much as a
romance itself.
18 **briers** literally, prickly, thorny bushes or
shrubs; figuratively, troubles, difficulties
or vexations
22 **weep** This last line, ending on *weep*, is
the first hint that the play to come may not
be as light-hearted as its title suggests.
1.1 Location: upstairs in Oldrents' house
(Hearty says, on exiting, that he will await

Oldrents' coming down, 108). The space
appears to abut the beggars' barn, which
is revealed by pulling back a curtain.
1 The play begins in mid-conversation;
Oldrents has just told Hearty that he has
been visiting a fortune-teller. The idea
that past events overshadow present
ones is introduced here, as is the topsy-
turvy theme of the play, in which those
expected to be happy are sad and vice
versa. The technique of beginning a play
mid-conversation to pique the audience's
interest was often adopted; Shakespeare
used it for *AYL* and *AC*.
3–4 **That . . . you** i.e. who could be so lacking in religious piety as to obtain an astrological prognostication about yourself
3 **curious** anxious, concerned

1.1] (*Actus Primus.*)   0 SD *Enter*] *Dodsley*   OLDRENTS *and*] *Dodsley;* OLDRENTS *Q1*

To tempt a judgement on you; to give ear,
And faith, too, by your leave, to fortune-tellers,   5
Wizards and gypsies!
OLDRENTS   I have since been frighted
With't in a thousand dreams.
HEARTY   I would be drunk
A thousand times to bed, rather than dream
Of any of their riddlemy riddlemies.
If they prove happy, so; if not, let't go: 10
You'll never find their meaning till the event
(If you suppose there was, at all, a meaning) –
As the equivocating devil had when he
Cozened the monk to let him live soul-free
Till he should find him sleeping between sheets;   15

4   **tempt . . . you** (1) reach a decision about a future event deduced from the positions of the heavenly bodies (*OED* judgement *n.* 5b), rather than 'piously' from God; (2) invite God to punish you

6   **gypsies** from 'Egyptians' (see *OED* gipsy *n.* 1a). John Cowell describes 'Egyptians' as 'a counterfeit kinde of roagues, that being English or Welch people, accompany themselves together, disguising themselves in straunge roabes, blacking their faces and bodies, and framing to themselves an unknowne language, wander up and downe, and under pretence of telling of Fortunes, curing diseases, and such like, abuse the ignorant common people, by stealing all that is not too hote or too heavie for their cariaage' (sig. 2b1ʳ); John Florio adds, 'counterfaite egiptians . . . are thought by their witchcraft to bewitch folks purses, and by secret meanes to pick away and cosen them of their monie' (1611, 615).

9   **riddlemy riddlemies** riddles, puzzles or enigmas (*OED* riddlemy riddlemy *n.* cites this line as only recorded usage); a reduplication of 'riddle me' or 'riddle my', or a corruption of 'riddle me my riddle'

10   **they** i.e. the prognostications
     happy apt; successful

11   'You'll never find out what they mean until what was prophesied occurs.'

13–20 The *whim* or 'play on words' is that the devil's bargain allowed the monk to live *free* of *soul* (free of mortality, or free of religious duties) up until the time he went to sleep *between sheets*; the monk avoided sleeping in a bed thereafter, but was caught by the devil as he dozed over the *sheet-leaves* of his book. A source has not been located for the story, which appears to have been invented for this play. The pun on *sheets* was often employed in the drama of the period. In *Atheist's Tragedy*, Levidulcia offers to write 'a word or two' to reconcile Sebastian with his father; Sebastian, who is seducing her, responds, 'That you doe for mee, will not be contain'd in lesse then the compasse of two sheetes' (sig. F1ʳ).

14–15 i.e. duped the monk that he (the devil) would let him (the monk) live *soul-free* until he (the devil) should find him (the monk) sleeping *between sheets*

4 To] *Dodsley;* Yo *Q1*

The wary monk, abjuring all such lodging,
At last, by overwatching in his study,
The foul fiend took him napping with his nose
Betwixt the sheet-leaves of his conjuring book.
There was the whim or double meaning on't.   20
But these fond fortune-tellers, that know nothing,
Aim to be thought more cunning than their master,
The foresaid devil, though truly not so hurtful.
Yet, trust 'em? Hang 'em! Wizards? Old blind
    buzzards!
For once they hit, they miss a thousand times,   25
And most times give quite contrary, bad for good
And best for worst. One told a gentleman
His son should be a man-killer and hanged for't,
Who after proved a great and rich physician,
And with great fame i'th' university   30
Hanged up in picture for a grave example.
There was the whim of that. Quite contrary!
OLDRENTS   And that was happy. Would mine could so
    deceive my fears.
HEARTY
    They may, but trust not to't. Another schemist   35

17 **overwatching** staying awake too long
21 **fond** foolish
22 **cunning** skilful; learned
24 **blind buzzards** stupid, senseless people.
    The phrase does not refer to the bird,
    which has good sight, but to the black
    beetle, which is clumsy, and whose fly-
    ing makes a buzzing sound. Dent lists
    'He is a blind buzzard' as proverbial
    (B792).
25 'For every one instance when they are
    correct, they are incorrect for a thousand.'
28 **man-killer** The precarious cures of
    physicians of the time regularly killed
    patients. See the anonymous *Two Wise
    Men*, where Gulato 'can passe for a

Physician . . . and kill as many as the best
Doctor of them all' (sig. F3ʳ ᵛ).
31 **grave example** (1) serious example; (2)
    example who leads people to the grave
33 **happy** lucky; fortunate
35 **schemist** framer of 'schemes' or horo-
    scopes; an astrologer; *OED n.* 1 cites this
    passage as first recorded usage. The
    derogatory term reflected the profession's
    reliance on 'schemes' or written horo-
    scopes, which were often used for tricking
    the gullible. Subtle, in Ben Jonson's
    Alchemist, 4.4.18–19, pretends to Dame
    Pliant that he has learned that 'By this
    my scheme you are to undergo / An
    honourable fortune very shortly'.

Found that a squint-eyed boy should prove a notable
Pickpurse and afterwards a most strong thief,
When he grew up to be a cunning lawyer
And at last died a judge. Quite contrary!
How many have been marked out by these wizards   40
For fools, that after have been pricked for sheriffs?
Was not a shepherd-boy foretold to be
A drunkard, and to get his living from
Bawds, whores, thieves, quarrellers and the like?
And did he not become a suburb justice,   45
And live in wine and worship by the fees
Racked out of such delinquents? There's the
    whim on't.
Now I come to you. Your figure-flinger finds
That both your daughters, notwithstanding all
Your great possessions, which they are coheirs of,   50

36 **squint-eyed** literally, affected with a squint; cross-eyed – see *Advertisements*: 'a squint-ey'd look, wherewith while she seems to look fixedly upon one, she is very intent in observing another' (sig. 3g'). By extension, the phrase came to refer to a double-dealer.

37–8 **Pickpurse ... thief ... lawyer** Lawyers were said to empty their clients' purses of money very readily; Thomas Wilson catechizes, 'I praie you who getteth the money? The lawyers ... Undoubtedly the lawyer never dieth a begger' (*Rhetoric*, sig. E4').

41 **fools ... sheriffs** Local sheriffs were notoriously unintelligent; *City Madam*, 5.2.72–3, contains a description of 'a foolish creature / Call'd an Under-sheriffe'. These dramatic stereotypes were popular in a country overwhelmed with petty officialdom (see Kent).

    pricked selected; from the habit of indicating who, in a list, had been chosen by pricking the paper or parchment next to their names. The word was particularly used for the process of the sovereign's choosing a sheriff; see *OED* prick v. 21. Raphael Holinshed, in his *Chronicles*, explains how 'the Prince ... foorthwyth pricketh some suche one of them ... who hereupon is Shirife of that shyre, for one whole yeare' (sig. K2').

43–7 **drunkard ... delinquents** Suburban justices were notorious drinkers, as the depiction of Justice Clack will illustrate.

45 **suburb justice** a suburban Justice of the Peace, typically a grandiose person who profits from his role within his minor community; *Sparagus Garden* refers to 'some Suburbe Justice, that sits o'the skirts o'the City, and lives by't' (sig. D2').

47 **Racked out** literally, extracted while on the rack; figuratively, obtained or extorted

48 **figure-flinger** contemptuous synonym for 'figure-caster', or astrologer: someone who casts (flings) numbers around in order to make astrological predictions. William Perkins warns desperate people 'not to seeke for helpe or remedie at the hands of Astrologers, commonly called *Figure casters*' (sig. F4').

Shall yet be beggars. May it not be meant
(If, as I said, there be a meaning in it)
They may prove courtiers, or great courtiers' wives,
And so be beggars in law?
Is not that the whim on't, think you? You shall think   55
no worse on't.

OLDRENTS
Would I had your merry heart.

HEARTY   I thank you, sir.

OLDRENTS
I mean the like.

HEARTY   I would you had, and I
Such an estate as yours. Four thousand yearly,
With such a heart as mine, would defy Fortune   60
And all her babbling soothsayers. I'd as soon
Distrust in Providence as lend a fear
To such a destiny for a child of mine
While there be sack and songs in town or country.
Think, like a man of conscience – now I am serious –   65
What justice can there be for such a curse
To fall upon your heirs? Do you not live
Free, out of law or grieving any man?

51–4 **May . . . law** i.e. may they not 'beg' suits and favours in a courtly fashion? That courtiers were high-class beggars was a poignant conceit for Brome, author of *Court Beggar*. See 426–7, 2.1.376–7 and 5.1.560–4. In Thomas Heywood's *Royal King*, the Captain declares, 'were I a begger, I might be a Courtiers fellow: / Could I begge suites my Lord as well as you' (sig. C1ᵛ).

61 **babbling soothsayers** chattering prognosticators; prating claimants to the power of foretelling the 'sooth' or truth

62 **lend** hold out; cf. *JC*, 3.2.74: 'lend me your ears'.

64 **sack** from 'sec', meaning 'dry'; sack is a general name used for a class of white wines imported from Spain and the Canaries (see *OED n.*³ 1). The subject of acquiring happiness artificially, often through a combination of drinking sack and singing songs, is a preoccupation of this play.

65 **conscience** sense or understanding; cf. *Tim*, 2.2.175–6: 'Canst thou the conscience lack, / To think I shall lack friends?'

66 **justice** propriety; conformity to reason (*OED n.* 3)

68 **out of law** not engaged in legal action

54–6] *this edn; Q1 lines* that / worse on't /

Are you not th'only rich man lives unenvied?
Have you not all the praises of the rich   70
And prayers of the poor? Did ever any
Servant or hireling, neighbour, kindred, curse you,
Or wish one minute shortened of your life?
Have you one grudging tenant? Will they not all
Fight for you? Do they not teach their children,   75
And make 'em, too, pray for you morn and evening,
And in their graces too, as duly as
For King and realm? The innocent things would think
They ought not eat else.

OLDRENTS   'Tis their goodness.

HEARTY

It is your merit. Your great love and bounty   80
Procures from heaven those inspirations in 'em.
Whose rent did ever you exact? Whose have
You not remitted, when by casualties
Of fire, of floods, of common dearth or sickness,
Poor men were brought behindhand? Nay,
         whose losses   85
Have you not piously repaired?

OLDRENTS   Enough.

HEARTY

What heriots have you ta'en from forlorn widows?
What acre of your thousands have you racked?

---

72 **hireling** hired servant
76–7 **pray . . . duly** a foreshadowing of 'duly and truly pray for you', the refrain that the disguised gentry will use as beggars when they attempt to extract money from gentlemen
77 **graces** short prayers either asking a blessing before, or rendering thanks after, a meal (*OED* grace *n.* 20)
81 **inspirations** exalted impulses – with some suggestion that they are brought about by the spirit of God

82 **exact** demand and enforce the payment of
83 **remitted** deferred, diminished or possibly abandoned altogether (*OED* remit *v.* 13, 5a, 5b)
84 **dearth** scarcity
85 **behindhand** late; in arrears
86 **repaired** restored
87 **heriots** in English law, the custom that the best live beast or dead chattel should be paid to the landlord when a tenant died (*OED* heriot *n.* 2, citing this line)
88 **racked** charged an excessive rent for (*OED* rack *v.*[1], citing this line)

OLDRENTS

Good friend, no more.

HEARTY   These are enough, indeed,

To fill your ears with joyful acclamations   90

Where'er you pass: 'Heaven bless our landlord,
     Oldrents;

Our master, Oldrents; our good patron, Oldrents.'

Cannot these sounds conjure that evil spirit

Of fear out of you, that your children shall

Live to be beggars? Shall Squire Oldrents' daughters   95

Wear old rents in their garments – there's a whim,
     too –

Because a fortune-teller told you so?

OLDRENTS

Come, I will strive to think no more on't.

HEARTY

Will you ride forth for air, then, and be merry?

OLDRENTS

Your counsel and example may instruct me.   100

HEARTY

Sack must be had in sundry places, too.

For songs, I am provided.

---

91 **Heaven** pronounced in this play with one syllable, i.e. 'Heav'n'

93 **conjure** convey away

96 **old rents** Hearty's pun reminds the audience that most names in this play are themselves 'whims' or double meanings. So far, 'old rents' has appeared to be a comment on Oldrents' source of wealth; here is the first suggestion that it might refer to ancient tears or holes and thus also predict poverty.

101–2 **Sack . . . songs** This theme either exemplifies or parodies Robert Burton's idea that to cure melancholy there is 'in my Judgment none so present, none so powerfull, none so apposite as a cup of strong drinke, mirth, Musick, and merry company' (372).

101 **sundry** several

102 **am provided** have a supply

91 Oldrents] *Haaker; Oldrent Q1*   92 Oldrents . . . Oldrents] *Haaker; Oldrent . . . Oldrent Q1*   95 Oldrents']
Haaker; Oldrent's Q1

Enter SPRINGLOVE *with books and papers*[;]
he lays them on the table.

OLDRENTS

Yet here comes one brings me a second fear,
Who has my care the next unto my children.

HEARTY

Your steward, sir, it seems has business with you.   105
I wish you would have none.

OLDRENTS   I'll soon dispatch it,
And then be for our journey instantly.

HEARTY

I'll wait your coming down, sir.   *Exit.*

OLDRENTS

But why, Springlove, is now this expedition?

SPRINGLOVE

Sir, 'tis duty.   110

OLDRENTS

Not common among stewards, I confess,
To urge in their accounts before the day
Their lords have limited. Some that are grown
To hoary hairs and knighthoods are not found
Guilty of such an importunity.   115
'Tis yet but thirty days, when I give forty

104 **has my care** (1) has my regard; (2) needs my protection
105 **steward** described by Thomas Thomas as 'one that hath the charge of his masters monie' (sig. E6ᵛ), and in *OED* (*n.* 1a) as an official who controls the domestic affairs of a household, supervising the service of his master's table, directing the domestics and regulating household expenditure
108 **coming down** The exit from the house is understood to be downstairs from the room in which the characters are currently situated.
109 **expedition** haste
110 **duty** that which one ought or is bound to do
112 **urge in** impress upon the attention (of their employers)
113 **limited** specified; delimited
115 **an importunity** unseasonableness
116 **give** gave – but Oldrents' use of the present tense shows how immediate the event is to him.

112+ accounts] *(Accompts)*

After the half-year-day, Our Lady last.
Could I suspect my trust were lost in thee,
Or doubt thy youth had not ability
To carry out the weight of such a charge,   120
I then should call on thee.
SPRINGLOVE   Sir, your indulgence,
I hope, shall ne'er corrupt me. Ne'ertheless,
The testimony of a fair discharge,
From time to time, will be encouragement
To virtue in me.

(*Springlove turns over the several books
to his master.*)

You may then be pleased   125
To take here a survey of all your rents
Received, and all such other payments as
Came to my hands since my last audit, for
Cattle, wool, corn, all fruits of husbandry.
Then, my receipts on bonds and some new leases,   130
With some old debts, and almost desperate ones,
As well from country cavaliers as courtiers.

117 **half-year-day** one of two days spaced
half a year apart on which rents became
due. As Lady Day, 25 March, is the
accounting day referred to, the other
accounting day in the Oldrents' household must be its counterpart, Michaelmas
Day, 29 September. Springlove presents
his accounts a mere thirty days after
Lady Day (so on 24 April), though he had
been allowed forty days to close his
accounts.
123 **discharge** fulfilment; performance
126 **survey** Garrett A. Sullivan points out that
'Springlove's surveying pun . . . involves
not the remeasuring or revaluing of
Oldrents' lands, but simply the landlord's
scrutiny of the work performed and

information collected by the steward'
(160); it does, however, predict the journey
Springlove will take 'to survey and
measure lands abroad' in 2.2.61.
129 **fruits of husbandry** results of careful
management. Cf. *Mac*, 2.1.4–5: 'There's
husbandry in heaven; / Their candles are
all out.'
131 **desperate** irretrievable; irreclaimable
132 **As well from . . . as** both from . . . and
from
cavaliers gentlemen trained to arms,
courtly gentlemen, gallants (*OED* cavalier
n. and *adj.* 2a). The word was already
being used reproachfully of seventeenth-
century Royalists, thought of as swash-
bucklers who enjoyed the prospect of

125 SD] *this edn; after 124 Q1*

Then here, sir, are my several disbursements
In all particulars for yourself and daughters,
In charge of housekeeping, buildings and repairs,   135
Journeys, apparel, coaches, gifts, and all
Expenses for your personal necessaries.
Here, servants' wages, liveries and cures,
Here for supplies of horses, hawks and hounds,
And lastly, not the least to be remembered,   140
Your large benevolences to the poor.

OLDRENTS

Thy charity there goes hand in hand with mine,
And, Springlove, I commend it in thee, that
So young in years art grown so ripe in goodness.
May their heaven-piercing prayers bring on thee   145
Equal rewards with me.

SPRINGLOVE   Now here, sir, is
The balance of the several accounts,
Which shows you what remains in cash, which added
Unto your former bank, makes up in all –

OLDRENTS

Twelve thousand and odd pounds.

SPRINGLOVE   Here are the keys   150
Of all. The chests are safe in your own closet.

OLDRENTS

Why in my closet? Is not yours as safe?

---

fighting for the King. *OED* cavalier *n.* and *adj.* 3 quotes Edward Montagu, Earl of Manchester, who, in *The Right Honorable the Lord Kimbolton his Speech in Parliament on Tuesday the Third of January 1641* (1642), refers to 'Ill affected cavaleers and commanders about the Court'. The term was later used for followers of the King during the Civil War.

133 **disbursements** expenditures

135 **In charge of** in the care of

138 **cures** (1) cares, duties; (2) medical treatments

141 **benevolences** contributions for the support of the needy

142 **hand in hand** side by side; concurrently (*OED* hand in hand *adv.* 1b cites this line)

145 **their** i.e. the poor's

149 **bank** sum of money; amount (*OED n.*³ II 3, citing this line)

151 **closet** private repository of valuables (*OED n.* 3a)

SPRINGLOVE

   Oh, sir, you know my suit.

OLDRENTS   Your suit? What suit?

SPRINGLOVE

   Touching the time of year.

OLDRENTS   'Tis well-nigh May.   154

   Why, what of that, good Springlove?   *Nightingale sings.*

SPRINGLOVE

   Oh, sir, you hear I'm called.

OLDRENTS   Fie, Springlove, fie.

   I hoped thou hadst abjured that uncouth practice.

SPRINGLOVE

   You thought I had forsaken nature, then.

OLDRENTS

   Is that disease of nature still in thee

   So virulent? And, notwithstanding all   160

   My favours – in my gifts, my cares and counsels,

   Which to a soul ingrateful might be boasted –

   Have I first bred thee, and then preferred thee, from

   I will not say how wretched a beginning,

   To be a master over all my servants?   165

   Planted thee in my bosom? And canst thou,

   There, slight me for the whistling of a bird?

SPRINGLOVE

   Your reason, sir, informs you, that's no cause,

   But 'tis the season of the year that calls me.

---

153 **suit** supplication; petition

154 **well-nigh** very nearly

155 SD i.e. the sound of a nightingale is made, presumably using a whistle as 167 suggests. As each of Brome's birdcalls is different, a number of whistles or other instruments will have been needed in the tiring-house to make the separate noises. John Bate, in *Mysteries*, describes 'long white boxes' from France that could give up to eleven different birdcalls, and also explains ways of making instruments which he calls 'The Cooko Pipe' and 'A Call for small Birds' (82).

157 **abjured** foresworn; repudiated
    uncouth strange, unpleasant or distasteful (*OED adj.* and *n.* 4, citing this line)

162 **ingrateful** not feeling or showing gratitude

163 **preferred** advanced

155 SD] *Haaker; opp. 155–6 Q1*

101

What moves her notes provokes my disposition   170
By a more absolute power of nature than
Philosophy can render an account for.

OLDRENTS

I find there's no expelling it, but still
It will return. I have tried all the means,
As I may safely think, in humane wisdom,   175
And did, as near as reason could, assure me
That thy last year's restraint had stopped forever
That running sore on thee, that gadding humour:
When, only for that cause, I laid the weight
Of mine estate in stewardship upon thee,   180
Which kept thee in that year, after so many
Summer vagaries thou hadst made before.

SPRINGLOVE

You kept a swallow in a cage that while.
I cannot, sir, endure another summer
In that restraint, with life: 'twas then my torment,   185

---

170 **her notes** Spring was often feminized because it is a time of birth and fruitfulness.

172 **Philosophy** learning; knowledge
render . . . for Springlove describes the season using terms from his stewarding profession; his love of nature is tempered by his other job and vice versa.

173 **still** invariably

175 **humane** civilizing (*OED adj.* 2)

177 **last year's restraint** Oldrents prevented Springlove's expedition the previous year by making him steward of the estate, which increased his workload and obliged him to be present on the two half-yearly accounting days (see 117n. and 179–82).

178 **running sore** weeping wound. Though used figuratively to mean constant irritation, the phrase draws attention to the

fact that beggar life involves untended diseases.
gadding humour disposition to wander

182 **vagaries** vag'ries; excursions

183 **swallow . . . cage** A swallow represented spring. See *Love and Eloquence*: 'Q. what birds of all others are the most perfect heralds of the Spring? / A. The Swallow and the Cuckow' (sig. N8ʳ). Caging the swallow, however, denies spring, while suggesting that the homes of the gentry are a form of imprisonment. In Thomas Jordon's 'Meditation on a Bird', a caged bird is described as a '*little prisoner*' who 'hops about / Her wyrie *Cage*' (sig. F4ʳ). The caged bird analogy is turned on its head in 2.1.231–4.

184–5 **I cannot . . . life** 'Another summer under such restraint will kill me.'

175 humane] human *Haaker*

But now my death. Yet, sir, my life is yours
Who are my patron; freely may you take it.
[*Kneels.*] Yet pardon, sir, my frailty, that do beg
A small continuance of it on my knees.

OLDRENTS

Can there no means be found to preserve life   190
In thee but wandering like a vagabond?
Does not the sun as comfortably shine
Upon my gardens as the opener fields?
Or on my fields as others far remote?
Are not my walks and greens as delectable   195
As the highways and commons? Are the shades
Of sycamore and bowers of eglantine
Less pleasing than of bramble or thorn-hedges?
Or of my groves and thickets than wild woods?
Are not my fountain-waters fresher than   200
The troubled streams where every beast does drink?
Do not the birds sing here as sweet and lively

190–207 The passage reworks one in *Old Fortunatus*, 2.2.400–6, where Shadow asks, 'what can you see abroad that is not at home? The same Sunne cals you up in the morning, and the same man in the Moone lights you to bed at night, our fields are as greene as theirs in summer, and their frosts will nip us more in winter: Our birds sing as sweetly, & our women are as fair.' In each of Oldrents' instances, 'the first element in the comparison signifies exclusivity and order, while the second is a common space defined either by its uncultivated nature (bramble, wild woods) or its general accessibility (open fields, commons)' (Sullivan, 162).

191 **wandering ... vagabond** leading a nomadic life – a reference to the Beggars'

Act, originally published in 1598 and regularly reissued, which detailed the members of society who constituted 'Rogues, Vagabonds, and Sturdy Beggars' and how they were to be punished
wandering wand'ring
195 **greens** grassy spots
196 **highways** public roads forming ordinary routes between one town or city and another
commons undivided land belonging to the members of a local community
197 **eglantine** eglantine rose or sweet brier, a scented plant combining flowers and thorns which had associations with pleasure and pain. It symbolized the suffering of love, and, because Elizabeth I had used it as an emblem, also represented England at her most courtly.

188 SD] *this edn*   191 wandering] *(wandring)*

As any other where? Is not thy bed more soft,
And rest more safe, than in a field or barn?
Is a full table, which is called thine own,   205
Less curious or wholesome than the scraps
From others' trenchers, twice or thrice translated?

SPRINGLOVE
Yea, in the winter season, when the fire
Is sweeter than the air.

OLDRENTS   What air is wanting?

SPRINGLOVE
Oh, sir, you've heard of pilgrimages and   210
The voluntary travels of good men.

OLDRENTS
For penance or to holy ends? But bring
Not those into comparison, I charge you.

SPRINGLOVE
I do not, sir. But pardon me to think
Their sufferings are much sweetened by delights,   215
Such as we find by shifting place and air.

OLDRENTS
Are there delights in beggary? Or, if to take
Diversity of air be such a solace,
Travel the kingdom over, and if this
Yield not variety enough, try further,   220
Provided your deportment be gentle.

---

205 **full table** literally, a table covered with food; figuratively, 'full board', the full provision of food for meals
206 **curious** exquisitely prepared. John Stephens writes, 'The inviter . . . cannot well provide . . . One dish so curious, as may please each tast' (*Satirical*, sig. A7ᵛ).
207 **trenchers** wooden platters, used as plates
    translated transferred

209 **What . . . wanting** Springlove likes to stay on the estate in wintertime when the fire is more pleasant than the (cold) air; Oldrents asks what the air in his estate lacks currently. Alternatively, Oldrents, concerned that he has no 'heir', mishears what Springlove is saying.
221 **deportment** bearing; demeanour
    gentle (1) gentlemanly; genteel; (2) kind

215 sweetened] *(sweetned)*   221 gentle] *(gentile)*

Take horse, and man and money: you have all,
Or I'll allow enough.   *Sing nightingale, cuckoo, etc.*
SPRINGLOVE   Oh, how am I confounded!
[*Rises.*] Dear sir, retort me naked to the world
Rather than lay those burdens on me which   225
Will stifle me. I must abroad or perish.
OLDRENTS [*aside*]
I will no longer strive to wash this Moor,
Nor breathe more minutes so unthriftily
In civil argument against rude wind,
But rather practise to withdraw my love   230
And tender care, if it be possible,
From that unfruitful breast, incapable
Of wholesome counsel.
SPRINGLOVE   Have I your leave, sir?
OLDRENTS
I leave you to dispute it with yourself.
I have no voice to bid you go or stay;   235
My love shall give thy will pre-eminence,
And leave th'effect to time and Providence.   *Exit.*
SPRINGLOVE
I am confounded in my obligation
To this good man; his virtue is my punishment,
When 'tis not in my nature to return   240
Obedience to his merits. I could wish
Such an ingratitude were death by th' law,

---

223 **allow** bestow
223 SD **nightingale, cuckoo, etc.** heralds of
the spring; '*etc.*', often used to mean
'repeat', suggests the sound continues for
some time. For methods of creating these
sounds, see 155 SDn.
223 **confounded** put into mental confusion
224 **retort me** throw me out, reject me (*OED*
retort v.¹ 8 cites this line)

227 i.e. I will no longer attempt to perform an
impossible task. The lines are a variant
of the proverbial 'To wash an Ethiope'
(Dent, E186), which is explained by
Thomas Dekker: 'I wash an Aethiope,
who will never be the whiter for all
the water I spend upon him' (*Rod*, sig.
B4ʳ).
232–3 **incapable / Of** unable to take in

224 SD] *this edn*   227 SD] *Lawrence*

And put in present execution on me,
To rid me of my sharper suffering.
Nor, but by death, can this predominant sway   245
Of nature be extinguished in me. I
Have fought with my affections by th'assistance
Of all the strengths of art and discipline
(All which I owe him for in education too)
To conquer, and establish my observance,   250
As in all other rules, to him in this –
This inborn strong desire of liberty
In that free course, which he detests as shameful
And I approve my earth's felicity –
But find the war is endless and must fly.   255
What must I lose then? A good master's love.
What loss feels he that wants not what he loses?
They'll say I lose all reputation.
What's that, to live where no such thing is known?
My duty to a master will be questioned?   260
Where duty is exacted it is none,
And among beggars, each man is his own.

Enter RANDALL *and three or four* Servants *with*
a great kettle, and black jacks and a baker's
basket, all empty.

245 **sway** bias (*OED n.* 4)
247 **affections** emotions, feelings (as opposed to reason)
248 **art and discipline** learning and instruction
254 **approve ... felicity** attest my life's happiness
256–62 Springlove parodies the catechism, a device in religion for indoctrinating students, teaching them correct responses through question and answer; he thus illustrates the education he has had, while showing the audience that he has thought objectively through to his conclusion – he has counter-arguments for every objection to his actions.

261 i.e. enforced submission (submission only brought about because Springlove is a servant to Oldrents) is not real submission.
262 **each ... own** i.e. each man belongs to himself – a variant on the proverb 'Every man for himself' (Dent, M112).
262.2 **kettle** pot or cauldron for boiling water over a fire; subsequent dialogue reveals this to be a *beef-kettle* (266) for heating large joints. This kind of kettle was to be found in brass amongst the grander families; one features amongst the 'Brass' holdings of the Fairfax family (Peacock, 145).
black jacks large leather jugs, blackened and sealed with tar

106

Now fellows, what news from whence you came?

[Servants] exeunt with all. Randall remains.

RANDALL   The old wonted news, sir, from your
guesthouse, the old barn. We have unloaden the   265
bread-basket, the beef-kettle and the beer-bombards
there, amongst your guests, the beggars. And they
have all prayed for you and our master, as their
manner is, from the teeth outward; marry, from the
teeth inwards 'tis enough to swallow your alms, from   270
whence I think their prayers seldom come.

SPRINGLOVE   Thou shouldst not think uncharitably.

RANDALL   Thought's free, Master Steward, an it please
you. But your charity is nevertheless notorious, I
must needs say.   275

SPRINGLOVE   Meritorious, thou meantest to say.

RANDALL   Surely, sir, no; 'tis out of our curate's book.

SPRINGLOVE   But I aspire no merits, nor popular thanks.
'Tis well if I do well in it.

264 **wonted** customary
265 **guesthouse . . . barn** The tradition of letting begging crews sit out the winter in a landowner's subsidiary buildings is also referred to in *Spring's Glory*, where the beggars are staged coming out of 'an old Barne' (sig. C2ʳ). For this as a literary cliché, see Sanders, 'Commonwealths', 6.
266 **beer-bombards** leather containers or bottles for holding beer, probably named after their resemblance to early cannons or 'bombards'. Jonson refers to 'a bombard of broken beer' (*Masque of Augurs*, 97–8); Shakespeare writes of 'a foul bombard that would shed his liquor' (*Tem*, 2.2.21). Such containers are described in *Philocothonista*: 'small Jacks wee have in many Alehouses of the Citie, and Suburbs, tipt with silver, besides the great black Jacks, and bombards at the Court, which when the *French-men* first saw, they reported at their returne into their Countrey, that the *English-men* used to drinke out of their Bootes' (45).
269 **from . . . outward** outwardly but not internally; insincerely. John Withals translates 'Lingua amicus' as 'A friend from the teeth outward' (562).
270 **alms** things given in charity
273 **Thought's free** 'You can think what you please'; proverbial (Dent, T244)
274 **notorious** (1) well known; (2) infamous
277 **curate's book** A curate was thought to be learned; his book was deemed to be the repository of good words.
278 **aspire** have an ardent desire for; pant or long for (*OED v.* 4, citing this example)

RANDALL   It might be better though – if old Randall, 280
whom you allow to talk, might counsel – to help to
breed up poor men's children, or decayed labourers
past their work or travel, or towards the setting up of
poor young married couples, than to bestow an
hundred pound a year (at least you do that, if not all 285
you get), besides our master's bounty, to maintain in
begging such wanderers as these – that never are out
of their way, that cannot give account from whence
they came, or whither they would, nor of any
beginning they ever had, or any end they seek, but 290
still do stroll and beg till their bellies be full, and then
sleep till they be hungry.

SPRINGLOVE   Thou art ever repining at those poor
people! They take nothing from thee but thy pains,
and that I pay thee for, too. Why shouldst thou 295
grudge?

RANDALL   Am I not bitten to it every day by the
six-footed bloodhounds that they leave in their litter,
when I throw out the old to lay fresh straw for the
newcomers at night? That's one part of my office. 300
And you are sure, though your hospitality be but for
a night and a morning for one rabble, to have a new
supply every evening. They take nothing from me
indeed; they give too much.

---

283 **travel** (1) travel; (2) travail. Both words were interchangeable in spelling; in this instance either might be meant. Brome will later pun on the two; see 2.2.169.
293 **repining** grumbling; complaining
294 **pains** labours; troubles

296 **grudge** grumble; complain
298 **six-footed bloodhounds** fleas and/or lice, both of which suck blood and have six feet **litter** straw, rushes or the like, serving as bedding (*OED n.* 3)
300 **office** service or task to be performed

286 our] your *Dodsley*   291 do] *Q2;* to *Q1*   301 sure,] *this edn;* sure that *Q1*

SPRINGLOVE Thou art old Randall still! Ever grumbling, 305
but still officious for 'em.

RANDALL Yes, hang 'em, they know I love 'em well
enough; I have had merry bouts with some of 'em.

SPRINGLOVE What sayest thou, Randall?

RANDALL They are indeed my pastime. I left the merry 310
grigs, as their provender has pricked 'em, in such
a hoigh yonder! Such a frolic! You'll hear anon, as
you walk nearer 'em.

SPRINGLOVE Well, honest Randall, thus it is. I am for a
journey. I know not how long will be my absence. 315
But I will presently take order with the cook, pantler
and butler for my wonted allowance to the poor, and
I will leave money with thee to manage the affair till
my return.

RANDALL Then up rise Randall, bailie of the beggars. 320

SPRINGLOVE And if our master shall be displeased –
although the charge be mine – at the openness of the

---

306 **officious** eager to help; obliging (*OED adj.* 2)

308 **bouts** contests; matches – probably here with the specific sense 'drinking sessions', though *OED* dates that meaning to 1670

310–11 **merry grigs** extravagantly lively people, full of frolic and jest; 'merry grig' and 'merry Greek' appear to have been interchangeable. See *OED* grig *n.*[1] 5.

311 **as ... 'em** 'as their food has rendered them', but a play on the proverbial phrase 'provender pricks – ' ('abundance of food stimulates and creates high spirits in –'). See *OED* prick *v.* 9b.

312 **hoigh** excitement (*OED n.* cites this line)
anon forthwith; instantly

316 **take order** take measures or steps
pantler servant in a large household in charge of the bread or pantry. Cf. *2H4*,

2.4.238: 'A would have made a good pantler, a would ha' chipped bread well.'

317 **butler** from Anglo-Norman French *butuiller* (derived from Latin *buticula* = bottle); the servant who has charge of the wine cellar and dispenses the liquor

320 **up rise** a play on the terminology used by the monarch when knighting someone, 'rise up'
bailie a humorous variant of 'bailiff'. Mistress Birdlime, in *Westward Ho*, 2.2.51, declares, 'I'me but your Baily'. 'Bailiff' was another name for a landholder's steward: he managed the estate and superintended the husbandry of the farm.

322 **charge** (1) expense; (2) responsibility
openness open-handedness; generousness

entertainment, thou shalt then give it proportionably in money and let them walk farther.

RANDALL   Pshaw! That will never do't, never do 'em   325
good. 'Tis the seat, the habitation, the rendezvous, that cheers their hearts. Money would clog their consciences. Nor must I lose the music of 'em in their lodging.

SPRINGLOVE   We will agree upon't anon. Go now about   330
your business.

RANDALL   I go. Bailie? Nay, steward and chamberlain of the rogues and beggars!   *Exit.*

SPRINGLOVE

I cannot think but with a trembling fear
On this adventure. In a scruple which   335
I have not weighed with all my other doubts,
I shall in my departure rob my master.
Of what? Of a true servant; other theft
I have committed none. And that may be supplied,
And better too, by some more constant to him.   340
But I may injure many in his trust,

323–4 **thou . . . money** 'You can hand over the same proportion in money.'

325 **Pshaw** an expression of impatience. Though *OED* does not record this word before 1760 it is in fact found in other plays of Brome's period: *Old Law* (thought to have been written in the 1610s), 4.1.15, has 'Pshaw, I'm too fearful', and *John Swabber*, written in the 1650s, gives 'Pshaw, this has ner'a beard' (in *Acteon*, 39).

326–7 **'Tis . . . hearts** i.e. it is the nature of Oldrents' estate that cheers them.

326 **seat** residence, situation
rendezvous meeting place

327–8 **clog their consciences** hamper or weigh down their moral judgements; 'to clog the conscience' was a standard phrase.

332 **chamberlain** literally, the high steward or factor of a nobleman

335 **scruple** literally, a small unit of weight or measurement, but also carrying the sense of 'doubt'. Springlove's uncertainty is due to his realization that he will, by absenting himself, be effectively robbing his master (of his steward).

341–2 Springlove fears that Oldrents will be more sparing of his trust towards others in the future.

325 Pshaw] *(Pseugh)*   335 adventure. In] *this edn;* adventure, in *Q1*

Which now he cannot be but sparing of.
I rob him, too, of the content and hopes
He had in me, whom he had built and raised
Unto that growth in his affection   345
That I became a gladness in his eye,
And now must be a grief or a vexation
Unto his noble heart.
                    (*a noise and singing within*)
                              But hark! Ay, there's
The harmony that drowns all doubts and fears.
A little nearer –   350

                         SONG

BEGGARS [*Sing within.*]
        From hunger and cold who lives more free,
            Or who more richly clad than we?
        Our bellies are full; our flesh is warm;
            And against pride our rags are a charm.
        Enough is our feast, and for tomorrow   355
            Let rich men care: we feel no sorrow.
                No sorrow, no sorrow, no sorrow, no sorrow.
            Let rich men care: we feel no sorrow.
SPRINGLOVE   The emperor hears no such music, nor
        feels content like this!   360

351–8 The tune and words, with minor variants, are printed by John Wilson under
   the title 'The Jovial Begger' (*Select Airs*,
   no. 64); they can also be found in British
   Library MS Harley 3991, fol. 145ʳ⁻ᵛ,
   where the composer is said to be 'J. G.'
   (possibly John Goodgroome?). See p. 257.
   Inverting binaries throughout, this is a
standard 'merry beggar' song, in which
   the delights of poverty are romanticized.
352 **richly clad** (1) expensively dressed
   (ironic); (2) plentifully dressed (ironic)
355 **Enough . . . feast** a variant on the proverb
   'Enough is as good as a feast' (Dent,
   E158)
356 **care** worry

348 SD] *after 347 Q1*   351 SP] *this edn; not in Q1*   SD *Sing*] *this edn*   *within*] *Brome Online subst.*

[SONG]

BEGGARS [*Sing within.*]
    Each city, each town and every village
        Affords us either an alms or pillage
    And, if the weather be cold and raw,
        Then in a barn we tumble in straw;
    If warm and fair, by yea-cock and nay-cock,   365
        The fields will afford us a hedge or a haycock.
            A haycock, a haycock, a haycock, a haycock,
            The fields will afford us a hedge or a haycock.

SPRINGLOVE
    Most ravishing delight! But in all this
    Only one sense is pleased: mine ear is feasted.   370
    Mine eye, too, must be satisfied with my joys.
    The hoarding usurer cannot have more
    Thirsty desire to see his golden store
    When he unlocks his treasury than I
    The equipage in which my beggars lie.   375

362 **an alms or pillage** charitable relief or the opportunity to plunder the place
364 **tumble** roll about, but with the suggestion of potential sexual activity
365 **yea-cock and nay-cock** combination of 'by yea and nay' (*OED* yea *adv.* and *n.* 3b), the oath 'by cock' or 'by God', and a weathercock. The sense is either that the weathercock determines 'yea' or 'nay' for fair weather, or that the tumbling is determined, yes or no, by the weather.

The stress on *cock*, which continues over the next three lines, also suggests that nature offers sexual compensations for the harshness of beggar life. See p. 259.
366 **haycock** conical heap of hay in a field
373 **golden store** money
375 **equipage** accoutrements; trappings
    my beggars Springlove suggests that the beggars are his – both because he is, yearly, one of them, and because he is king over them – see 378.

360 SD] *this edn*   361 SP] *this edn; not in Q1*   SD] *this edn*

He opens the scene; the BEGGARS[*, including* SCRIBBLE,
LAWYER, SOLDIER, COURTIER *and* PATRICO,] *are
discovered in their postures; then they* [*all*] *issue
forth; and last, the Patrico.*

ALL BEGGARS
Our master, our master! Our sweet and comfortable
master.

SPRINGLOVE
How cheer my hearts?

SCRIBBLE   Most crouse, most caperingly.
Shall we dance, shall we sing, to welcome our king?
Strike up, piper, a merry, merry dance,

375.1 **the scene** a portion of the stage wall, known as the 'scene' (now usually known by its Latin name, *frons scenae*), that divides the tiring-house from the stage. *If It Be Not Good*, 1.2.158, has the SD 'Narcisso *stepping in before in the Scene, Enters here*'; in *Covent Garden*, characters enter and leave through 'the right Scoene' and 'the left Scoene' (sigs B1ʳ, B2ᵛ) – meaning by the right and left door of the *frons scenae*. The term comes from '*scena*', defined by Thomas Thomas as 'the frunt of the theater, the place where players make them readie, being trimmed with hangings, out of which they enter upon the stage' (sig. 3G3ᵛ). That the *frons scenae* had a central curtained 'discovery space' within which tableaux such as this could be shown is often maintained. Alexander Leggatt believes this moment of stage action is ironic: 'The effect is of a "discovery" in a court masque, the lowest reaches of society presented by a device that entertained the highest' (170).

375.3 **postures** poses or attitudes. The beggars seem to been revealed posed in an illustrative 'tableau'. Cf. *Northern Lass*, when Squelch rehearses Humphrey in the postures that make up a gentleman usher: 'Fall to your Postures *Humfrey*. Your Garbe. *(He does his postures)* So. Your Pace. So. Your Congie. So. Hand your Lady. Good. Arme your Lady. Good still. Side your Lady. Very good. Draw out your Lady. Excellent. Present your Lady. Singular well, good *Humfrey*' (sig. I1ʳ ᵛ).

376 **comfortable** comforting; cheering

377 **crouse** confidently; vivaciously (northern British dialect)
caperingly cap'ringly; in capering or dancing fashion (*OED* capering *adj.*, citing this example)

379 **Strike up** begin to play (the music). It is likely that the piper was to set the tune and that other instruments – probably the fiddlers of the *dramatis personae*, who are not mentioned in SDs – would then join in.

375.1–2 SD *including . . .* PATRICO] *this edn*   375.3 *all*] *this edn*   376 SP] *Brome Online; All. Q1*   377+ SP2] *Brome Online; 1 Beg. Q1*

113

That we on our stampers may foot it and prance,   380
To make his heart merry as he has made ours,
As lustick and frolic as lords in their bowers.

Music. [*Beggars*] *dance.*

SPRINGLOVE   Exceeding well performed.

SCRIBBLE   'Tis well if it like you, master. But we have
not that rag among us that we will not dance off to do   385
you service, we being all and only your servants,
most noble sir. Command us, therefore, and employ
us, we beseech you.

SPRINGLOVE   Thou speakest most courtly.

LAWYER   Sir, he can speak, and could have writ as well.   390
He is a decayed poet, newly fallen in among us, and
begs as well as the best of us. He learned it pretty
well in his own profession before and can the better
practise it in ours now.

SPRINGLOVE   Thou art a wit too, it seems.   395

SOLDIER   He should have wit and knavery too, sir, for
he was an attorney till he was pitched over the bar.
And from that fall he was taken up a knight o'the
post, and so he continued till he was degraded at the

---

380 **stampers** *cant* shoes or feet, cited in *OED*
stamper *n.* 4, referring to this line. For
early modern definitions of cant words,
see Appendix 2.
foot it dance

382 **lustick** merry or jolly, chiefly used with
reference to drinking (*OED adj.* and
adv. A cites this line)

382 SD The music is presumably played by a
piper, as requested in 379. Which beggar
is the piper is unclear; possibly an instru-
mentalist enters onto the stage to play the
tune for this dance. The piper will be
requested again at 4.2.167.

384 **like** pleases

390 **Sir . . . speak** This is the start of a series
of descriptive vignettes about the beggars

and their previous professions. Each
beggar's past life is described in turn by
a fellow beggar.

391 **decayed** reduced in fortune

397 **pitched . . . bar** disbarred (playing on
the legal and literal sense of *bar*); see
OED pitch *v.*² which cites this line.

398–9 **knight o'the post** i.e. 'knight' of the
whipping-post or pillory; hence a notorious
perjurer, one who got his living by giving
false evidence, a false bail. See *OED*
knight of the post *n.*, which cites this line.
Brome employs the term derogatively
elsewhere. *Damoiselle* has 'He takes me
for a common Bail; a Knight o'th Post'
(sig. C5ᵛ).

---

382 SD *Beggars*] *this edn*   390+ SP] *Brome Online; 2 Beg. Q1*   396+ SP] *Brome Online; 3 Beg. Q1*

whipping-post, and from thence he ran resolutely 400
into this course. His cunning in the law, and the
other's labour with the muses, are dedicate to your
service; and for myself, I'll fight for you.

SPRINGLOVE   Thou art a brave fellow and speakest like
a commander. Hast thou borne arms?   405

COURTIER   Sir, he has borne the name of a Netherland
soldier, till he ran away from his colours and was
taken lame with lying in the fields by a sciatica – I
mean, sir, the strappado. After which, by a second
retreat – indeed running away – he scambled into this   410
country, and so scaped the gallows, and then snapped
up his living in the city by his wit in cheating,

400 **whipping-post** a post set up, usually in a public place, to which offenders were tied to be whipped
resolutely determinedly
402 **labour . . . muses** i.e. poetic and other artistic creations
dedicate dedicated
404 **brave** handsome
406–7 **Netherland soldier** The Soldier may have been a mercenary for one of the armies involved in the Dutch War of Independence, 1566–1648. Cf. *Witch of Edmonton*, 3.1.39–40, where Clown asks whether 'any Souldier . . . ever received his pay but in the Low Countries'. Alternatively, he is a 'netherland' soldier, because he was found lying with his nether regions on the land.
407 **his colours** (1) the standard of his regiment, pluralized, *Brome Online* suggests, for reasons of heraldic significance; (2) his enemies (see *OED* colour n.¹ P7, where 'fear no colours' means 'to be afraid of no enemy or opponent')
408–9 **sciatica . . . strappado** i.e. the real cause of his lameness was that he had been punished with the strappado, rather than, as he maintained, struck down by illness.

408 **a sciatica** an attack of a disease characterized by pain in the great sciatic nerve and its branches. 1 Gentleman asks Mistress Overdone, in *MM*, 1.2.54–5, 'How now, which of your hips has the most profound sciatica?'
409 **strappado** a form of punishment or torture used to extort confession (*OED n.* 1). Cf. Thomas Coryate: 'I saw . . . Two men tormented with the strapado, which is done in this manner. The offender having his hands bound behind him, is conveighed into a rope that hangeth in a pully, and after hoysed up in the rope to a great heigth with two severall swinges, where he sustaineth so great torments that his joynts are for the time loosed and pulled asunder; besides such abundance of bloud is gathered into his hands and face, that for the time he is in the torture, his face and hands doe looke as red as fire' (254).
410 **retreat** (1) military signal to retire; (2) the act of running away
scambled stumbled along (*OED* scamble *v.* 4)
411–12 **snapped up** caught up, seized

406+ SP] *Brome Online; 4 Beg. Q1*   410 this] *Dodsley; his Q1*

pimping and suchlike arts, till the cart and the pillory showed him too publicly to the world. And so, begging being the last refuge, he entered into our 415 society, and now lives honestly, I must needs say, as the best of us.

SPRINGLOVE　Thou speakest good language too.

SCRIBBLE　He was a courtier born, sir, and begs on pleasure, I assure you, refusing great and constant 420 means from able friends to make him a staid man. Yet, the want of a leg notwithstanding, he must travel in this kind against all common reason, by the special policy of Providence.

SPRINGLOVE　As how, I prithee? 425

SCRIBBLE　His father, sir, was a courtier, a great court beggar, I assure you; I made these verses of him and his son here.

A courtier begged – by covetise, not need –
From others that which made them beg indeed. 430
He begged till wealth had laden him with cares
To keep – for's children and their children – shares,
While the oppressed, that lost that great estate,
Sent curses after it unto their fate.
The father dies, the world says, very rich; 435
The son, being gotten while, it seems, the itch
Of begging was upon the courtly sire,
Or bound by fate, will to no wealth aspire –
Though offered him in money, clothes or meat –
More than he begs or instantly must eat. 440

413 **cart and pillory** The first was a vehicle for the public exposure and chastisement of offenders; the second was a device for further exposure and punishment, consisting of a wooden framework mounted on a post, with holes or rings for trapping the head and hands. Carts often took offenders to pillories.

416 **honestly** as honestly
421 **staid** settled
423 **kind** fashion
424 **policy** contrivance
426–7 **court beggar** See 51–4n.
429 *covetise* inordinate desire for the possession of wealth
432 *shares* i.e. shares in the estate

Is not he heavenly blessed that hates earth's treasure,
And begs with 'What's a gentleman but's pleasure'?
Or say it be upon the heir a curse:
What's that to him? The beggar's ne'er the worse.
For of the general store that heaven has sent,   445
He values not a penny till't be spent.

ALL BEGGARS   A Scribble, a Scribble!

LAWYER   What city or court poet could say more than
our hedge-musemonger here?

SOLDIER   What say, sir, to our poet Scribble here?   450

SPRINGLOVE   I like his vein exceeding well, and the
whole consort of you.

LAWYER   Consort, sir? We have musicians, too, among
us: true merry beggars indeed that, being within the
reach of the lash for singing libellous songs at   455
London, were fain to fly into our covey, and here
they sing all our poet's ditties. They can sing anything
most tunably, sir, but psalms. What they may do

---

441 **heavenly** heav'nly
447 **A** prefixed to a proper name as a cheer
or rallying war cry. *OED int.*[2] cites '*John
Clappam* an Esquire and servant to *Warwicke* displaied his Lords Colours with
his *white-beare*, and from an eminent
place cried a *Warwicke*, a *Warwicke'*
(Speed, 679).
449 **hedge-musemonger** muse-trader, or
second-rate poet, of the hedges. The term
musemonger is created from 'muse' and
the 'monger' of fishmonger or ironmon-
ger; it is also found in *Humour out of
Breath*, which refers to 'The Iron-pated
Muse-mongers about the towne' (sig.
A2ʳ).
451 **his vein** the characteristic style of his
language or expression (see *OED* vein
n. 12, citing this line); the particular
strain of his talent
452 **consort** (1) company; (2) musical group

455 **lash . . . songs** The punishment for singing or posting libels was often a lashing
or whipping; hence John Stephens's
reference to 'Libell-lashing measures'
(*Essays*, sig. C31ʳ).
456 **covey** literally, a hatch of partridges;
figuratively, a party or set. The connection between beggars' life and birds'
freedom is underlined here by choice of
vocabulary. See 183n.
457 **ditties** compositions intended to be set
to music
458–9 **What . . . expected** probably a reference to a song in *Bloody Brother* by
John Fletcher *et al.*; in its second quarto,
Rollo (1640), the words are, 'Three merry
boyes, and three merry boyes, / and three
merry boyes are we, / As e're did sing
three parts in a string, / All under the
triple tree' (42; the words are 'gallows
tree' in other editions of the play).

447 SP] *this edn*; All *Q1*   450 SP] *Brome Online; 2 Beg. Q1; 3 Beg. Dodsley*

117

hereafter under a triple tree is much expected. But
they live very civilly and gently among us.   460

SPRINGLOVE   But what is he there? That solemn old
fellow that neither speaks of himself, nor anybody
for him.

LAWYER   Oh, sir, the rarest man of all. He is a prophet.
See how he holds up his prognosticating nose. He is   465
divining now.

SPRINGLOVE   How? A prophet?

LAWYER   Yes, sir, a cunning man and a fortune-teller.
'Tis thought he was a great clerk before his decay,
but he is very close, will not tell his beginning, nor   470
the fortune he himself is fallen from. But he serves
us for a clergyman still, and marries us, if need be,
after a new way of his own.

SPRINGLOVE   How long have you had his company?

LAWYER   But lately come amongst us, but a very ancient   475
stroll all the land over, and has travelled with gypsies,
and is a patrico. Shall he read your fortune, sir?

SPRINGLOVE   If it please him.

PATRICO   Lend me your hand, sir.
By this palm, I understand   480
Thou art born to wealth and land

---

459 **triple tree** name given to Tyburn gallows,
which was made up of a horizontal
wooden triangle supported by three legs,
one at each corner, so that it could suspend
people from three sides at once. 'In virtue
of its three interlocking cross-beams' it
was thus capable of hanging up to twenty-
four felons simultaneously (see Kaufman-
Osborn, 66).

465 **prognosticating nose** literally, presag-
ing nose, but seemingly also a way of
describing a large or unattractive nose.
In *Scornful Lady*, 4.1.319–20, Abigail is

described as having 'a face as olde as
Erra Pater' together with 'such a prognosticating nose'.

466 **divining** soothsaying; prophesying

468 **cunning man** fortune-teller; conjurer

469 **clerk** churchman; clergyman. The Patrico
is the only beggar whose name represents
his current, rather than his previous,
profession.

470 **close**   reserved;   uncommunicative;
secretive

476 **stroll** stroller

477 **patrico** *cant* a vagabond priest

460 gently] *Haaker;* gentily *Q1;* genteelly *Dodsley*

And, after many a bitter gust,
Shalt build with thy great-grandsire's dust.

SPRINGLOVE   Where shall I find it? But come, I'll not
    trouble my head with the search.   485

LAWYER   What say, sir, to our crew? Are we not well
    congregated?

SPRINGLOVE   You are a jovial crew; the only people
    whose happiness I admire.

SOLDIER   Will you make us happy in serving you? Have   490
    you any enemies? Shall we fight under you? Will
    you be our captain?

LAWYER   Nay, our king.

SOLDIER   Command us something, sir.

SPRINGLOVE   Where's the next rendezvous?   495

SCRIBBLE

Neither in village nor in town,
But three mile off at Mapledown.

SPRINGLOVE   At evening there I'll visit you.

---

482 **gust** experience or foretaste (though *OED*
  *n.*² 7 only traces this meaning to 1658)
484 **Where . . . it** Springlove does not know
  who his grandfather is, so cannot understand the Patrico's prognostication.
487 **congregated** assembled; gathered together
488 **jovial crew** used to describe carefree
  drinking companions, and often found
  in titles or choruses of risqué drinking
  songs; its use in this play to describe a
  company of beggars is purposely jarring,
  particularly as *jovial* still bore Jove-like
  assumptions of thunder as well as joy and
  happiness. The use of the phrase may
  have been inspired by a song by John
  Ford, 'What hoe we come to be merry, /
  Open the doores a Joviall crew', found in
  Lady's Trial, sig. H1ᵛ; this song contains

the phrase 'We drinke till all looke blew',
which seems to be picked up on in the
grey-beards' song later in the play, at
4.1.260. See p. 269.
493 **king** The beggars, having been praised
  for their liberty, immediately start projecting a monarchical system.
497 **Mapledown** The play is later said to take
  place in Nottinghamshire (see 5.1.172),
  so Ann Haaker's suggestion (34) that the
  story is located in Mapledown, Kent,
  appears to be a misapprehension. Julie
  Sanders runs through a number of potential locations for the play, concluding
  that Maplebeck in Sherwood Forest, with
  its associations with Robin Hood (and
  hence with 'outlaw literature'), is the
  most likely ('Commonwealths', 5).

483 great-grandsire's] *(great Gransires)* 488–9] *Dodsley; Q1* lines people / admire. /   497 Mapledown]
Haaker; Maple-down *Q1;* Maplebeck *conj. Sanders*

SONG

BEGGARS [*Sing.*]

> Come, come away: the spring,
> By every bird that can but sing　　　　　　　500
> Or chirp a note, doth now invite
> Us forth to taste of his delight.
> In field, in grove, on hill, in dale,
> But above all the nightingale,
> Who in her sweetness strives t'outdo　　　　505
> The loudness of the hoarse cuckoo.
>
> 'Cuckoo', cries he; 'Jug Jug Jug', sings she
> From bush to bush, from tree to tree;
> Why in one place then tarry we?
>
> Come away; why do we stay?　　　　　　　510
> We have no debt or rent to pay,
> No bargains or accounts to make,
> Nor land or lease to let or take,
> Or if we had, should that remore us,
> When all the world's our own before us?　　515
> And where we pass and make resort,
> It is our kingdom and our court.

'Cuckoo', cries he, *etc.*　　　　*Exeunt* [*all Beggars*] *singing.*

499 **Come, come away** The song, like others of its kind, compares two omens of spring – the nightingale, whose melancholy tune recalls the ravished Philomela, and the cuckoo, whose ugly cry threatens married men with cuckoldry. The words keep the sexual side of the play to the forefront, suggesting that the beggars' urge to travel is also an urge to mate. Songs beginning 'Come' or 'Come away' were popular in the period, and were often pastoral or Orphic in theme. There does not appear to be extant music for this song. See p. 260.

514 **remore** hinder; impede. *OED v.* cites this as its only recorded usage. *Brome Online*, however, suggests the word should actually be 'reward'.

518 *etc.* used to indicate that the singing should continue

518 SD **singing. Brome gives his SD in Latin at this point, '*Exeunt Cantantes*', probably because he was thinking about 'canting', the language of the beggars; both words have a root in *cantus* = singing, song, chant. In this instance Brome appears to have been employing 'whims' of his own.

499 SP] *this edn; not in Q1*　SD] *this edn*　514 remore] reward *Brome Online*　518 SD all Beggars] *this edn*　singing] *(Cantantes)*

SPRINGLOVE

So, now away.

They dream of happiness that live in state, 520

But they enjoy it that obey their fate. [*Exit.*]

2.1 [*Enter*] VINCENT, HILLIARD, MERIEL [*and*] RACHEL.

VINCENT I am overcome with admiration at the felicity
they take!

HILLIARD Beggars! They are the only people can boast
the benefit of a free state, in the full enjoyment of
liberty, mirth and ease, having all things in common 5
and nothing wanting of nature's whole provision
within the reach of their desires. Who would have
lost this sight of their revels?

VINCENT How think you, ladies? Are they not the only
happy in a nation? 10

MERIEL Happier than we, I'm sure, that are pent up
and tied by the nose to the continual steam of hot
hospitality here in our father's house, when they
have the air at pleasure in all variety.

2.1 Location: Oldrents' house

1 **admiration** wonderment

4 **a free state** (1) a state or position of
freedom; (2) a state which is governed by
some form of representative democracy,
rather than by a sovereign or similar ruler
(see *OED* free state *n.*)

5–7 **having … desires** sharing everything
and lacking none of nature's whole/
wholesome provision that their desires
can conceive

12 **tied … steam** forced to work in the
close air emanating from the hot food and
drink prepared for entertaining. Possibly

an analogy is being drawn between the
women and turnspit dogs. These dogs
were pent up inside a wheel that rotated
the spit on which meat was roasted
over the fire; they worked in the steam
released by the cooking food. The speech
seems to look forward to Randall's
description of his first job as turnspit boy
(see 4.1.115). Oldrents' daughters, like
his servants, are constantly at work in the
cause of entertainment; 'hot hospitality'
might also refer to the ardent attentions
of the men so entertained.

521 SD] *Lawrence* **2.1**] (Actus Secundus.) 0 SD *Enter*] *Dodsley* *and*] *Brome Online*

RACHEL   And though I know we have merrier spirits   15
than they, yet to live thus confined stifles us.

HILLIARD   Why, ladies, you have liberty enough, or may
take what you please.

MERIEL   Yes, in our father's rule and government, or by
his allowance. What's that to absolute freedom such   20
as the very beggars have, to feast and revel here
today and yonder tomorrow, next day where they
please, and so on still, the whole country or kingdom
over? There's liberty! The birds of the air can take no
more.   25

RACHEL   And then at home here, or wheresoever he
comes, our father is so pensive – what muddy spirit
soe'er possesses him, would I could conjure't out –
that he makes us even sick of his sadness, that were
wont to 'see my gossip's cock today', 'mould cockle-   30

---

20 **allowance** permission

24–5 **The birds . . . more** a continuation of the notion that beggars are as free as birds; see 1.1.183n.

27 **muddy** gloomy

28 **conjure't out** get rid of it; Hearty likewise had hoped to conjure Oldrents out of his mood in 1.1.93–4. The suggestion that supernatural power is needed hints at the mystical origin of Oldrents' unhappiness.

30 **'see . . . today'** *OED* gossip *n*. 2a, citing this line, writes that it is apparently 'the name of some rustic game or dance'. Another, later, allusion to a dance of a similar name is in *Hercules Buffoon* (1684), where Bowman lists the dancing accomplishments of the northern heiress: 'they say she plays at several Sports, as *Ramp-scattle, Clapper-depouch*, and *Come mother, saw you my cock to day?*' (12). Like the other dances enumerated by Meriel, this dance, which seems to be sexual, may explain the 'hot hospitality' offered by the girls to their father's guests (12–13) and the kisses they are asked to give (71–2).

30–1 **'mould cockle-bread'** a dance that involved revealing the buttocks and simulating sexual activity: 'Young wenches have a wanton sport, wch they call moulding of Cocklebread; viz. they gett upon a Table-board, and then gather-up their knees & their coates with their hands as high as they can, and then they wabble to and fro with their Buttocks, as if the[y] were kneading of Dowgh with their A——, and say these words, viz.: "My Dame is sick & gonne to bed, / And I'le go mowld my cockle-bread." In Oxfordshire the maids . . . say thus: "My granny is sick, and now is dead, / And wee'l goe mould some cockle-bread. / Up wth my heels, and down wth my head, / And this is the way to mould cocklebread"' (Aubrey, 43–4). A further context is supplied in Thomas D'Urfey's poem 'June's Canto', in *Pendragon*: 'She gets across a Chair to ride, / With her divided Legs astride; / She challenges them All to leap, / And straddle widest at a Step; / From that, to molding Cocklebread' (77).

bread', dance 'clutterdepouch' and 'hannykin booby', 'bind barrels' or do anything before him, and he would laugh at us.

MERIEL Now he never looks upon us but with a sigh, or tears in his eyes, though we simper never so   35
sanctifiedly. What tales have been told him of us, or what he suspects, I know not. God forgive him: I do, but I am weary of his house.

RACHEL Does he think us whores, trow, because sometimes we talk as lightly as great ladies? I can   40
swear safely for the virginity of one of us, so far as word and deed goes; marry, thought's free.

---

31 **'clutterdepouch'** Called 'an obsolete dance' by *OED* (clutter *n.* 6, citing this line), it also had obvious sexual ramifications. In *Hey for Honesty*, Clodpole relates how 'My *Jane* and I full right merrily, this jollity will avouch, / To witnesse our mirth upon the green earth, together we'll dance a clatter-do-pouch. clatter-de-pouch, clatter, &c.' (24). *Hercules Buffoon* spells out the name's explicit sexual connotation: 'we have play'd at *Clapperdeponch* [*sic*] together; therefore 'tis too late to break off the Match' (49).

31–2 **'hannykin booby'** an obsolete dance, presumably sexual and probably humorous, as 'booby' and 'Hankin' (from the Dutch for 'little Hans') both meant 'clown'. John Skelton's poem 'Ware the Hawk', in *Certain Books*, mentions the dance: 'Wyth troll, cytrace and trovy / They rangyd hankyn bovy / My churche all a bowte' (sig. B7ʳ). John Playford published a dance called 'Halfe Hannikin'; as it is to be performed by men and women together, however, it may not relate closely to 'Hannykin Booby', which appears, like the other dances, to have been for women only (*English*, 43).

32 **'bind barrels'** literally, to secure barrels with strengthening material, but appar-

ently the name of an obsolete and sexual dance or game. Its nature is suggested by Richard Head in *The English Rogue*, where, describing being attacked by a boar, Guzman records how he was forced 'to claspe my armes about the sides of him, with all the might and force I could. And as if we had playd at binding of barrels . . . giving him many a rap at the wrong doore . . . he carried me' (51–2).

32–3 **or . . . us** 'or if we did anything in front of him he would laugh at us'

35–6 **simper so sanctifiedly** 'smile in ever such a devout manner'

39 **trow** do you suppose

40 **as lightly . . . ladies** as merrily or easily as noblewomen, whose wanton speech contrasted powerfully with diatribes against 'profane swearing' written by Puritans. Queen Elizabeth I was said to have sworn 'like a man' and to have counted 'God's wounds' amongst her favourite oaths; 'she never spared an oath in public speech or private conversation when she thought it added energy to either'. See *Swearing*, 81.

41 **one of us** i.e. herself

42 **thought's free** See 1.1.273n. Rachel explains that she is virginal in reality though her thoughts have ranged.

MERIEL   Which is that one of us, I pray? Yourself or me?

RACHEL   Good sister Meriel, charity begins at home.
But I'll swear I think as charitably of thee, and not   45
only because thou art a year younger, neither.

MERIEL   I am beholden to you. But for my father, I
would I knew his grief and how to cure him, or that
we were where we could not see it. It spoils our
mirth, and that has been better than his meat to us.   50

VINCENT   Will you hear our motion, ladies?

MERIEL   Pshaw, you would marry us presently out of his
way, because he has given you a foolish kind of
promise. But we will see him in a better humour first
and as apt to laugh as we to lie down, I warrant him.   55

HILLIARD   'Tis like that course will cure him, would
you embrace it.

RACHEL   We will have him cured first, I tell you. And
you shall wait that season and our leisure.

MERIEL   I will rather hazard my being one of the devil's   60
ape-leaders than to marry while he is melancholy.

---

44 **charity ... home** proverbial (Dent, C251). Usually the phrase is used to propose being generous to one's family before helping others; Rachel, however, is using it to imply that she can only, in fairness, trust herself.

50 **meat** food

51 **motion** inclination; desire

55 **apt ... lie down** a reference to the proverb and card game 'Laugh and lay (lie) down' (Dent, L92), in which the player who holds the winning combination of cards lays them down and laughs at his success. The phrase was often, as here, given a sexual turn.

56–7 'It is likely that that proceeding (i.e. marriage) would cure him were you to adopt it.'

59 **season** period

60 **hazard** risk

60–1 **the devil's ape-leaders** An old maid was said to lead apes in hell. See Delia in *School of Compliment*, who explains: 'keeping my maiden-head till it was stale, I am condemn'd to lead Apes in hell' (40). The phrase was proverbial, and seems to arise from the notion that married women had children to lead to heaven – or to lead them to heaven – but unmarried women had none. Further examples are supplied in Dent, M37.

52 Pshaw] *Brome Online;* Psew *Q1*

RACHEL   Or I to stay in his house to give entertainment
to this knight, or tother coxcomb, that comes to cheer
him up with eating of his cheer: when we must fetch
'em sweetmeats, and they must tell us, 'ladies, your   65
lips are sweeter', and then fall into courtship, one in
a set speech taken out of old Breton's works, another
with verses out of *The Academy of Compliments*, or
some or other of the new poetical pamphleters,
ambitious only to spoil paper and publish their names   70
in print. And then to be kissed and sometimes
slavered. Faugh!

MERIEL   'Tis not to be endured. We must out of the
house. We cannot live but by laughing, and that
aloud, and nobody sad within hearing.   75

---

63   **coxcomb** foolish, conceited, showy person; originally named after the cap worn by professional fools which resembled a cock's comb in shape and colour. See also 5.1.403.

63–4   **cheer ... cheer** 'keep him happy by eating his food'. Rachel highlights the fact that the guests who come to *cheer* their father in fact simply succeed in consuming his *cheer* or bounty.

65   **sweetmeats** cakes or confectionery, given as hospitality but often also seen as sexual come-ons. Hence Prusius, in *The Siege*, wants to ransack foreign cities for 'the best Conserves, and tenderst Virgins', concluding 'Sweetmeats and Maidenheads are all I aime at' (Cartwright, *Comedies*, sig. G8ʳ).

67   **old Breton's works** writings by the prolific poet and pamphleteer Nicholas Breton (1554/5–*c*. 1626). Books by or said to be by him often concern love; amongst works attributed to him are *Breton's Bower of Delights* (1591), *The Arbor of Amorous Devices* (1597) and

An Old Man's Lesson and a Young Man's Love (1605).

68   *Academy of Compliments* a compendium by J[ohn]. G[ough]. (1639). Its full title was *The Academy of compliments wherein ladies, gentlewomen, schollers, and strangers may accommodate their courtly practice with most curious ceremonies, complemental, amorous, high expressions, and forms of speaking, or writing.*

69   **pamphleters** writers of pamphlets, pamphleteers (*OED* pamphleter *n.*). The vogue for poetic love pamphlets, said to be written by 'specious pretenders, but most wretched performers of what they undertook', is critiqued in *Love and Eloquence*, sigs A3ᵛ–A4ʳ.

72   **slavered** drooled over, the hallmark of being kissed by old people, as William in *All for Money* suggests: 'She is an olde croust none would marie her for love, / Her mouth would slaver ever when I did her kisse' (sig. D2ᵛ)
Faugh! an exclamation of abhorrence or disgust

67 Breton's] *Dodsley & Reed; Britains Q1*

125

VINCENT   We are for any adventure with you, ladies.
Shall we project a journey for you? Your father has
trusted you and will think you safe in our company,
and we would fain be abroad upon some progress
with you. Shall we make a fling to London and see   80
how the spring appears there in the Spring Garden,
and in Hyde Park to see the races, horse and foot; to
hear the jockeys crack, and see the Adamites run
naked afore the ladies?

RACHEL   We have seen all already there, as well as they,   85
last year.

HILLIARD   But there ha' been new plays since.

---

77 **project** plan; contrive; scheme
79 **fain** gladly
    progress journey. Robert Burton writes,
    'The most pleasing of all outward pas-
    times, is . . . to make a petty progresse, a
    merry journey . . . with some good com-
    panions' (227).
80 **fling** hasty or impetuous trip. *OED n.*
    3 cites this line to illustrate 'a hasty,
    reckless, or wanton movement', but does
    not address the sense of journey that the
    term also contains.
81 **Spring Garden** Adjoining the palace of
    Whitehall, and situated to the north-west
    of St James's Park, Spring Garden was
    originally named after its fountain, which
    sprang into life every time the spectator
    set foot on its hidden machinery. The
    garden was turned into a bowling green
    in 1630, but 'put down' sometime after
    1634 because of its expensive tavern and
    quarrelling customers. The tavern was
    reopened later, for on 13 June 1649 John
    Evelyn wrote a diary entry in which he
    recorded: 'I treated divers Ladys of my
    relations in *Spring Gardens*' (2.556).
    Brome, however, might have chosen to
    name the place as part of his play's
    emphasis on 'spring'; he contrasts the
    contrived gardens of London with the
    actual season.

82 **Hyde Park** Expropriated from the
    Church as a game park in 1536 by Henry
    VIII, the park, situated a little further to
    the west of Whitehall, was thrown open
    to the public in 1632. In Brome's time
    it was known as a site of aristocratic
    pleasure, where foot- and horse-races –
    spectacularizations of the hunting and
    blood sports that had originally typified
    the place – were held. See *Hyde Park*,
    where Bonavent asks, 'Be there any races
    here?', and Lacy replies, 'Yes, Sir, horse
    and foot' (sig. E4'); the play also high-
    lights the continued connection there
    between horse-racing and flirtation (see
    Graham).
83 **crack** boast; brag
    Adamites a nonconformist sect of
    'imitators of Adam' who chose to live
    nude like Adam and Eve and 'Cast off
    their petticoats and breeches' (Colvil,
    46). Mentioned with relish in pamphlets
    from 1641 onwards, Adamites, or tales
    of them, illustrated the cultural, political
    and religious confusion of the period;
    whether they really existed or were
    simply part of the literary tradition of
    burlesque is considered by David Cressy
    ('Adamites').

RACHEL   No, no; we are not for London.

HILLIARD   What think you of a journey to the Bath,
then?   90

RACHEL   Worse than tother way. I love not to carry my
health where others drop their diseases. There's no
sport i'that.

VINCENT   Will you up to the hilltop of sports, then, and
merriments: Dover's Olympics or the Cotswold   95
Games?

MERIEL   No, that will be too public for our recreation.
We would have it more within ourselves.

HILLIARD   Think of some course yourselves, then. We
are for you upon any way, as far as horse and money   100
can carry us.

89 **Bath** A Somerset city, site of several natural hot and warm springs, Bath had first come into prominence under the Romans. Its waters had from then onwards been thought potentially curative if imbibed or bathed in. William Camden records how 'Within the Citie . . . buble and boile up three springs of hote water' which 'are very medicinable and of great vertue to cure bodies over-charged and benummed . . . with corrupt humors' (233). Queen Anne's 1613 and subsequent trips to Bath for her gout had given the place the sobriquet 'the loyal city'; Charles I had himself visited Bath in 1628 (see Hembry, 55). The eleven eminent doctors – and many quacks – recorded there in the 1640s are testament to the place's increasing importance in Brome's time. Tobias Venner wrote, 'These famous hot Waters are of singular force, not only against diseases gotten by cold . . . but also bring, in time of health, exceeding comfort and profit to all cold, moist, and corpulent bodies' (*Baths*, sig. A4ʳ).

93 **sport** diversion; entertainment

95–6 **Dover's . . . Games** First organized by attorney Robert Dover in 1612, the Cotswold Games, also known, after their originator's name, as Dover's Olympics, took place on a hill above Chipping Camden in north Gloucestershire at Whitsun. They consisted of standard athletic competitions together with horse-racing, greyhound-racing, coursing, hunting, wrestling, throwing the sledge and spurning the bar (throwing a long pole); women's dances were also included. A collection of thirty-three poems – including poems by Drayton, Jonson and Heywood – was gathered in their honour by Matthew Walbancke in *Annalia Dubrensia* (1636). In that book's introduction, written to 'my worthy Friend Mr Robert Dover' (sig. A2ʳ·ᵛ), Walbancke writes, 'you . . . have in these your Famous . . . yearly Celebrations, not only revived the memory of [the original Greek Olympics], but adorned these your Cotswald Hills with such Ovations and Triumphs, as may continue their memorie to all posteritie'.

97 **recreation** activity or pastime pursued for pleasure or instruction

98 **within** amongst

100 **for you** willing to go along with you

VINCENT   Ay, and if those means fail us, as far as our
legs can bear or our hands can help us.

RACHEL *(aside)*   And we will put you to't. *[to Meriel]*
Come aside, Meriel. *[Rachel and Meriel step aside.]*   105

VINCENT   Some jeer, perhaps, to put upon us.

HILLIARD   What think you of a pilgrimage to Saint
Winifred's Well?

VINCENT   Or a journey to the wise woman at Nantwich
to ask if we be fit husbands for 'em?   110

HILLIARD   They are not scrupulous in that, we having
had their growing loves up from our childhoods, and
the old squire's good will before all men.

RACHEL, MERIEL   Ha, ha, ha –

VINCENT   What's the conceit, I marvel?   115

RACHEL, MERIEL   Ha, ha, ha, ha –

HILLIARD   Some merry one it seems.

---

104 **put you to't** require or force you to hold
   to it
106 **jeer** jibe; taunt
   put upon trick or dupe
107–8 **Saint Winifred's Well** a healing
   spring in Holywell, Flintshire, Wales,
   said to have burst into being on the spot
   where the nun Winifred was beheaded by
   Caradog in the seventh century, and long
   a popular place of Catholic pilgrimage.
   In 1632 Archbishop Abbot warned the
   King that 'There hath been these Two last
   Years past . . . Papists frequenting *Holy-
   Well* or St. *Winifred's* Well in *Wales*'; he
   admonished, 'it is not to be forgotten,
   that at that Well a great part of the
   Powder Treason was hatched' (see Laud,
   519–20). The well continued to retain
   Catholic and hence disestablishment
   associations during the interregnum.
   Thomas Gage, in 1648, describes how

'most of the Papists of the Land . . . doe
yearly resort thither to bee washed and
healed upon any light occasion either of
Head-ach, Stomack-ach, Ague, want of
children, where they blindly phansie a
speedy remedy for all maladies, or wants
of this World' (5). This is the first of
several Catholic references in the play.

109 **Nantwich** famous for its salt and salt-
   springs. Though no other reference to a
   particular wise woman there survives, the
   area was said to have healing properties
   and may have attracted quacks and 'wise
   women' as a consequence. Alternatively,
   Brome may be playing on the name of
   the place, perhaps suggesting that the
   wise woman is nothing but an 'antic'
   witch, or perhaps that she 'an't' (is not)
   really a witch.

111 **scrupulous** doubtful; chary
115 'What's the turn of thought, I wonder?'

104 SD] *this edn; after 105 Q1*   SD2] *this edn*   105 SD] *this edn*

RACHEL   And then, sirrah Meriel [*whispering to Meriel*]
    – Hark again [*whispering to Meriel*] – ha, ha, ha –
VINCENT   How they are taken with it!   120
MERIEL   Ha, ha, ha – Hark again, Rachel. [*Whispers to
    Rachel.*]
HILLIARD   Some wonderful nothing, sure. They will
    laugh as much to see a swallow fly with a white
    feather imped in her tail.
VINCENT   They were born laughing, I think.   125
RACHEL, MERIEL   Ha, ha, ha –
VINCENT   If it be not some trick upon us, which they'll
    discover in some monstrous shape, they cozen me.
    Now, ladies, is your project ripe? Possess us with the
    knowledge of it.   130
RACHEL   It is more precious than to be imparted upon a
    slight demand.
HILLIARD   Pray let us hear it. You know we are your
    trusty servants.
VINCENT   And have kept all your counsels ever since we 135
    have been infant playfellows.
RACHEL   Yes, you have played at all kinds of small
    game with us, but this is to the purpose. Ha, ha, ha –

118 **sirrah** a term used to stress the authority of the speaker (and thus the lack of authority of the person addressed). It was usually employed when speaking to children or women: Rachel's use of the word may arise from the fact that Meriel is her younger sister.
124 **imped** engrafted. New feathers were *imped* into the wing or tail feathers of a hunting bird to improve or restore its powers of flight; the idea of altering a brown swallow's appearance by imping white feathers into its tail, however, was absurd.

128 **discover** reveal
    cozen dupe; beguile
129 **ripe** ready
129–30 **Possess . . . of** provide us with the knowledge of; apprise us of
137–8 **small game** game where the stakes are low – but with a *double entendre*. Corisca, in *Bondman*, 2.2.41–4, records how 'some great women . . . in a dearth of Visitants, / Rather then be idle, have beene glad to play / At small game'.
138 **to the purpose** about the matter in hand

118, 119, 121 SDs] *this edn*

HILLIARD   It seems so by your laughing.

RACHEL   And asks a stronger tongue-tie than tearing of   140
books, burning of samplers, making dirt-pies, or piss
and paddle in't.

VINCENT   You know how and what we have vowed: to
wait upon you any way, any how, and any whither.

MERIEL   And you will stand to't?   145

HILLIARD   Ay, and go to't with you, wherever it be.

MERIEL   Pray tell't 'em, sister Rachel.

RACHEL   Why gentlemen – ha, ha – Thus it is – tell it
you, Meriel.

VINCENT   Oh, is that all?   150

MERIEL   You are the elder. Pray tell it you.

RACHEL   You are the younger. I command you tell it.
Come, out with it. They long to have it.

HILLIARD   When?

VINCENT   When?   155

MERIEL   In troth you must tell it, sister, I cannot. Pray
begin.

RACHEL   Then, gentlemen, stand your ground.

VINCENT   Some terrible business, sure!

RACHEL   You seemed, e'en now, to admire the felicity   160
of beggars.

---

140 **tongue-tie** that which ties the tongue, or restrains speech (*OED n.* 1, citing this line); here specifically an oath of silence. Rachel refers to a series of childhood pranks that were to be kept secret.

141 **samplers** beginners' exercises in embroidery, often containing the alphabet or prayers and mottoes worked in with various decorative devices

141–2 **piss . . . in't** The reference seems to be to a children's dare; Brome also referred to it in the play he co-wrote with Thomas Heywood, *Late Lancashire Witches*: 'yeou shall as soone pisse and paddle in't, as lap me in the mouth with

an awd Petticoat . . . to be whyet' (sig. C3ʳ ᵛ).

145 **stand to't** abide by it, with a bawdy quibble

146 **go to't** go ahead; 'get cracking'; also with a bawdy quibble

154, 155 **When** an exclamation of impatience

158 **stand your ground** refuse to be pushed backwards, i.e. hold fast to what you swore (to be ready for 'any adventure with you, ladies', 76).

160 **felicity** Rachel quotes back at Vincent what he said of beggars at the opening of the scene: 'I am overcome with admiration at the felicity they take!' (1–2).

MERIEL   And have engaged yourselves to join with us in
any course.

RACHEL   Will you now, with us and for our sakes, turn
beggars?   165

MERIEL   It is our resolution and our injunction on you.

RACHEL   But for a time and a short progress.

MERIEL   And for a spring trick of youth, now, in the
season.

VINCENT   Beggars! What rogues are these?   170

HILLIARD   A simple trial of our loves and service!

RACHEL   Are you resolved upon't? If not, God b'w'y'.
We are resolved to take our course.

MERIEL   Let yours be to keep counsel.

   [*Meriel and Rachel start to leave.*]

VINCENT

   Stay, stay. Beggars! Are we not so already?   175
   Do we not beg your loves and your enjoyings?
   Do we not beg to be received your servants,
   To kiss your hands, or, if you will vouchsafe,
   Your lips? Or your embraces?

HILLIARD   We now beg
   That we may fetch the rings and priest to marry us.   180
   Wherein are we no beggars?

RACHEL   That will not serve. Your time's not come for
that yet. You shall beg victuals first.

---

162 **engaged yourselves** undertaken

166 **injunction** emphatic admonition

167 **progress** See 79n. There may also be a comic reversal here: the term often referred to a state or royal journey undertaken so that noblemen across the land could shelter, feed and entertain their monarch; on this journey, however, it is the beggars who will provide shelter, food and entertainment for the nobility.

168 **spring trick** springtime hoax or piece of roguery

170 **rogues** Here the term is applied affectionately to the women, though the juxtaposition of *Beggars* and *rogues* foreshadows frequent references to the statute against rogues and beggars.

172 **God b'w'y'** 'God be with ye': 'goodbye'

173 **take our course** (1) proceed in such a way; (2) take our path (to the beggars)

174 **keep counsel** keep the secret

176 **your enjoyings** opportunities to enjoy you

178 **vouchsafe** condescend

183 **victuals** food or provisions of any kind

174 SD] *this edn*

VINCENT   Oh. I conceive your begging progress is to
ramble out this summer among your father's tenants,   185
and 'tis in request among gentlemen's daughters
to devour their cheese-cakes, apple pies, cream-
custards, flapjacks and pan puddings.

MERIEL   Not so, not so.

HILLIARD   Why, so we may be a kind of civil beggars.   190

RACHEL

I mean stark, errant, downright beggars. Ay,
Without equivocation, statute beggars.

MERIEL

Couchant and passant, guardant, rampant beggars.

VINCENT

Current and vagrant –

184–8 For the habit of eating tenants' home-cooking, see *Bartholomew Fair*, 1.4.56–7, where Wasp complains that Cokes runs 'up and down the country . . . to beg puddings and cake-bread of his tenants'.

186 **in request** the fashionable thing to do

187 **their** i.e. the tenants'
   cheese-cakes defined by Randle Cotgrave as 'a Tart, or cake made of egges, and cheese' (sig. 4f6ʳ)

187–8 **cream-custards** from 'crustades', rich pies, made of meat, eggs, herbs, spices, etc., enclosed in a crust. Cream-custards were open pies containing pieces of meat or fruit covered with a broth made of eggs that had been sweetened and seasoned with spices.

188 **flapjacks** apple turnovers or flat tarts, 'apple-jacks' (*OED* flapjack *n*. b, citing this line)
   pan puddings heavy, savoury puddings cooked in a pan, seemingly something like British Yorkshire puddings

190 Hilliard's idea is to redefine what they are already doing as civil beggary.

191 **stark** (1) unqualified; (2) naked
   errant (1) wandering; (2) wicked
   downright (1) outright; (2) right about being downcast or dejected

192 **Without equivocation** without ambiguities, double meanings or 'whims' – ironic, in view of the double meanings in all the descriptive words she has just used
   statute beggars a reference to Statute 39 Eliz., c. 3 (1597/98) that determined which people were to be defined as beggars. It listed, amongst others, wandering scholars, seafarers or ex-prisoners obliged to beg, fortune-tellers, unlicensed players and quack doctors.

193 **Couchant . . . rampant** allusions to and parodies of heraldic animals, continuing the suggestion here that *beggar-errants* are a form of *knight-errants* (cf. 3.1.43, 42 and nn.). *Couchant* is lying down; *passant* is walking and looking ahead, with three paws on the ground and the dexter (right) forepaw raised; *guardant* is having the full face towards the spectator; *rampant* is standing on the sinister (left) hind foot with the forepaws in the air, the sinister above the dexter. The effect is to define beggars in heraldic but also in animal terms.

194 **Current and vagrant** Seemingly a continuation of the 'heraldic' list, these words actually have nothing to do with heraldry and have been chosen by Vincent

HILLIARD   Stockant, whippant beggars!

VINCENT

Must you and we be such? Would you so have it?   195

RACHEL

Such as we saw so merry, and you concluded
Were th'only happy people in a nation.

MERIEL

The only free men of a commonwealth –
Free above scot-free – that observe no law,
Obey no governor, use no religion   200
But what they draw from their own ancient custom
Or constitute themselves, yet are no rebels.

RACHEL

Such as, of all men's meat and all men's money,
Take a free part and, wheresoe'er they travel,
Have all things gratis to their hands provided.   205

VINCENT

Coarse fare, most times.

RACHEL   Their stomach makes it good,
And feasts on that which others scorn for food.

MERIEL

The antidote, content, is only theirs

for their sounds. *Current* is 'present';
vagrant is 'roaming'; both are thus
descriptions of real beggary.
Stockant, whippant further parodies
of heraldic vocabulary that are actually
descriptions of the life of the beggar.
These words have been created to mean
'frequently put in the stocks' (see *OED*
stockant *adj.*, citing this line as only
recorded usage) and 'frequently whipped'
(see *OED* whippant *adj.*, citing this line
as only recorded usage).
196–7 Rachel quotes back Vincent's own
   words spoken in 9–10.
198 **free men** (1) men who are free; (2)
   'freemen', who enjoy the rights and
   liberties of a free society in a commonwealth, republic or democratic state, as

opposed to under a tyrannical regime or
totalitarian rule
199 **scot-free** free above even the petty
   concerns of tavern payments. A scot was
   a tavern score or fine; Thomas Blount
   described how 'when goodf[e]llows meet
   at the Tavern or Alehouse, they at parting,
   call for a Shot, Scot, or reckoning: And
   he is said to go Scot-free, that pays not
   his part or share towards the reckoning'
   (1656, sig. 2m6ʳ).
200 **use** practise
202 **constitute** create; determine
205 **gratis** free; out of favour or kindness
206 **Coarse fare** ordinary or harsh diet; but
   see 2.2.289n.
208 **antidote** medicine. The palliative of
   contentment makes the food digestible.

And, unto that, such full delights are known
That they conceive the kingdom is their own.   210
VINCENT [*to Hilliard*]   'Fore heaven I think they are in
   earnest, for they were always mad.
HILLIARD [*to Vincent*]   And we were madder than they,
   if we should lose 'em.
VINCENT [*to Hilliard*]   'Tis but a mad trick of youth, as   215
   they say, for the spring, or a short progress, and mirth
   may be made out of it, knew we how to carry it.
RACHEL   Pray, gentlemen, be sudden.   *Cuckoo* [*sings.*]
   Hark – you hear the cuckoo.
HILLIARD   We are most resolutely for you in your   220
   course.
VINCENT   But the vexation is how to set it on foot.
RACHEL   We have projected it. Now if you be perfect
   and constant lovers and friends, search you the
   means. [*to Meriel*] We have puzzled 'em.   225
MERIEL [*to Rachel*]   I am glad on't. Let 'em pump.
VINCENT   Troth, a small stock will serve to set up withal.
   This doublet sold off o'my back might serve to
   furnish a camp-royal of us.

---

209 **unto that** with that aim
210 **conceive** believe
215 **trick of youth** youthful trait; a proverb
   (see Dent T519.11)
216 **progress** journey; period of time. See
   79n.
217 **carry it** conduct matters
218 **sudden** speedy; prompt
218 SD The cuckoo's song is requested in
   other Cockpit plays of the time, including
   Dekker and Ford's *The Sun's Darling*
   and Shirley's *Hyde Park*. Presumably the
   company had a prop capable of creating
   a cuckoo's sound. See 1.1.155 SDn.
220–1 'We are decidedly in favour of your
   choice of action.'

222 **on foot** in motion – but also with the
   literal suggestion that, from now on, the
   lovers will be travelling on foot
223–5 **We ... means** 'We've come up with
   it intellectually: you must arrange the
   practical side of it.'
225 **puzzled** perplexed; confounded (*OED*
   puzzle *v.* 1a cites this line)
226 **Let 'em pump** 'Let them exert themselves' (*OED* pump *v.* 8 *intr.* A)
227 **Troth** i.e. 'by my troth'; 'upon my truth'
   stock sum of money
228 **doublet** close-fitting buttoned jacket,
   with or without sleeves, worn by men
229 **camp-royal** great body of troops, here
   used to mean 'a large number of us',

211, 213, 215 SDs] *Brome Online*   218 SD] *this edn; after 219 Q1*   sings] *this edn*   225, 226 SDs] *Lawrence*

HILLIARD   But how to enter or arrange ourselves into   230
the crew will be the difficulty. If we light raw and
tame amongst 'em – like cage-birds among a flight
of wild ones – we shall never pick up a living but
have our brains pecked out.

VINCENT   We want instruction dearly.   235

Enter SPRINGLOVE.

HILLIARD   Oh, here comes Springlove. His great
benefactorship among the beggars might prefer us
with authority into a ragged regiment presently. Shall
I put it to him?

RACHEL   Take heed what you do. His greatness with my   240
father will betray us.

VINCENT   I will cut his throat then. [*to Springlove*]
My noble Springlove – the great Commander of the

though any army reference in a play of this period darkly foreshadows the future. *OED* camp *n.*² c cites this line.

231–4 **light . . . out** In this analogy, the tame gentlefolk, who have lived like birds in a cage, will be unable to fend for themselves when freed into the wild: the beggars, presented as aggressive wild birds, will peck out their brains. This is a restatement of the idea introduced by Springlove, that gentry are encaged in their houses while beggars are free; see 1.1.183n. Yet it leaves unclear which of the two states is desirable. As George Pettie explicates, 'the birde inclosed in cage, the cage doare beeing set open, and the Hauke her ennemy sitting without . . . standeth in doubt whether it bee better stil to remaine in prison, or to goe forth to bee a pray for the hauke' (72).

231 **light** alight; descend
raw unfamiliar; naive

237 **benefactorship** office or action of a benefactor (*OED n.*, citing this line as first recorded usage)
prefer advance

238 **ragged regiment** a jocular term for a group of beggars, perhaps additionally attractive to Brome because of the army connotations of *regiment*: the *ragged regiment* is both the opposite of an army and an army in itself. In *Jew's Tragedy*, a similar 'regiment' is projected when the 'brave Captain of the ragged Regiment' enters with a band of 'Mechanicks' whom he addresses as his 'bilbow blades . . . roaring Renegadoes, and . . . ragged Ruffians', offering, 'I will instruct ye in the Rudiments of war' (43).

240 **greatness** intimacy. *Noble Gentleman*, 3.3.35, has Longaville refer to the Duke's 'greatnesse with the people'.

242 SD] *this edn*

Maunders and King of Canters – we saw the gratitude
of your loyal subjects in the large tributary content   245
they gave you in their revels.

SPRINGLOVE   Did you, sir?

HILLIARD   We have seen all with great delight and
admiration.

SPRINGLOVE   I have seen you, too, kind gentlemen and   250
ladies, and overheard you in your quaint design to
new create yourselves out of the worldly blessings
and spiritual graces heaven has bestowed upon you,
to be partakers and co-actors, too, in those vile
courses, which you call delights, ta'en by those   255
despicable and abhorred creatures.

VINCENT

Thou art a despiser – nay, a blasphemer –
Against the maker of those happy creatures
Who, of all humane, have priority
In their content, in which they are so blessed   260
That they enjoy most in possessing least.
Who made 'em such, dost think? Or why so happy?

RACHEL   He grows zealous in the cause; sure he'll beg
indeed.

HILLIARD

Art thou an hypocrite, then, all this while,   265
Only pretending charity, or using it
To get a name and praise unto thyself,

---

244 **Maunders** *cant* beggars
King Springlove was described as king
of the beggars at 1.1.378 and asked to be
king of the beggars at 1.1.493.
Canters *cant* those who use the 'cant' of
beggars, thieves and gypsies. Dekker, in
Lantern, writes, 'Stay and heare a *Canter*
in his own language, making Rhithmes'
(sig. C1ʳ).

245 **tributary content** pleasure they gave
you as tribute
251 **quaint** characterized by cleverness or
ingenuity (*OED adj.* cites this line)
259 **all humane** all that has humanity
259–60 **priority ... content**   precedence
over others in happiness

259 humane] human *Haaker*

And not to cherish and increase those creatures
In their most happy way of living? Or
Dost thou bestow thine alms with a foul purpose,   270
To stint their begging and, with loss, to buy
And slave those free souls from their liberty?

MERIEL
They are more zealous in the cause than we!

SPRINGLOVE
But are you, ladies, at defiance too
With reputation and the dignity   275
Due to your father's house and you?

RACHEL   Hold thy peace, good Springlove, and, though
you seem to dislike this course and reprove us for it,
do not betray us in it; your throat's in question. I tell
you for good will, good Springlove.   280

MERIEL   What wouldst thou have us do? Thou talkest
o'th' house. 'Tis a base, melancholy house. Our
father's sadness banishes us out on't. And, for the
delight thou takest in beggars and their brawls, thou
canst not but think they live a better life abroad than   285
we do in this house.

SPRINGLOVE   I have sounded your faith, and I am glad I
find you all right. And, for your father's sadness, I'll
tell you the cause on't. I overheard it but this day in
his private discourse with his merry mate, Master   290
Hearty. He has been told by some wizard that you
both were born to be beggars –

---

271 **stint** stop
272 **slave** enslave
279 **your . . . question** (the health of) your
throat is in danger. If Springlove reveals
their secret, Vincent will cut his throat
(see 242).

285 **abroad** away from home; hence *2H4*,
1.2.94–7: 'I am glad to see your lordship
abroad, I heard say your lordship was
sick. I hope your lordship goes abroad by
advice.'
287 **sounded** ascertained; tested

277–80] *Dodsley; Q1 lines Springlove, / it, / question. / Springlove. /*   281–3 What . . . on't] *Dodsley; Q1
lines do? / House. / House. / on't. /*   292 beggars –] *Brome Online; Beggars. Q1*

ALL   How? How?

SPRINGLOVE   – for which he is so tormented in mind
that he cannot sleep in peace nor look upon you but   295
with heart's grief.

VINCENT   This is most strange.

RACHEL   Let him be grieved, then, till we are beggars.
We have just reason to become so now. And what we
thought on but in jest before, we'll do in earnest now.   300

SPRINGLOVE   Oh, I applaud this resolution in you;
would have persuaded it; will be your servant in't.
For, look ye, ladies: the sentence of your fortune
does not say that you shall beg for need, hungry or
cold necessity. If, therefore, you expose yourselves   305
on pleasure into it, you shall absolve your destiny
nevertheless and cure your father's grief. I am
overjoyed to think on't, and will assist you faithfully.

ALL   A Springlove! A Springlove!

SPRINGLOVE

I am prepared already for th'adventure   310
And will, with all conveniences, furnish
And set you forth; give you your dimensions,
Rules and directions. I will be your guide,
Your guard, your convoy, your authority.
You do not know my power; my command   315
I'th' beggars' commonwealth.

VINCENT   But how? But how, good Springlove?

SPRINGLOVE

I'll confess all. In my minority
My master took me up a naked beggar,

---

293 **How?** exclamation to attract attention –
equating to the modern 'What?'
304 **for** because of
304–5 **hungry . . . necessity** need brought
about by hunger or cold

309 **A** See 1.1.447n.
311 **furnish** supply
312 **dimensions** measurements (by which to
understand distances)
314 **convoy** conductor (often of troops)

---

294 – for] *Brome Online;* For *Q1*   298–300] *Dodsley; Q1 lines* Beggars, / now: / before, / now. /   301–3
Oh . . . ladies] *Dodsley; Q1 lines* you; / in't. / Ladies: /

Bred me at school, then took me to his service,   320
You know in what good fashion. And, you may
Collect to memory, for seven late summers –
Either by leave, pretending friends to see
At far remote parts of the land, or else
By stealth – I would absent myself from service   325
To follow my own pleasure, which was begging,
Led to't by nature. My indulgent master,
Yet ignorant of my course, on my submission,
When cold and hunger forced me back at winter,
Received me still again. Till, two years since –   330
He being drawn by journey towards the north
Where I then quartered with a ragged crew
On the highway, not dreaming of him there –
I did accost him with a 'good your worship,
The gift of one small penny to a creeple',   335
For here I was with him [*limping*], 'and the good Lord
To bless you and restore it you in heaven'.

ALL   Ha, ha, ha.

SPRINGLOVE

My head was dirty clouted, and this leg
Swaddled with rags, the other naked, and   340
My body clad like his upon the gibbet.

322 **Collect to memory** recollect
   seven sev'n
328 **ignorant** ign'rant
   on my submission when I submitted
334–7 **'good … heaven'** These lines, and
   others that are to be spoken in a wheed-
   ling 'beggar's whine', are often visually
   separated from genuine speech or beggars'
   cant in Brome's text by being printed in
   italics. Brome also attempts to reproduce
   phonetically the beggars' pronunciation
   of certain words.
335 **creeple** cripple. The spelling, which is
   Brome's, indicates the beggar pronunciation of this word.

339 **dirty clouted** covered with a dirty cloth
   or clout, from 'clout' ('patch'), a material
   made from patched cloth, or a scrap of
   material
340 **Swaddled** swathed; bandaged
341 **his … gibbet** that of a man hanging
   from a gallows. Hanged men wore rags,
   as one of the hangman's perks was the
   clothes of his victims. *Gamester* refers to
   gentlemen who 'let their clothes enrich
   the hangmans wardrobe' (sig. A4ᵛ); and
   the ballad 'An Excellent New Medley'
   (1620) has the couplet, 'The Broker hath
   gay clothes to sell, / Which from the
   hangman's budget fell.'

335 gift of] *Dodsley;* gift *Q1*   336 SD] *this edn; Halts Q1*

Yet he, with searching eyes, through all my rags
And counterfeit postures made discovery
Of his man Springlove; chid me into tears
And a confession of my forespent life.   345
At last, upon condition that vagary
Should be the last, he gave me leave to run
That summer out. In autumn, home came I
In my home clothes again and former duty.
My master not alone conserved my counsel,   350
But lays more weighty trust and charge upon me.
Such was his love to keep me a home man
That he conferred his steward's place upon me,
Which clogged me, the last year, from those delights
I would not lose again to be his lord.   355

ALL   A Springlove! A Springlove!

SPRINGLOVE

Pursue the course you are on, then, as cheerfully
As the inviting season smiles upon you.
Think how you are necessitated to it
To quit your father's sadness and his fears   360
Touching your fortune. Till you have been beggars,
The sword hangs over him. You cannot think

---

344 **man** employee
  chid rebuked
345 **forespent** spent previously (*OED adj.*
  cites this line)
346 The scansion here is awkward. Presumably *condition* is to be pronounced as a
  four-syllable word and *vagary* as a two-
  syllable one – though another solution is
  that there is an additional 'that' missing
  before *vagary*.
  that vagary that that wandering journey
347–8 **run . . . out** see that summer through
  to its end
350 **not . . . counsel** did not simply keep my
  counsel (see *OED* conserve *v.* 3, citing
  this line)

351 **lays** The move from past to present
  tense signifies the immediacy with which
  Springlove is reliving the experience.
352 **home man** man associated with the home
  or employed at home (*OED n.*, citing this
  line)
354 **clogged** hindered or impeded; from
  'clog', the block or heavy piece of wood
  that was attached to imprisoned men or
  beasts to prevent escape
359 **necessitated to it** (1) obliged to do it;
  (2) predetermined to do it
360 **quit** get rid of
362 **sword . . . him** an allusion to the legend
  of Damocles, a courtier to King Dionysius
  I of Syracuse, who was allowed to dine at

Upon an act of greater piety
Unto your father than t'expose yourselves
Brave volunteers, unpressed by common need,   365
Into this meritorious warfare; whence,
After a few days or short season spent,
You bring him a perpetual peace and joy
By expiating the prophecy that torments him.
'Twere worth your time in painful, woeful steps,   370
With your lives' hazard, in a pilgrimage
So to redeem a father. But you'll find
A progress of such pleasure, as I'll govern't,
That the most happy courts could never boast
In all their tramplings on the country's cost;   375
Whose envy we shall draw, when they shall read
We out-beg them, and for as little need.

ALL   A Springlove! A Springlove!

SPRINGLOVE

Follow me, gallants, then, as cheerfully
As –   *Birds singing*
Hark! We are summoned forth.   380

ALL   We follow thee. *Exeunt.*

---

the King's table if he sat throughout, in danger of his life, under a sword hanging by a single hair. By analogy, Oldrents can enjoy nothing as he is constantly tortured by fear.

365 **volunteers, unpressed** The group are to opt for the begging life, not be impressed (conscripted) into it. These military metaphors are an ironic reflection of the troubled times in which Brome was writing. Charles I was heavily reliant on pressed troops made up of unskilled labourers including beggars. Reversing the paradigm, the beggars here are conceived of as an army engaged in 'meritorious warfare' into which the gentry can be impressed or choose to volunteer.

369 **expiating** averting the evil portended by (a prodigy or prophecy). *OED* expiate *v.* 1 cites this line.

373 **progress** Here the term is used more explicitly than at 79, referring not just to a journey, but to an official visit made by a monarch. See 79n. and 167n.

375 **tramplings** from 'trample'. Springlove trivializes stately courtly progresses that take place at the country's expense.

377 **out-beg them** outdo them in begging; the suggestion is that courtiers, who beg for preferment and favours, are beggars themselves. See 1.1.51–4n.

little need a further dig at courtly extravagance

[2.2]   *Enter* RANDALL, *a purse in his hand.*

RANDALL   Well, go thy ways. If ever any just or
charitable steward was commended, sure thou shalt
be at the last quarter-day. Here's five and twenty
pounds for this quarter's beggar-charge. And, if he
return not by the end of this quarter, here's order to a   5
friend to supply for the next. If I now should venture
for the commendation of an unjust steward and turn
this money to mine own use – Ha, dear devil, tempt
me not: I'll do thee service in a greater matter! But to
rob the poor, a poor trick, every churchwarden can   10
do't! Now something whispers me that my master,
for his steward's love, will supply the poor, as I may
handle the matter. Then I rob the steward if I restore
him not the money at his return. Away, temptation,
leave me! I am frail flesh, yet I will fight with thee.   15
But say the steward never return? Oh, but he will return.
Perhaps he may not return? Turn from me, Satan;

2.2 Location: outside, by the beggars' barn

1–3 **If ... quarter-day** Randall addresses the absent Springlove, conflating the commendation Oldrents will give Springlove at the last quarter-day with the commendation God will give at the Last Judgement.

3   **quarter-day** one of the four days that marked off the quarters of the year, on which tenancies, payments and other quarterly charges fell due and meetings were held. In England and Ireland the traditional quarter-days were Lady Day (25 March), Midsummer Day (24 June), Michaelmas (29 September) and Christmas Day (25 December).

3–4 **five and twenty pounds** equivalent to over half Randall's lifetime savings of forty pounds (see 4.1.117).

10   **poor ... poor** The 'whim', in this instance a pun, is on the two meanings of *poor*: destitute ... unworthy.

churchwarden lay officer who attended to certain secular matters such as care of church property. Churchwardens were proverbially lovers of money and robbers of the poor. Julio, in *Knave*, asks, 'How much of the poores money was found in one of the Churchwardens purchase last day?' (sig. C3^r). In *Queen's Exchange*, Brome has Jeffrey refer to how 'covetous . . . a Churchwarden / May be, when I am dead and gone' (sig. D3^v).

11–18 **Now ... conscience** Randall sets up a catechismical argument with himself that is reminiscent of the debate between the good and bad angels in Marlowe's *Doctor Faustus*: his good and bad sides are in conflict with one another. Cf. Springlove at 1.1.256–62.

2.2] *Haaker*

strive not to clog my conscience: I would not have
this weight upon't for all thy kingdom. [*Walks aside.*]

      Enter HEARTY *singing, and* OLDRENTS.

HEARTY [*Sings.*]
Hey down, hey down a down, *etc.*   20

Remember, sir, your covenant to be merry.
OLDRENTS   I strive, you see, to be so. Yet something
pricks me within, methinks.
HEARTY
No further thought, I hope, of Fortune's tell-tales.
OLDRENTS
I think not of 'em. Nor will I presage   25
That when a disposition of sadness
O'erclouds my spirits, I shall therefore hear
Ill news or shortly meet with some disaster.
HEARTY
Nay, when a man meets with bad tidings, why
May not he then compel his mind to mirth,   30
As well as puling stomachs are made strong

18 **clog my conscience** See 1.1.327–8 (and n.), where Randall argued that money would *clog* the *consciences* of the beggars: here money is in danger of clogging his conscience too.

20 **Hey down** a standard phrase representing singing. In Florio, 'Filibustacchina' is defined as 'the burden of a country song, as we say hay doune a doune douna' (1598, 131); in Blount, 'Caroll' is glossed with the explanation that 'when men were jocund, they were wont to sing *Rola, Rola*, as sometimes they now do, *Hey down, derry derry*' (1656, sig. H2r).

etc. used here to indicate that the actor should carry on in the same vein. For comparable uses of 'etc.' in playtexts see Stern, 251.

21 **covenant** undertaking; promise
23 **pricks** torments
24 **Fortune's tell-tales** (1) Fortune's malicious disclosures; (2) Fortune's tattlers, i.e. the fortune-teller
25 **presage** predict
31–2 **puling . . . appetite** That the sick should be encouraged to eat was a strongly held belief. Michael Drayton describes a search made for foods to tempt an ill man: Dover's cliffs are raided for 'Sampyre, to excite / His dull and sickly taste, and stirre up appetite' (300).
31 **puling** ailing; sickly (*OED adj.* 2, citing this instance)

19 SD1] *Brome Online*   20 SP] *Haaker; not in Q1*   SD] *this edn*

143

By eating against appetite?

OLDRENTS

Forced mirth, though, is not good.

HEARTY

It relishes not, you'll say. No more does meat
That is most savoury to a long-sick stomach,   35
Until, by strife and custom, 'tis made good.

OLDRENTS

You argue well. But [*pointing to Randall*] do you see
    yond fellow?

HEARTY

I never noted him so sad before.
He neither sings nor whistles.

OLDRENTS   Something troubles him.
Can he force mirth out of himself now, think you?   40

HEARTY

What? Speak you of a clod of earth, a hind
But one degree above a beast, compared
To th'airy spirit of a gentleman?

OLDRENTS

He looks as he came laden with ill news
To meet me on my way.

HEARTY   'Tis very pretty.   45
Suppose the ass be tired with sadness? Will you
disburden him to load yourself? Think of your
covenant to be merry in spite of Fortune and her
riddle-makers.

---

34 **relishes** (1) savours (of food, continuing
    the food analogy); (2) pleases
41–3 Hearty's idea that true sadness is the
    prerogative of gentlemen will be ques-
    tioned throughout this play.
41 **hind** servant or country person
42 **But one degree** just one step, i.e. just
    minimally

43 **th'airy** the lofty
45 **pretty** nicely done
46 **ass** Hearty, continuing the insulting
    animal imagery, now sees Randall as an
    ass carrying a heavy load (of sadness).
    He warns Oldrents that relieving Randall
    of sorrow will burden him yet further.

37 SD] *this edn*   46–9] *Dodsley; Q1 lines* him / merry / riddle-makers. /

OLDRENTS Why, how now, Randall? Sad? Where's 50
Springlove?

HEARTY [*aside*]
He's ever in his care. But that I know
The old squire's virtue, I should think Springlove
Were sure his bastard.

RANDALL [*to Oldrents*] Here's his money, sir.
I pray that I be charged with it no longer. 55
The devil and I have strained courtesy these two
hours about it. I would not be corrupted with the trust
of more than is mine own. Master Steward gave it
me, sir, to order it for the beggars. He has made me
steward of the barn and them, while he is gone, he 60
says, a journey to survey and measure lands abroad
about the countries: some purchase, I think, for your
worship.

OLDRENTS I know his measuring of land. He is gone his
old way. And let him go. Am not I merry, Hearty? 65

HEARTY Yes, but not hearty merry. There's a whim
now.

OLDRENTS The poor's charge shall be mine. Keep you
the money for him.

RANDALL Mine is the greater charge, then. Knew you 70
but my temptations and my care, you would discharge
me of it.

OLDRENTS Ha, ha, ha.

---

56 **strained courtesy** treated (one another) with less than due consideration
59 **order** manage
64 **his . . . land** Oldrents' meaning combines assessing of land (surveying), with walking the countryside (joining the beggars).

66 **hearty** heartily. The reversion of name and mood is Hearty's 'whim', showing that he knows Oldrents' 'merriment' is put on.
68–71 **charge . . . discharge** further use of 'whim' that plays on the meanings of *charge* and *discharge*: expense, burden . . . release

52 SD] *Dodsley*   54 SD] *Brome Online*   58 Master] *Brome Online;* Mr *Q1*   70–2] *Dodsley; Q1 lines* then. / care, / it. /

RANDALL   I have not had it so many minutes as I have
    been in several minds about it and most of them   75
    dishonest.
OLDRENTS   Go, then, and give it to one of my daughters
    to keep for Springlove.
RANDALL   Oh, I thank your worship –   *Exit.*
OLDRENTS   Alas, poor knave! How hard a task it is to   80
    alter custom!
HEARTY   And how easy for money to corrupt it. What a
    pure treasurer would he make!
OLDRENTS   All were not born for weighty offices –
    which makes me think of Springlove. He might have   85
    ta'en his leave, though.
HEARTY   I hope he's run away with some large trust.
    I never liked such demure downlooked fellows.
OLDRENTS
    You are deceived in him.
HEARTY   If you be not,
    'Tis well. But this is from the covenant.   90
OLDRENTS
    Well, sir, I will be merry. I am resolved
    To force my spirit only unto mirth.
    Should I hear now my daughters were misled
    Or run away, I would not send a sigh
    To fetch 'em back.
HEARTY   Tother old song for that.   95

81 **custom** habit
86 **ta'en his leave** departed with some
    expression of farewell; bid farewell
88 **demure** reserved
    downlooked having downward or down-
    cast looks; guilty-looking (*OED adj.*,
    citing this line)
90 **this . . . covenant** i.e. this disagreement
    about Springlove distracts from the

covenant – the promise *to be merry* – that
Oldrents referred to at 21.
94–5 **send . . . back** The notion of sending a
    sigh to fetch a loved person was commonly
    employed in literature. George Herbert,
    in 'The Search', 'sent a sigh to seek
    thee' (*Temple*, 156); and Cartwright's
    Comedies included a verse called 'A sigh
    sent to his absent Love' (sig. O8^{r-v}).

80–8] *Dodsley; Q1 lines* Custome! / it. / make! / Offices. / *Springlove.* / tho'. / Trust, / Fellows. /   89–90]
Brome Online; prose Q1   95 Tother] *(*To'ther*)*

SONG

[*Sings.*]   There was an old fellow at Waltham Cross,
Who merrily sung when he lived by the loss.
He never was heard to sigh with 'hey ho',
But sent it out with a 'hey trolly lo'.
He cheered up his heart when his goods went
    to wrack,   100
With a 'hem boy, hem' and a cup of old sack.

OLDRENTS
Is that the way on't? Well it shall be mine, then.

Enter RANDALL [*with a letter*].

RANDALL   My mistresses are both abroad, sir.
OLDRENTS   How? Since when?

96–101 Music for this song, with the title 'A Catch within a Catch', by John Hilton, is printed in Hilton (1652). See p. 263 for verbal differences.

96 **Waltham Cross** one of twelve 'Eleanor crosses' set up by Edward I to mark the place where the body of his wife, Queen Eleanor of Castile (d. 1290), had rested on its journey from Nottinghamshire to London for burial. This monument was erected in Walthamstow, Hertfordshire, in 1291–2.

97 **by the loss** while losing money; from the proverb 'He buys and sells and lives by the loss' (Tilley, L459)

98 **'hey ho'** The term represented a sigh, and is sometimes said to mimic the sound a sigh makes, as when Petillus, in *Bonduca*, 1.2.140–1, opines that 'Aymees and hearty hey-hoes, / Are Sallets fit for soldiers.' The closeness between a sad sigh, *hey ho*, a shout of joy, *a-hey* (used regularly by Clack) or *hey toss* (used by Springlove), and a merry song, *hey down* or *hey trolly*

lo (both used by Hearty), will be continually pointed out.

99 **'hey trolly lo'** the burden to a merry song, often about drinking. In *Trial of Treasure* the character Lust sings, 'like a gallant', a song beginning, 'Hey rowse, fill all the pottes in the house . . . Hey how troly lowe, hey dery, dery' (sig. A3ʳ); in *Late Lancashire Witches*, the parody drinking song chanted by the witches to their familiars includes, 'Suck our blouds freely, and with it be jolly, / While merrily we sing, Hey Trolly lolly' (sig. L4ʳ). If Brome's song was sung to the music supplied in Appendix 1, it included a thrice-repeated refrain of 'hey trolly lolly lolly lo', a 'catch' in which Oldrents will have joined. It is possible that Clack, too, later sings a snatch of the refrain. See 5.1.251–2n. and p. 264.

101 **'hem . . . hem'** an interjectional utterance to attract attention from the *boy* who is to serve the sack

96 SD] *this edn*   99 hey] *(Haigh)*   101 hem] *(heghm)*   102 SD *with a letter*] *Brome Online*

147

RANDALL   On foot, sir, two hours since, with the two   105
    gentlemen their lovers. Here's a letter they left with
    the butler. And there's a muttering in the house.
OLDRENTS
    I will not read nor open it, but conceive
    Within myself the worst that can befall them:
    That they are lost and no more mine. What follows?   110
    That I am happy; all my cares are flown.
    The counsel I anticipated from
    My friend shall serve to set my rest upon,
    Without all further helps to jovial mirth,
    Which I will force out of my spleen so freely   115
    That grief shall lose her name where I have being,
    And sadness, from my furthest foot of land,
    While I have life, be banished.
HEARTY   What's the whim now?
OLDRENTS
    My tenants shall sit rent-free for this twelvemonth,
    And all my servants have their wages doubled;   120
    And so shall be my charge in housekeeping.
    I hope my friends will find and put me to't.
HEARTY
    For them I'll be your undertaker, sir.
    But this is overdone: I do not like it.

---

107 **muttering** something muttered; a rumour
108 **conceive** imagine
113 **set ... upon** set my stake upon: a metaphor from the card game Primero, meaning to stand by the cards in your hand in the hope that they are better than your adversary's; hence to make up your mind or be determined on a subject
115 **spleen** abdominal organ regarded as the seat of both laughter and melancholy.

Cf. 'Why this would vex / The resolution of a suffering spleene' (*Jeronimo*, sig. E3ᵛ), and 'Such matter as will make you laugh your fill, if you have a laughing spleene' (Camden, 464). Though Oldrents declares he will force mirth from his spleen, what emerges may actually be another version of sorrow.
123 **For ... undertaker** 'I'll undertake for them'; 'I'll speak for them'.
124 **overdone** exaggerated

107 muttering] (muttring)

OLDRENTS

And for thy news, the money that thou hast 125
Is now thine own. I'll make it good to Springlove.
Be sad with it and leave me. For I tell thee,
I'll purge my house of stupid melancholy.

RANDALL

I'll be as merry as the charge that's under me:

*A confused noise [is made] within of laughing
and singing, and one crying out.*

The beggars, sir. D'ye hear 'em in the barn? 130

OLDRENTS

I'll double their allowance too, that they may
Double their numbers and increase their noise.
These bear not sound enough, and one, methought,
Cried out among 'em.

RANDALL

By a most natural cause. For there's a doxy 135
Has been in labour, sir. And 'tis their custom
With songs and shouts to drown the woman's cries,
A ceremony which they use not for
Devotion but to keep off notice of
The work they have in hand. Now she is in 140
The straw, it seems, and they are quiet.

127–8 Oldrents' belief that money causes
sadness undercuts his generosity, while
raising questions about the connection
between wealth and happiness.

129 **the charge . . . me** i.e. the beggars, but
also a pun on the idea of 'charge' as (1)
responsibility; (2) pecuniary expense

135 **doxy** *cant* unmarried mistress of a beggar
or rogue

140–1 **in / The straw** in childbed; probably
referring to the straw mattress on which

women gave birth. See *Rich Closet*,
which describes 'How . . . the child-bed
womans bed ought to be furnished': 'A
large boulster made of linnen cloth, must
be stuffed with straw, and be spread on
the ground, that her upper part may lye
higher than her lower' (9). Alternatively
the phrase is traceable to the straw laid
down to deaden noise during labour,
or even to the straw in which cows lie
to calve. Here the term has particular

129.1 *is made*] *this edn*   130+ D'ye] *this edn*; Do'e *Q1*; Do you *Dodsley*

HEARTY   The straw!
That's very proper there. That's Randall's whim.

OLDRENTS
We will have such a lying-in and such
A christening, such up-sitting and gossiping!
I mean to send forty miles circuit at the least   145
To draw in all the beggars can be found,
And such devices we will have for jollity
As fame shall boast to all posterity.
Am I not merry, Hearty? Hearty merry?

HEARTY
Would you were else. I fear this overdoing.   150

OLDRENTS
I'll do't for expiation of a crime
That's charged upon my conscience till't be done.

HEARTY   What's that? What says he?

OLDRENTS   We will have such a festival month on't,
Randall –   155

---

resonance because literal straw, in the form of haybales, will constitute the childbed. It recalls the earlier reference to beggars 'tumbling' in straw of which births such of this will be the result; see 1.1.364.

142 **Randall's whim** Randall has used the conventional phrase to indicate that the woman is in childbed; it is a 'whim' as she is literally in the straw in the barn.

143 **lying-in** the formalities of being in childbed. 'The lying-in of a woman in childbed' is described in Florio (1611) as being 'when she is finely drest and trimmed up in her bed curiously expecting her friends to come to visite and gossip with her' (120). Thomas Middleton's *Chaste Maid*, 2.3, depicts the kind of celebration that might take place when gossips visit a woman in childbed.

144 **up-sitting** the occasion of a woman's first sitting up to receive company after a confinement (*OED n.* 1, citing this line). For the up-sitting, which usually took place three days after the birth, a woman was confined to her chamber but was allowed to leave her bed; a feast would celebrate the occasion.

gossiping christening or christening-feast, at which female friends – known as gossips from 'god sib', kin in God – chatted, drank and celebrated the recovery of the mother and the birth of the child

147–8 Oldrents plans to celebrate the beggar birth as though it were a noble one.

147 **devices** events devised or fancifully invented for dramatic representation

151 **crime** The nature of Oldrents' crime will be made apparent at the play's conclusion.

154 **festival month** A month of celebration at home succeeded a birth; only after this period was a (well-born) woman allowed out of the house to be 'churched'.

RANDALL

Sir, you may spare the labour and the cost:
They'll never thank you for't. They'll not endure
A ceremony that is not their own,
Belonging either to the child or mother.
A month, sir? They'll not be detained so long   160
For your estate! Their work is done already:
The bratling's born, the doxy's in the strummel –
Laid by an autem mort of their own crew
That served for midwife – and the childbed woman
Eating of hasty pudding for her supper,   165
And the child part of it for pap,
I warrant you, by this time. Then to sleep,
So to rise early to regain the strength
By travel which she lost by travail.

HEARTY   There's Randall again.   170

OLDRENTS   Can this be?

RANDALL   She'll have the bantling at her back tomorrow
that was today in her belly, and march a-footback
with it.

HEARTY   Art there again, old Randall?   175

---

162 **bratling** little brat, infant (*OED n.* cites this line as first recorded usage)

162–3 **strummel ... autem mort** *cant* straw ... married woman; the first sustained example of beggars' cant in *A Jovial Crew*, and a sign of the effect the beggars have already begun to have on Randall's vocabulary and thinking

165 **hasty pudding** Famously thick and hot, hasty pudding was made by stirring flour and spices into boiling cream, milk or water.

166 **for pap** for food. 'Pap' was bland, soft or moist food suitable for babies and invalids.

169 **travel ... travail** a 'whim' on two words pronounced and sometimes spelled the same way: *travel*, meaning a journey, and *travail*, meaning work or labour – in this instance the labour pangs of a woman in childbirth. Blount describes 'paritude' as 'the time of travail or deliverance of childe or yong' (1656, sig. 2f3ᵛ).

170 i.e. Randall has made another 'whim'.

172 **bantling** young or small child; often used depreciatively as a synonym for bastard

173 **a-footback** on foot; a humorous backformation from 'a-horseback'

175 Hearty observes that Randall has indulged in yet more wordplay.

RANDALL

And for their gossiping, now you are so nigh,
If you'll look in, I doubt not but you'll find 'em
At their high feast already.

HEARTY   Pray, let's see 'em, sir.

Randall opens the scene. The BEGGARS *discovered*
at their feast. After they have scrambled a while
at their victuals, this song.

BEGGARS [*Sing.*]

Here, safe in our skipper, let's cly off our peck
And bowse in defiance o'th' harman-beck.   180
Here's pannum, and lap and good poplars of
    yarrum
To fill up the crib and to comfort the quarrom.
Now bowse a round health to the go-well and
    come-well
Of Cicely Bumtrinket that lies in the strummel.

178.1 **opens the scene... discovered** See
1.1.375.1n.

178.2–3 **scrambled... victuals** contended
with one another for a share of food

179–84 **cant** 'Here, safe in our barn
⌊*skipper*⌋, let's seize ⌊*cly off*⌋ our food
[*peck*] / And drink [*bowse*] in defiance of
the constable [*harman-beck*]. / Here's
bread [*pannum*], and butter [*lap*] and
good milk pottage [*poplars of yarrum*] /
To fill up the basket [*crib*] and comfort
the body [*quarrom*]. / Now drink [*bowse*]
a round health to the delivery [*go-well*
and come-well] / Of Cicely Bumtrinket
that lies in the straw [*strummel*].'

182 **crib** according to *OED n.* 6b, which cites
this line, a dialect word meaning a light
meal or snack. As that does not make
sense in context, the *crib* referred to here
is probably a wickerwork basket, pannier
or the like (*OED n.* 7a).

183 **the go-well and come-well** literally, the
successful going and coming; by extension, the delivery. *OED*'s suggestion that
'go-well' means 'prosperous journey
outwards', though it cites this instance,
seems to have missed the point (go *v.*
compounds).

184 **Cicely Bumtrinket** an insulting, low-
class name. It is found in *Shoemaker's*,
1.4.32–3: 'wheres *Cisly Bumtrinket* your
maide? she has a privie fault, she fartes
in her sleepe', and is also employed in a
list of insults applied to Mistress Miniver
in *Satiromastix*, 3.1.186–9 (to which
she responds, 'Why dost call mee such
horrible ungodlie names . . . ?').

179 SP] *this edn; not in Q1*   SD] *this edn*   182 quarrom] *this edn;* Quarron *Q1*

Now bowse a round health to the go-well and
   come-well   185
Of Cicely Bumtrinket that lies in the strummel.

Here's ruffpeck, and casson and all of the best,
And scraps of the dainties of gentry cove's feast.
Here's grunter and bleater, with tib-of-the-butt'ry,
And margery-prater, all dressed without slutt'ry.   190
For all this bene cribbing and peck let us then
Bowse a health to the gentry cove of the ken.
Now bowse a round health to the go-well and
   come-well
Of Cicely Bumtrinket that lies in the strummel.

OLDRENTS   Good heaven, how merry they are!   195
HEARTY   Be not you sad at that.
OLDRENTS

Sad, Hearty, no – unless it be with envy
At their full happiness. What is an estate
Of wealth and power, balanced with their freedom,
But a mere load of outward compliment,   200
When they enjoy the fruits of rich content?
Our dross but weighs us down into despair,

187–92 *cant* 'Here's bacon [*ruffpeck*], and cheese [*casson*] and all of the best, / And scraps of the dainties of the gentleman's [*gentry cove's*] feast. / Here's pork [*grunter*] and lamb [*bleater*], with goose [*tib-of-the-butt'ry*], / And chicken [*margery-prater*], all cleanly prepared [*without slutt'ry*]. / For all this good assortment [*bene cribbing*] and provisions [*peck*] let us then / Drink [*Bowse*] a health to the gentleman [*gentry cove*] of the house [*ken*].' For more on the lyrics, see p. 265; for lengthier definitions of the cant words, see Appendix 2.

190 **dressed without slutt'ry** prepared in the cleanest fashion

191 **cribbing** Though *OED* claims this is thieves' cant for 'provender, provisions' (*OED n.* 5, citing this line as sole recorded usage), 'cribbing' is not to be found in canting dictionaries of the period. The word was probably coined by Brome from 'crib'; it seems to mean the collection of food gathered in the basket – see 182n.

192 **gentry** pronounced with three syllables

200 **compliment** ceremony; formality (*OED* complement *n.* 8b, citing this instance)

202 **dross** worthless, impure matter; particularly, in alchemy, the extraneous matter thrown off from metals in the process of melting

While their sublimed spirits dance i'th' air.

HEARTY

I ha' not so much wealth to weigh me down,

Nor so little, I thank chance, as to dance naked.   205

OLDRENTS

True, my friend Hearty; thou, having less than I,

Of which I boast not, art the merrier man.

But they exceed thee in that way so far

That, should I know my children now were beggars –

Which yet I will not read – I must conclude   210

They were not lost, nor I to be aggrieved.

HEARTY

If this be madness, 'tis a merry fit.

Enter PATRICO. *Many of the Beggars look out.*

PATRICO

Tour out with your glaziers; I swear by the ruffin,

That we are assaulted by a queer cuffin.

RANDALL

Hold! What d'ye mean, my friends? This is our

   master: 215

The master of your feast and feasting-house.

PATRICO   Is this the gentry cove?

---

203 **sublimed** refined. In alchemy, 'sublimed' meant having gone through a process of sublimation, in which a solid substance is converted by means of heat into vapour, which resolidifies on cooling.

spirits . . . air Oldrents reverses Hearty's statement at 43 that only 'th'airy spirit of a gentleman' can feel real emotion.

205 **chance** absence of design or assignable cause; fortuity (*OED n.*, citing this example)

dance naked probably a reference to Adamites; see 2.1.83n. on *Adamites*.

208 **they** i.e. the beggars

210 **I will not read** Oldrents refers back to his decision not to read the letter about his children; see 108–9.

212 **fit** paroxysm of lunacy

212 SD **look out** i.e. peep their heads through the curtain that separates the stage-space from the tiring-house. This curtain will have covered either a 'discovery space' or one of the entrance doors.

213 **Tour out . . . glaziers . . . ruffin** *cant* look out . . . eyes . . . devil

214 **queer cuffin** *cant* churlish fellow or Justice of the Peace

217 **gentry cove** *cant* gentleman

ALL BEGGARS   Lord bless his worship! His good worship!
    Bless his worship!   [*Exeunt*] *Beggars*; *Patrico remains.*
PATRICO
    Now, bounteous sir, before you go,   220
    Hear me, the beggar 'patrico',
    Or 'priest', if you do rather choose
    That we no word of canting use.
    Long may you live, and may your store
    Never decay nor balk the poor,   225
    And as you more in years do grow,
    May treasure to your coffers flow,
    And may your care no more thereon
    Be set than ours are, that have none.
    But as your riches do increase,   230
    So may your heart's content and peace.
    And, after many, many years,
    When the poor have quit their fears
    Of losing you, and that with heaven
    And all the world you have made even,   235
    Then may your blessed posterity,
    Age after age, successively,
    Until the world shall be untwined,
    Inherit your estate and mind.
    So shall the poor to the last day,   240
    For you, in your succession, pray.

223 **canting** *cant* speaking in cant
224 **store** plenty; abundance (of food or necessaries as well as money)
225 **balk** disappoint (expectations, or anyone in his expectations) (*OED v.*¹ III 5c, citing this example)
227 **coffers** boxes in which money was kept
235 **made even** settled accounts – a tellingly financial metaphor for death
236 **blessed posterity** i.e. descendants

238 **untwined** dissolved; destroyed – a figurative use of the word found, for instance, in 'The world cannot untwine / The joyfull union of His heart, and Mine' (Quarles, sig. C2ʳ)
240 **last day** Judgement Day
241 **succession** descendants. This is the second time that the Patrico has referred to Oldrents' descendants in the same speech: the reason why will emerge at the end of the play.

219 SD *Exeunt*] Dodsley; *Exit* Q   *remains*] *(manet)*

155

HEARTY   'Tis a good vote, Sir Patrico, but you are too
grave. Let us hear and see something of your merry
grigs, that can sing, play gambols and do feats.

PATRICO

Sir, I can lay my function by   245
And talk as wild and wantonly
As Tom or Tib, or Jack or Jill,
When they at bowsing ken do swill.
Will you therefore deign to hear
My autem mort, with throat as clear   250
As was Dame Annis' of the name.
How sweet in song her notes she'll frame
That, when she chides, as loud is yawning
As chanticleer waked by the dawning.

HEARTY

Yes, pray let's hear her. What, is she your wife?   255

PATRICO

Yes, sir. We of our ministry,

---

242 **vote** prayer
Sir Placed before a common noun, 'sir'
forms a term of address, as in 'sir clerk',
'sir king', etc.
243–4 **merry grigs** See 1.1.310–11n.
244 **gambols** leaps or springs in dancing;
capers (*OED* gambol *n.* 2, citing this
instance)
feats actions; surprising tricks
245 **lay . . . by** set aside my profession
247 **Tom . . . Tib** common names used in
much the same manner as Jack and
Jill. Taylor, in 'Goose Faire at Stratford
Bowe, the Thursday after Whitsontide',
writes, 'There is ran tan Tom Tinker and
his Tib, / And there's a Jugler with his
fingers glib' (*Works*, 110).
248 **bowsing ken** *cant* boozing house, i.e.
alehouse or tavern
251 **Dame Annis'** This was the name of a
spring-fed well, also known as Dame
Agnes', St Agnes' or St Agnes Le Clare's

Well, near Paul Street, Finsbury (now
St Agnes Terrace). Richard Johnson
explains the origin of the well's name. It
was 'called by the name of a rich London
widow, called *Annis Clare*, who matching
herself with a riotous Courtier in the time
of *Edward* the first, who vainely con-
sumed all her wealth, and leaving her in
much povertie, there drowned she herself,
being then but a shallow ditch or running
water' (*Moorfields*, sig. B2ᵛ); the *clear*
waters that resulted were traced both to
the spirit of Annis or Agnes Clare and to
the name, as Agnes meant 'pure' or 'holy',
and 'clare' was a homonym for 'clear'.
253 **yawning** gaping; uttering with a wide
open mouth (*OED* yawn *v.* 4c, though the
earliest recorded usage supplied there is
1718)
254 **chanticleer** sometimes used as a proper
name for a cock or rooster, from the
French for 'clear singer'

As well as those o'th' presbytery,
Take wives and defy dignity.   *Exit.*

HEARTY

A learned clerk in verity!

Enter PATRICO *with* [AUTEM MORT] *his old wife,
with a wooden bowl of drink. She is drunk.*

PATRICO

By Sol'mon, I think   260
My mort is in drink.
I find by her stink
And the pretty, pretty pink
Of her neyes that half wink,
That the tippling feast,   265
With the doxy in the nest,
Hath turned her brain
To a merry, merry vein.

AUTEM MORT   Go fiddle, Patrico, and let me sing. First
set me down here on both my prats. Gently, gently,   270
for cracking of my wind now I must use it. Hem, hem.

---

257 **presbytery** the body of presbyters, elders, or priests. In the church system of Presbyterianism, no higher order is recognized.

258 'reject the dignity of formal church marriage'. Presbyterian weddings, not sanctioned by the Church of England, had to be held without banns or a licence. They often took place by night and in barns. In Scotland, Presbyterian marriages were declared illegal by Archbishop Laud in 1632; in Ireland, all Presbyterian church activity was made illegal in 1639, and a 'Black Oath' was introduced forcing Presbyterians to swear loyalty to the King. Couples married by Presbyterian ministers risked excommunication.

259 **in verity** in truth

260 **By Sol'mon** *cant* an inviolable oath amongst the canting crew. A rogue 'will not . . . falsifie his oath, if he swear by his *Solomon* (which is the *Mass*) though you hang him' (Head, 140). See pp. 277–8.

264 **neyes . . . wink** eyes that are half shut

265 **tippling feast** drinking celebration

266 **nest** bed or snug lodging in which one can nestle; the wife in Heywood's *Dialogue* says, 'Husband . . . I wold we were in our nest' (sig. F4ʳ)

269 **fiddle** play the fiddle (violin)

270 **prats** *cant* buttocks

271 **for cracking . . . wind** (1) in case my breath is hoarse; (2) in case I fart
Hem an interjectional utterance, here used to signify a clearing of the throat. See also 4.2.182n. on *Ahem, ahem.*

259.1 AUTEM MORT] *this edn*   260 Sol'mon] *Brome Online;* salmon *Q1*   269 SP] *Haaker;* MORT *Q1*

(*She sings.*)   This is bene bowse, this is bene bowse,
                    Too little is my skew.
                  I bowse no lage, but a whole gage
                    Of this I'll bowse to you.   275

                  This bowse is better than rombowse,
                    It sets the gan a-giggling;
                  The autem mort finds better sport
                    In bowsing than in niggling.

                  This is bene bowse, *etc.*   280
            She tosses off her bowl, falls back, and is carried out.
PATRICO
    So, so; your part is done.   *Exit.*
HEARTY   How find you, sir, yourself?
OLDRENTS   Wondrous merry, my good Hearty.

                        Enter PATRICO.

PATRICO
    I wish we had, in all our store,
    Something that could please you more.   285
    The old or autem mort's asleep,
    But before the young ones creep
    Into the straw, sir, if you are –

272–89 *cant* 'This is good drink [*bene bowse*], this is good drink, / Too little is my cup [*skew*]. / I drink [*bowse*] no water [*lage*], but a whole quart-pot [*gage*] / Of this I'll drink to you. / This drink is better than wine [*rombowse*], / It sets the mouth [*gan*] a-giggling; / The married woman [*autem mort*] finds better sport / In drinking [*bowsing*] than in sex [*niggling*].' For more on the lyrics, see pp. 266–7; for lengthier definitions of the cant words, see Appendix 2.

280 *etc.* an instruction to repeat the chorus and perhaps more. As Head (131–2) contains a third verse to this song, it is possible that *etc.* signifies the singing of further verses not recorded in this text. See p. 266.

280 SD *tosses off* energetically drinks
    is carried out Either one of the beggars re-enters to carry out the Autem Mort, or a players' boy or other stage-hand has to do this job.

272 bene] *(Bien)*   281 SD] *this edn; Exit with her Q1*

As gallants sometimes love coarse fare,
So it be fresh and wholesome ware –   290
Disposed to doxy, or a dell
That never yet with man did mell,
Of whom no upright-man is taster,
I'll present her to you, master.

OLDRENTS   Away. You would be punished. Oh!   295

HEARTY   How is it with you, sir?

OLDRENTS   A sudden qualm overchills my stomach. But
'twill away.

Enter [BEGGARS *who are*] *dancers.*

PATRICO

See, in their rags, then, dancing for your sports,
Our clapperdudgeons and their walking morts.   300

[Music. Beggars] dance.

PATRICO

You have done well. Now let each tripper
Make a retreat into the skipper,
And couch a hogshead till the darkmans's passed;
Then all, with bag and baggage, bing awast.

Exeunt Beggars.

289 **coarse fare** In 2.1.206 the gentry had dreamed of beggars' coarse fare, which they took to mean rough food; now an alternative meaning – sex with a coarse or unrefined woman – is revealed.
291 **doxy . . . dell** *cant* unmarried mistress . . . virgin
292 **mell** *cant* mix; have sexual intercourse
293 **upright-man** *cant* chief or high-class vagabond; probably with *double entendre*
297 **qualm** (1) sickening pang; (2) scruple of conscience. Oldrents is reminded of his past misdeeds.
stomach used (like 'heart', 'bosom', 'breast') to designate the inward seat

of emotion, as well as the site of digestion
300 **clapperdudgeons** *cant* born beggars
walking morts *cant* vagrant or walking women, older than doxies, who profess themselves widows
301 **tripper** dancer
302 **skipper** *cant* barn
303 **couch a hogshead** *cant* lie down and sleep
darkmans's *cant* night is
304 **bag and baggage** Originally a military phrase denoting all the property of an army collectively, the phrase came more generally to mean 'all belongings'.
bing awast *cant* hurry away

298 SD BEGGARS *who are*] *this edn*   300 SD *Music. Beggars*] *this edn*   303 darkmans's] *this edn; dark man's Q1*

RANDALL

I told you, sir, they would be gone tomorrow.   305
I understand their canting.

OLDRENTS   Take that amongst you. *Gives money.*

PATRICO

May rich plenty so you bless,
Though you still give, you ne'er have less.

HEARTY

And as your walks may lead this way,
Pray strike in here another day.   310
So you may go, Sir Patrico –   *Exit [Patrico].*
How think you, sir? Or what? Or why do you think
at all, unless on sack and supper time? Do you fall
back? Do you not know the danger of relapses?

OLDRENTS   Good Hearty, thou mistakest me. I was   315
thinking upon this Patrico. And that he has more soul
than a born beggar in him.

HEARTY   Rogue enough, though, to offer us his what-
d'ye-call-its? His doxies. Heart and a cup of sack, do
we look like old beggar-nigglers?   320

OLDRENTS   Pray forbear that language.

HEARTY   Will you then talk of sack? That can drown
sighing. Will you in to supper and take me there your
guest? Or must I creep into the barn among your
welcome ones?   325

OLDRENTS

You have rebuked me timely and most friendly.   *Exit.*

HEARTY

Would all were well with him.   *Exit.*

---

310 **strike** make your way
319 **Heart** i.e. God's heart
320 **beggar-nigglers** *cant* people who have
sex with beggars. Hearty's knowledge of

the beggar phrase may indicate that he
has knowledge of the activity too.
322–3 **drown sighing** sink sighs

311 SD] *after 308 Q1   Patrico] this edn*   318–19 what-d'ye-call-its] *(what- d'ecalts)*

RANDALL It is with me;
For now these pounds are, as I feel them swag,
Light at my heart, though heavy in the bag. *Exit.*

3.1 [*Enter*] VINCENT *and* HILLIARD *in their rags.*

VINCENT Is this the life that we admired in others, with
envy at their happiness?

HILLIARD Pray let us make virtuous use of it and repent
us of that deadly sin, before a greater punishment
than famine and lice fall upon us, by steering our 5
course homeward. Before I'll endure such another
night –

VINCENT What? What wouldst thou do? I would thy
mistress heard thee.

HILLIARD I hope she does not. For I know there is no 10
altering our course before they make the first motion.

VINCENT Is't possible we should be weary already? And
before their softer constitutions of flesh and blood?

HILLIARD They are the stronger in will, it seems.

Enter SPRINGLOVE.

SPRINGLOVE How now, comrades! Repining already at 15
your fullness of liberty? Do you complain of ease?

328–9 i.e. the *pounds* (as weight and as financial sum) are now only heavy in the bag, not the conscience. Oldrents has let Randall legitimately keep the money that was tempting him before.
328 **swag** sway without control; get out of line (*OED v.* 1b, citing this usage)

3.1 Location: outside, near the beggars' camp
11 **first motion** first move
15 **comrades** chums; from the French *camarade*, originally meaning 'chamberful' but regularly used for 'chambermate'
Repining grumbling; complaining
16 **fullness** abundance
ease comfort, luxury

3.1] *(Actus Tertius)* 0.1 *Enter*] *Dodsley*

VINCENT   Ease, callest thou it? Didst thou sleep tonight?

SPRINGLOVE   Not so well these eighteen months, I swear – since my last walks.

HILLIARD   Lightning and tempest is out of thy litany.   20
Could not the thunder wake thee?

SPRINGLOVE   Ha, ha, ha!

VINCENT   Nor the noise of the crew in the quarter by us?

HILLIARD   Nor the hogs in the hovel that cried till they
drowned the noise of the wind? If I could but once   25
ha' dreamt in all my former nights that such an
affliction could have been found among beggars,
sure I should never have travelled to the proof on't.

VINCENT   We looked upon them in their jollity and cast
no further.   30

HILLIARD   Nor did that only draw us forth, by your
favour, Vince, but our obedience to our loves, which
we must suffer till they cry home again. Are they not
weary yet, as much as we, dost think, Springlove?

SPRINGLOVE   They have more moral understanding than   35
so. They know, and so may you, this is your birthnight
into a new world. And we all know, or have been
told, that all come crying into the world, when the

---

17   **tonight** on the night just past; last night (*OED adv.* and *n.* 3, citing this line)

18   **Not . . . months** better than at any time over the last eighteen months

20   **litany** literally, liturgical prayers or supplications. Lightning and thunder do not need to feature in Springlove's prayers, as he does not mind or notice them.

23   **quarter** lodging

24   **hogs . . . hovel** literally, pigs in the sty. This might also be an insulting reference to beggars in the barn.

27   **affliction** grief; distress

28   **to the proof on't** to prove it

29   **cast** reckoned; calculated

33   **suffer** be subjected to
     cry beg for

36–7   **birthnight . . . world** the night of your birth into the world of beggary – though the term *birthnight* recalls that it is the literal night of birth for the beggar born in the previous act

38   **all come . . . the world** proverbial (Dent, W889). Here the tears that accompany birth – and that emphasize the melancholy in the rest of the play – are criticized; in *KL*, 4.6.174–9, they are said to be apt: 'We came crying hither . . . the first time that we smell the air / We wawl and cry . . . that we are come / To this great stage of fools.'

whole world of pleasures is before us. The world
itself had ne'er been glorious had it not first been a   40
confused chaos.

VINCENT   Well, never did knight-errants in all adventures
merit more of their ladies than we beggar-errants – or
errant beggars – do in ours.

SPRINGLOVE   The greater will be your reward. Think   45
upon that, and show no manner of distaste to turn
their hearts from you. You're undone then.

HILLIARD   Are they ready to appear out of their privy
lodgings, in the pigs' palace of pleasure? Are they
coming forth?   50

SPRINGLOVE   I left 'em almost ready, sitting on their
pads of straw, helping to dress each other's heads –
the one's eye is the tother's looking-glass – with the
prettiest coil they keep to fit their fancies in the most
graceful way of wearing their new dressings that you   55
would admire.

VINCENT   I hope we are as gracefully set out. Are we
not?

41 **confused chaos** According to Genesis,
1.2, in the beginning 'the earth was
without form, and void'; it was out of this
chaos that God structured the world and
the universe.
42 **knight-errants** knights of medieval
romance who wandered in search of
adventures to prove their chivalry (see
OED knight-errant *n.* 1, citing this
example)
43 **beggar-errants** a jocular back-formation
from *knight-errants*
44 **errant beggars** a 'whim' meaning simultaneously wandering, 'errant' beggars
and downright, 'arrant' beggars
47 **undone** ruined
48 **privy** (1) private; (2) intimate; (3)
lavatorial

49 **pigs' . . . pleasure** i.e. pigsty, but with
an ironic gesture towards the title of
William Painter's book *The Palace of
Pleasure* (1566), a compilation of stories
that provided sources for many playwrights. Cf. *Sparagus Garden*, where
Moneylack says, 'the house affords you
as convenient Couches to retyre to, as the
garden has beds for the precious plants
to grow in: that makes the place a pallace
of pleasure' (sig. D1ʳ⁻ᵛ).
52 **pads of straw** straw mattresses or cushions
dress comb, arrange
54 **coil . . . keep** 'to keep a coil' was to
continue a disturbance, fuss, or bustle
(*OED* coil *n.²* 4a), exemplified in *TNK*,
2.4.18: 'What a coil he keeps.' The
phrase was proverbial (Dent, C505).
57 **set out** displayed

SPRINGLOVE   Indifferent well. But will you fall to
practice? Let me hear how you can maund when you   60
meet with passengers.

HILLIARD   We do not look like men, I hope, too good to
learn.

SPRINGLOVE   Suppose some persons of worth or wealth
passing by now. Note me: good your good worship,   65
your charity to the poor, that will duly and truly pray
for you day and night –

VINCENT   Away, you idle rogue; you would be set to
work and whipped –

SPRINGLOVE   – that is lame and sick; hungry and   70
comfortless –

VINCENT   If you were well served –

SPRINGLOVE   – and even to bless you and reward you
for it –

HILLIARD   Prithee, hold thy peace – here be doleful   75
notes indeed – and leave us to our own genius. If we
must beg, let's let it go, as it comes, by inspiration.
I love not your set form of begging.

SPRINGLOVE   Let me instruct ye, though.

Enter RACHEL *and* MERIEL *in rags[, speaking to one another]*.

RACHEL   Have a care, good Meriel, what hearts or limbs   80
soever we have, and though never so feeble, let us set

---

59   **fall to** begin (*OED* fall, 'to fall to', *v.* 5)
60   **maund** *cant* beg
61   **passengers** foot-travellers; passers-by
65   **Note me** Study me carefully; pay attention to me.
65–74 **good your ... it** Springlove illustrates the vocal pitch and vocabulary used by beggars when trying to extract money.

68–9 Vincent replies in the persona of a potential patron.
     set ... whipped a further reference to the statute against beggars; see 2.1.192n.
72   **well served** treated appropriately
76   **notes** (1) examples for following; (2) speaking tones
76   **leave ... genius** i.e. allow us to use our own abilities.
78   **set form** fixed order of words

79 ye] you *Dodsley*   SD *speaking . . . another*] *this edn*

our best faces on't and laugh our last gasp out before
we discover any dislike or weariness to them. Let us
bear it out till they complain first and beg to carry us
home a-pick-pack.   85

MERIEL   I am sorely surbated with hoofing already,
  though, and so crupper-cramped with our hard
  lodging, and so bumfiddled with the straw, that –

RACHEL   Think not on't. I am numbed i'the bum and
  shoulders, too, a little, and have found the difference 90
  between a hard floor with a little straw and a down
  bed with a quilt upon't. But no words, nor a sour
  look, I prithee.

HILLIARD   Oh, here they come now, Madam Fewclothes
  and my Lady Bonnyrag.   95

VINCENT   Peace, they see us.

RACHEL, MERIEL   Ha, ha, ha!

VINCENT   We are glad the object pleases ye.

RACHEL   So does the subject.
  Now you appear the glories of the spring,   100
  Darlings of Phoebus and the summer's heirs.

HILLIARD
  How fairer than fair Flora's self appear,
  To deck the spring, Diana's darlings dear!

83 **discover** reveal
84–5 **beg ... home** The women want the
  men to *beg* – as in, plead – to go home.
85 **a-pick-pack** piggyback, i.e. on the back or
  shoulders; thought to originate in 'pack' and
  'pick', i.e. 'a pack pitched on the shoulders',
  or 'back' and 'pick', 'pitched on the back
  or shoulders' (see *OED* piggyback *n.*)
86 **surbated** footsore with much walking,
  from the Old French *sur*, 'exceedingly',
  and *batre*, 'to beat'. Edmund Spenser's
  Faerie Queene refers to dolphins per-
  mitted to stay in the water 'Least they
  their finnes should bruze, and surbate
  sore / Their tender feete upon the stony
  grownd' (p. 453).

hoofing going on foot (*OED* hoof *v.* 3,
  citing this example)
87 **crupper-cramped** cramped in the
  buttocks
88 **bumfiddled** tickled, as in Cudden's
  'Come, say you will play, or Ill ...
  Bumfiddle your ribs – ' (*Mr Anthony*, 35)
90 **found** discovered
101 **Phoebus** i.e. the sun; the Latin name of
  the Greek sun god Apollo, who also
  inspired music and poetry
102 **Flora** goddess of flowers and spring, and
  hence also a fertility goddess
103 **Diana's darlings** i.e. virgins. Diana was
  goddess of the moon, and – because
  women's cycles were said to relate to the

Oh, let us not, Actaeon-like, be strook –
With greedy eyes while we presume to look   105
On your half-nakedness, since courteous rags
Cover the rest – into the shape of stags.

RACHEL, MERIEL   Ha, ha, ha! – We are glad you are so
merry.

VINCENT   Merry and lusty, too. This night will we lie   110
together as well as the proudest couple in the barn.

HILLIARD   And so will we. I can hold out no longer.

RACHEL   Does the straw stir up your flesh to't,
gentlemen?

MERIEL   Or does your provender prick you?   115

SPRINGLOVE

What! Do we come for this? Laugh and lie down
When your bellies are full. Remember, ladies,
You have not begged yet, to quit your destiny,
But have lived hitherto on my endeavours.
Who got your suppers, pray, last night, but I,   120
Of dainty trencher-fees from a gentleman's house,

lunar movements – of virgins and chastity. She was the sister of Phoebus Apollo.

104 **Actaeon-like** Ovid's *Metamorphoses*, 3.138–52, tells how Actaeon came upon Diana bathing and was overwhelmed with her beauty. Diana turned him into a stag for trespassing on her privacy, and he was then hunted and torn apart by his own dogs.
strook turned as by enchantment (*OED* strike *v.* 46d, citing this usage)

106 **half-nakedness** That the women are scantily clad has already been suggested by the names Hilliard has used of them, *Madam Fewclothes* and *my Lady Bonnyrag* (94–5).

111 **proudest** most sexually excited, most lascivious. Cf. *Lucrece*, where 'The flesh being proud, Desire doth fight with Grace' (712). The men want to have sex

with the freedom enjoyed by all the other beggars in the barn.

112 **I . . . longer** Hilliard's statement that he can keep up no longer (the pretence of liking beggar life) is thought by the women to be a statement that he can no longer hold back his sexual urges.

113 **stir up** rouse; set in motion

115 **provender** food, especially dry food for animals, as in *1H6*, 1.2.10–11: 'They must be dieted like mules / And have their provender tied to their mouths.'
prick stimulate, with an obvious *double entendre*

118 **quit** requite; cancel

121 **trencher-fees** scraps of food given in alms (*OED* trencher *n.*¹ 7, citing this example). Such titbits were standard fare for beggars. Rime-well, in Cartwright's *Ordinary*, asks, 'No gleanings, James? No trencher-analects?' (*Comedies*, 49).

Such as the serving-men themselves sometimes
Would have been glad of! And this morning now,
What comfortable chippings and sweet buttermilk
Had you to breakfast!   125

RACHEL   Oh, 'twas excellent! I feel it good still, here.

MERIEL   There was a brown crust amongst it that has
made my neck so white, methinks. Is it not, Rachel?

RACHEL   Yes. You ga' me none on't. You ever covet to
have all the beauty. 'Tis the ambition of all younger   130
sisters.

VINCENT [*to Hilliard*]   They are pleased and never like
to be weary.

HILLIARD [*to Vincent*]   No more must we, if we'll be
theirs.   135

Enter two GENTLEMEN.

SPRINGLOVE   Peace. Here come passengers. Forget not
your rules, and quickly disperse yourselves, and fall
to your calling –   [*Exeunt Hilliard, Rachel and Meriel;
Vincent and Springlove walk aside.*]

---

124 **comfortable chippings** sustaining or
refreshing parings of bread-crust, often,
as here, in plural; see *OED* chipping *n.* 2.
The crust was thought, in finer house-
holds, to be an undesirable bit of the
loaf. Andrew Boorde points out that
'Burnt breade, and harde crustes, & pasty
crustes, doth ingendre color [choler]' and
advises, 'chyp the upper crust of your
breade' rather than eat it (sig. D4^v).

126 **here** Rachel suggests that the food is
lingering uncomfortably in her body:
she may indicate her throat, stomach or
buttocks.

127–8 **brown … white** a joke based on the
fact that facial washes to whiten the skin

were frequently made with white food-
stuffs, including soft white 'manchet'
bread, made of flour sifted through a fine
linen cloth. Girolamo Ruscelli recommends 'A verie good water' for the face,
which consists of calf's feet and rice that
are 'lette . . . seeth with crommes of fine
manchet breade stieped in milke, two
pound of freshe butter, and white of .x.
new laied egges, with their shelles & all'
(sig. K4^r). Brown 'maslan' bread, which
was made of mixed grains including
wheat and rye, was not only heavy and
tough to eat, but also would, as a facial
wash, have torn the skin.

137–8 **fall to** betake yourself to; begin

129–31] *Dodsley; Q1 lines* Beauty. / Sisters. /   132, 134 SDs] *Lawrence*   138 SD] *this edn; Meriel and Rachel exit in one direction, Hilliard in another* | Brome Online

167

1 GENTLEMAN [*to one within*]   Lead the horses down the
     hill! – The heat of our speed is over, for we have lost   140
     our journey.

2 GENTLEMAN   Had they taken this way, we had
     overtaken 'em, or heard of 'em at least.

1 GENTLEMAN   But some of our scouts will light on 'em,
     the whole country being overspread with 'em.   145

2 GENTLEMAN   There was never such an escape else.

VINCENT [*to Springlove*]   A search for us, perhaps. Yet I
     know not them, nor they me, I am sure. I might the
     better beg of 'em. But how to begin, or set the worst
     leg forwards, would I were whipped if I know now.   150

1 GENTLEMAN   That a young gentlewoman of her
     breeding and heir to such an estate should fly from so
     great a match and run away with her uncle's clerk!

2 GENTLEMAN   The old justice will run mad upon't, I
     fear.   155

VINCENT [*to Springlove*]   If I were to be hanged now,
     I could not beg for my life.

SPRINGLOVE [*to Vincent*]   Step forwards and beg
     handsomely. I'll set my goad i'your breech else.

VINCENT [*to Springlove*]   What shall I say?   160

139–40 **Lead ... hill** This instruction is presumably to a servant; it lets the audience know that the gentlemen have just dismounted.

140 **heat** fervour or vehemence, as in *Oth*, 1.2.40: 'It is a business of some heat'

140–1 **lost our journey** wasted or been defeated in our journey

144 **scouts** spies sent out to obtain information

145 **overspread** covered completely

149–50 **set ... forwards** playing on the proverb 'To set the best foot (leg) forward' (Dent, F570); *worst leg* refers to

the fact that beggars often affected to be lame (see 2.1.336).

158–9 Springlove's command, and his threat of punishment, illustrates the role reversal that has taken place. Springlove is king over the gentry as he is over the beggars.

159 **goad** cattle-prod or similar sharp stick; probably the stick he uses as a prop when claiming to be lame – see 2.1.336. Lame beggars are described by Thomas Harman as having 'cloutes bounde about theyr legs, and halting wyth their staffe in theyr handes' (sig. D1ᵛ).

139 +SP] *this edn*; 1. *Q1*   139 SD] *this edn*   142 +SP] *this edn*; 2. *Q1*   147 SD] *Lawrence*   156, 158, 160 SDs] *this edn*

SPRINGLOVE [*to Vincent*]   Have I not told you? Now
   begin.
VINCENT [*to Springlove*]   After you, good Springlove.
SPRINGLOVE   Good, your good worships –
1 GENTLEMAN   Away, you idle vagabond!   165
SPRINGLOVE   Your worships' charity to a poor critter
   welly starved –
VINCENT   – that will duly and truly prea for ye.
2 GENTLEMAN   You counterfeit villains, hence.
SPRINGLOVE   Good masters! Sweet worship, for the   170
   tender mercy of –
VINCENT   – duly and truly prea for you.
1 GENTLEMAN   You would be well whipped and set to
   work, if you were duly and truly served.
VINCENT [*to Springlove*]   Did not I say so before?   175
SPRINGLOVE   Good worshipful masters' worship, to
   bestow your charity, and to maintain your health and
   limbs –
VINCENT   – duly and truly pray for you.
2 GENTLEMAN   Begone, I say, you impudent, lusty   180
   young rascals.
1 GENTLEMAN   I'll set you going else.
                      [*Gentlemen*] *switch them.*
SPRINGLOVE   Ah, the goodness of compassion to soften
   your hearts to the poor!

166–7 **critter welly** 'creature well nigh',
   but the spelling suggests that an accent
   should be adopted for this phrase. *OED*
   welly *adv*. cites this example.
168 **prea** The unusual spelling suggests a
   pronunciation quirk: probably the word
   is said with a diphthong suggestive of
   northern British dialect.
169 **counterfeit** pretend; feigned. The heavy
   accents have led the gentlemen to guess
   that the beggars are not genuine.

174 **served** treated
175 Vincent refers to his own sentiment of
   149–50, when he was pretending to be
   a gentleman passer-by.
179 **pray** Vincent has lost the beggar
   pronunciation of 168 and 172.
182 SD *switch* lash with a thin stick ('switch'),
   here probably a riding-crop

161, 163, 175 SDs] *this edn*   177 and to] *Haaker; and* ——— *to Q1*   182 SD *Gentlemen*] *this edn*   them] ('*em*)

VINCENT [*aside to Springlove*]　Oh, the devil, must not　185
we beat 'em now? 'Sdeath –
SPRINGLOVE [*aside to Vincent*]　Nor show an angry look
for all the skin of our backs. [*to Gentlemen*] Ah, the
sweetness of that mercy that gives to all, to move
your compassion to the hungry when it shall seem　190
good unto you, and night and day to bless all that you
have. [*Gentlemen switch them.*] Ah, ah –
[*Exeunt Springlove and Vincent.*]
2 GENTLEMAN　Come back, sirrah. His patience and
humility has wrought upon me.

[*Enter* VINCENT.]

VINCENT　Duly and –　　　　　　　　　　　　　　195
2 GENTLEMAN　Not you, sirrah. The tother. You look like
a sturdy rogue.

[*Enter* SPRINGLOVE.]

SPRINGLOVE　Lord bless your master's worship.
2 GENTLEMAN　There's a halfpenny for you. [*Points at
Vincent.*] Let him have no share with you.　　　200
VINCENT [*aside*]　I shall never thrive o'this trade.
1 GENTLEMAN　They are of a fraternity and will share,
I warrant you.

---

186 **'Sdeath** God's death; an expletive
188 **for . . . backs** i.e. either despite all the
skin that has been flayed from our backs
already, or on account of all the skin that
may be flayed from our backs in the future
192 **Ah, ah!** Springlove cries out in mock
or real pain for the switching he has
received: this is also his warning to

Vincent to show suffering rather than
attempt revenge.
197 **sturdy rogue** statute beggar
201 **trade** occupation
202 **fraternity** brotherhood of men who
share occupations. The beggars were
presented in rogue literature as having
close fraternities. Dekker, in *O Per Se O,*

185 SD] *Brome Online*　186 'Sdeath] (Steth*)*　187 SD] *Brome Online*　188 SD] *this edn*　192 SD1]
this edn　SD2] *this edn;* SPRINGLOVE *and* VINCENT *run to escape the lashing.* | *Brome Online*　194 SD]
this edn　197 SD] *this edn*　198 your] *Dodsley;* you *Q1*　199–200 SD] *this edn*　201 SD] *Lawrence*

SPRINGLOVE   Never in our lives, trooly. He never
   begged with me before.   205
1 GENTLEMAN   But if hedges or hen-roosts could speak,
   you might be found sharers in pillage, I believe.
SPRINGLOVE   Never saw him before, bless you, good
   master, in all my life. [*to Vincent*] Beg for yourself.
   Your credit's gone else. [*to Gentlemen*] Good hea'en   210
   to bliss and prosper ye.   *Exit.*
2 GENTLEMAN   Why dost thou follow us? Is it your
   office to be privy to our talk?
VINCENT   Sir, I beseech you hear me. [*aside*] 'Slife,
   what shall I say? – I am a stranger in these parts and   215
   destitute of means and apparel.
1 GENTLEMAN   So methinks. And what o'that?
VINCENT Will you therefore be pleased, as you are worthy
   gentlemen and blessed with plenty –
2 GENTLEMAN   This is courtly!   220
VINCENT   – out of your abundant store, towards my
   relief in extreme necessity, to furnish me with a small
   parcel of money – five or six pieces, or ten, if you can
   presently spare it.
1 GENTLEMAN, 2 GENTLEMAN   Stand off! [*They*] *draw*   225
   [*swords*].

promises to show 'how they hang together in Fraternities, and what Articles of Brother-hood they are sworne too' (sig. M1ᵛ); in a later passage, 'Of their fraternities', he explains, 'There is no lustie Roague, but hath many both sworne Brothers, and the *Morts* his sworne Sisters: who vow themselves body and soule to the Divell to performe . . . tenne Articles' (sig N2ᵛ).
204 **trooly** Springlove returns to speaking in an accent.

207 **pillage** plunder; spoils
210 **credit's** credibility's
211 **bliss** bless
213 **office** position; post; task; duty
   privy to privately cognizant of
214 **'Slife** God's life
223 **parcel** part; portion
   pieces any of various English gold coins current in different periods; in particular, the unit of James I, the sovereign or the guinea. See *OED* piece *n.* 16c.
224 **presently** immediately

209 SD] *Lawrence*   210 SD] *Brome Online subst.*   214 SD] *Lawrence*   225 SD *They*] *Lawrence*   swords] this edn

VINCENT [*aside*]   I have spoiled all and know not how to
   beg otherwise.

1 GENTLEMAN   Here's a new way of begging!

VINCENT [*aside*]   Quite run out of my instructions.

2 GENTLEMAN   Some highway thief, o'my conscience,   230
   that forgets he is weaponless.

VINCENT   Only to make you merry, gentlemen, at my
   unskilfulness in my new trade. I have been another
   man i'my days. So I kiss your hands.   *Exit* [*running*].

1 GENTLEMAN   With your heels, do you?   235

2 GENTLEMAN   It had been good to have apprehended
   the rakeshame. There is some mystery in his rags.
   But let him go.

Enter OLIVER, *putting up his sword.*

OLIVER [*to one within*]   You found your legs in time.
   I had made you halt for something else.   240

1 GENTLEMAN   Master Oliver, well returned. What's the
   matter, sir?

OLIVER   Why, sir, a counterfeit lame rogue begged
   of me, but in such language the high sheriff's son
   o'the shire could not have spoke better, nor to have   245
   borrowed a greater sum. He asked me if I could spare
   him ten or twenty pound. I switched him; his cudgel

227 **otherwise** in any other way

229 **run out of** run through; exhausted

230 **highway thief** highwayman. Because highwaymen 'ride on horses well appointed, and goe in shew like honest men', they were thought 'Gent[lemen] robbers, or theeves' (Rid, sig. F4ᵛ).

235 **With your heels** i.e. Vincent's heels are kicking up because he is running away so quickly.

237 **rakeshame** a combination of 'rake' and 'shame'; a disreputable or dissolute person

239–40 Oliver shouts to Hilliard offstage.

240 **halt** limp

244–5 **high . . . shire** The high sheriff was the local representative of royal authority in the shire or province; his son would have been the most linguistically sophisticated non-aristocrat imaginable.

247 **ten . . . pound** This absurd sum is also a reference to *Aglaura*, in which Suckling had maintained that plays should not beg to be understood, for 'that has as bold a sound, / As if a beggar should aske

226, 229 SDs] *Lawrence*   234 SD *running*] *this edn*   239 SD] *this edn; Calling after him* | *Brome Online*

was up. I drew, and into the wood he scaped me, as
nimbly – but first he told me I should hear from him
by a gentleman to require satisfaction of me.   250

2 GENTLEMAN   We had such another begged of us. The
court goes a-begging, I think.

1 GENTLEMAN   Dropped through the clouds, I think;
more Lucifers, travelling to hell, that beg by the way.
Met you no news of your kinswoman, Mistress Amy?   255

OLIVER   No. What's the matter with her? Goes her
marriage forwards with young Master Tallboy? I
hastened my journey from London to be at the
wedding.

2 GENTLEMAN   'Twas to ha' been yesterday morning; all   260
things in readiness prepared for it. But the bride,
stolen by your father's clerk, is slipped away. We
were in quest of 'em, and so are twenty more, several
ways.

OLIVER   Such young wenches will have their own ways   265
in their own loves, what matches soever their
guardians make for 'em. And I hope my father will
not follow the law so close to hang his clerk for
stealing his ward with her own consent. It may breed
such a grudge may cause some clerks to hang their   270

---

twentie pound. / – Men have it not about
them' (sig. A2ʳ). As Brome now stages
a beggar asking for that sum, he agrees
with the sentiment while also indicating
that Suckling's play is indeed fully
understandable.

247–8 **his . . . up** his beggar's club, or
'filch', was raised. The cudgel was an
essential prop of the trade. Dekker, in
Penny Wise, refers to a man 'putting him-
selfe into ragges like a Begger, with a
short Cudgell in his hand' (sig. C4ʳ).

248 **drew** i.e. drew my sword

250 **require satisfaction** ask to satisfy his
honour by a duel: a 'gentleman's' response
to a threat

254 **Lucifers . . . hell** fallen 'rebel' angels on
their way to hell, their new home; by
extension, fallen courtiers on their way
to beggarly disgrace. As Lucifer had
rebelled against God, so the Gentleman
may imply that the courtly beggars are
anti-monarchists or rebels against the
earthly sovereign.

263 **several** separate; different

268 **hang his clerk** That stealing an heiress
and marrying her was punishable by
death is also referred to in *Heir*: 'You
know the law speakes death to any man /
That steales an Heire without her friends
consent' (sig. D4ᵛ).

masters that have 'em o'the hip of injustice. Besides,
Martin, though he be his servant, is a gentleman. But
indeed, the miserablest rascal! He will grudge her
meat when he has her.

1 GENTLEMAN   Your father is exceedingly troubled at   275
their escape. I wish that you may qualify him with
your reasons.

OLIVER   But what says Tallboy to the matter, the
bridegroom that should ha' been?

2 GENTLEMAN   Marry, he says little to the purpose, but   280
cries outright.

OLIVER   I like him well for that: he holds his humour. A
miserable wretch, too, though rich. I ha' known him
cry when he has lost but three shillings at mumchance.
But gentlemen, keep on your way to comfort my   285
father. I know some of his man's private haunts about
the country here, which I will search immediately.

1 GENTLEMAN   We will accompany you, if you please.

OLIVER   No, by no means: that will be too public.

2 GENTLEMAN   Do your pleasure.   290

                        [*Exeunt*] *1* [*and*] *2* [*Gentlemen*].

---

271 **o'the hip** at a disadvantage; in a position
in which one is likely to be overthrown.
The phrase is taken from wrestling.
273 **miserablest** most miserly; most stingy
276 **qualify** appease
282 **humour** The 'temper' was said to be
controlled by the four humours, yellow
bile, phlegm, blood and black bile,
producing people who were choleric,
phlegmatic, sanguine or melancholic. For
Jonson, from whom Brome inherited an
interest in writing 'humourous' characters, humour was, additionally, a deep-
seated characteristic responsible for the

behaviour and feelings of an individual.
Tallboy's *humour* is his mood, and also
his personality type.
283 **miserable** sad – but the word recalls
Martin, described in 273 as the 'miserablest rascal'. Amy's romantic choices
are both miserable.
284 **mumchance** a dice- or card-game
resembling hazard, for which silence –
keeping 'mum' – was a requisite: 'And
for Mum chance, how ere the chance
doe fall, / You must be mum, for feare of
marring all' (Breton, sig. B1ʳ).
286 **his man's** i.e. Martin's

290 SD *Exeunt*] *Dodsley & Reed; Exit Q1   and*] *this edn   Gentlemen*] *this edn*

OLIVER   My pleasure, and all the search that I intend, is, by hovering here, to take a review of a brace of the handsomest beggar-braches that ever graced a ditch or a hedge-side. I passed by 'em in haste, but something so possesses me that I must – what the 295 devil must I? A beggar? Why, beggars are flesh and blood, and rags are no diseases. Their lice are no French fleas. And there is much wholesomer flesh under country dirt than city painting, and less danger in dirt and rags than in ceruse and satin. I durst 300 not take a touch at London, both for the present cost and fear of an after-reckoning. But, Oliver, dost thou speak like a gentleman? Fear price or pox, ha? Marry, do I, sir; nor can beggar-sport be inexcusable in a young country gentleman short of means for 305 another respect, a principal one indeed: to avoid the punishment or charge of bastardy. There's no commuting with them, or keeping of children for them. The poor whores, rather than part with their own, or want children at all, will steal other folks' to 310

292 **review** general survey
  brace a pair – more usually used of animals than people
293 **beggar-braches** beggar-bitches. Oliver continues to describe the beggars as animals.
297–8 **lice ... fleas** Lice are not carriers of 'French pox' (syphilis), the lesions of which superficially resemble fleabites: 'The *Scots* ... when they have met, some part of this Disease, / They use in jest to say that they are bit with *Spanish Fleas*, / Because they leave red spots behinde, as Fleas doe used to doe, / And sure this jest is used in France, belike they use it too' (J. T., sig. B1ʳ⁻ᵛ). Brome makes a similar reference in *Damoiselle*: 'I have a white Skin ... Free from French Flea-bites' (sig. F5ᵛ).
299 **painting** cosmetics

300 **ceruse** Thomas Elyot explains, 'Ceruse, or whyte leade,' is a substance 'wherwith some women be paynted ... colde playsters be made of it' (xviii).
301 **take a touch** dabble in sex; *touch* was often used to describe a sexual encounter. Friar Peter says Angelo is 'as free from touch or soil with [Isabella] / As she from one ungot' (*MM*, 5.1.143–4).
301–2 **for ... after-reckoning** 'because of the immediate cost and for fear of a later one', i.e. of venereal disease
302–13 **But ... Oliver** Oliver enters into a disquisition with himself, as Springlove (at 1.1.256–62) and Randall (at 2.2.10–16) did earlier.
308 **commuting** having to redeem obligations with a monetary payment
310 **steal other folks'** Beggars, like gypsies, pirates and thieves, were said to steal

175

travel with and move compassion. He feeds a beggar-wench well that fills her belly with young bones. And these reasons considered, good Master Oliver – 'slid, yonder they are at peep. And now sitten down as waiting for my purpose.   315

Enter VINCENT.

Heart, here's another delay. I must shift him. [*to Vincent*] Dost hear, honest poor fellow? I prithee, go back presently, and at the hill-foot (here's sixpence for thy pains) thou shalt find a footman with a horse in his hand. Bid him wait there. His master will come   320
presently, say.

VINCENT   Sir, I have a business of another nature to you, which, as I presume you are a gentleman of right noble spirit and resolution, you will receive without offence and in that temper as most properly appertains   325
to the most heroic natures.

OLIVER   Thy language makes me wonder at thy person. What's the matter with thee? Quickly.

VINCENT   You may be pleased to call to mind a late affront which, in your heat of passion, you gave a   330
gentleman.

children. In the 'Persons of the Play' in *New Inn*, 'Frank' is described as '*Lord Frampul's younger daughter, stolen by a beggar-woman, shorn, put into a boy's apparel, sold to the Host, and brought up by him as his son*' (17–19).

312 **young bones** a baby or embryo, as in *King Leir*, where Leir excuses Gonorill's behaviour with 'She breeds yong bones!' (sig. D1ʳ)

313 **'slid** by God's (eye)lid

314 **at peep** in an act of peeping or giving furtive glances, especially through a narrow opening or out of a place of concealment (*OED* peep *n.*² 1b)

sitten rare past participle of sit, often associated with northern or Scottish dialect. Oliver may be speaking humorously, or may affectedly be failing to finish his words: 'sittin'.

316 **Heart** by God's heart

319 **footman** attendant or foot-servant, generally a runner who attended on a rider of rank

325 **properly** intrinsically

316–17 SD] *Lawrence*

176

OLIVER   What, such a one as thou art, was he?

VINCENT   True, noble sir. Who could no less in honour than direct me, his chosen friend, unto you, with the length of his sword, or to take the length of yours. 335 The place, if you please, the ground whereon you parted; the hour, seven the next morning. Or – if you like not these, in part, or all – to make your own appointments.

OLIVER   [*aside*] The bravest method in beggars that 340 ever was discovered! I would be upon the bones of this rogue now but for crossing my other design, which fires me. I must therefore be rid of him on any terms. – Let his own appointments stand. Tell him I'll meet him.   345

VINCENT   You shall most nobly engage his life to serve you, sir.

OLIVER   You'll be his second, will you?

VINCENT   To do you further service, sir, I have undertaken it.   350

OLIVER   I'll send a beadle shall undertake you both.

---

334 **his chosen friend** i.e. his second – the *gentleman* who would demand *satisfaction* as promised in 250

335 **length of his . . . yours** a request to know what sword-length is to be used for the forthcoming battle; in a duel 'it was vital to ensure that the swords were of equal length and type' (see Hopton, 65). Hamlet double-checks before fighting Laertes that 'these foils have all a length?' (*Ham*, 5.2.242).

339 **appointments** arrangements

340 **bravest method** most bold mode of procedure

341 **discovered** revealed
   be . . . of attack; hence, in 'A Cat and a Cock', '*Puss* had a Months Mind to be upon the Bones of him, but was not willing to pick a Quarrel' (*Fables*, 2).

342 **crossing** thwarting
   my other design i.e. his plan to debauch the women

343 **fires** enflames

346 **engage** bind by a pledge

348 **be his second** act as representative of the challenger (conveying the challenge, arranging the locality and declaring when the fight starts)

351 **beadle** warrant officer; under-bailiff
   undertake take in charge: a 'whim' picking up Vincent's *undertaken* (350) meaning 'agreed to'

340 SD] *Lawrence*

177

VINCENT Your mirth becomes the bravery of your mind
and dauntless spirit. So takes his leave your servant,
sir.   *[Exit.]*
OLIVER I think, as my friend said, the court goes   355
a-begging indeed. But I must not lose my beggar-
wenches.

Enter RACHEL *and* MERIEL.

Oh, here they come. They are delicately skinned and
limbed. There, there, I saw above the ham as the
wind blew. Now they spy me.   360
RACHEL Sir, I beseech you look upon us with the favour
of a gentleman. We are in a present distress and
utterly unacquainted in these parts, and therefore
forced by the calamity of our misfortune to implore
the courtesy, or rather charity, of those to whom we 365
are strangers.
OLIVER *[aside]* Very fine, this!
MERIEL Be therefore pleased, right noble sir, not only
valuing us by our outward habits, which cannot but
appear loathsome or despicable unto you, but as we   370
are forlorn Christians; and, in that estimation, be
compassionately moved to cast a handful or two of
your silver, or a few of your golden pieces unto us, to
furnish us with linen and some decent habiliments –
OLIVER *[aside]* They beg as high as the man-beggar   375
I met withal! Sure the beggars are all mad today, or

---

352 **becomes** befits
359 **ham** back of knee, but could describe the
upper part of the leg including the thigh,
or thigh and buttock collectively
367 **Very fine** may refer to the women's
language or appearance

369 **outward habits** outer garments
374 **habiliments** applied grandiloquently to
ordinary clothes
375 **high** loftily

354 SD] *this edn; He bows and exits.* | *Brome Online*   367, 375 SDs] *Lawrence*

bewitched into a language they understand not. The
spirits of some decayed gentry talk in 'em sure.

RACHEL   May we expect a gracious answer from you,
sir?   380

MERIEL   And that, as you can wish our virgin prayers to
be propitious for you –

RACHEL   – that you never be denied a suit by any
mistress.

MERIEL   Nay, that the fairest may be ambitious to place   385
their favours on you.

RACHEL   That your virtue and valour may lead you to
the most honourable actions, and that the love of all
exquisite ladies may arm you.

MERIEL   And that, when you please to take a wife, may   390
honour, beauty and wealth contend to endow her
most with.

RACHEL   And that with her you have a long and
prosperous life.

MERIEL   A fair and fortunate posterity.   395

OLIVER [*aside*]   This exceeds all that ever I heard and
strikes me into wonder. – Pray tell me, how long
have you been beggars, or how chanced you to be
so?

RACHEL   By influence of our stars, sir.   400

MERIEL   We were born to no better fortune.

OLIVER   How came you to talk thus, and so much above
the beggars' dialect?

378 **decayed** reduced in fortune
379 **gracious** kindly; benevolent
383 **suit** petition; supplication
389 **arm you** furnish you with protection

397 **strikes . . . wonder** bewitches, enchants
me
400–1 This is indeed the fortune that
Oldrents' daughters have been born to, as
foretold to Oldrents.

396 SD] *this edn*

RACHEL   Our speech came naturally to us, and we ever
loved to learn by rote as well as we could.   405

MERIEL   And to be ambitious above the vulgar, to ask
more than common alms, whate'er men please to
give us.

OLIVER [*aside*]   Sure some well-disposed gentleman as
myself got these wenches. They are too well-grown   410
to be mine own, and I cannot be incestuous with 'em.

RACHEL   Pray sir, your noble bounty.

OLIVER [*aside*]   What a tempting lip that little rogue
moves there! And what an enticing eye the tother.
I know not which to begin with. – What's this, a flea   415
upon thy bosom?

MERIEL   Is it not a straw-coloured one, sir?

OLIVER   Oh, what a provoking skin is there! That very
touch inflames me.

RACHEL   Sir, are you moved in charity towards us yet?   420

---

405 **by rote** by heart. Formal humanist education involved a large amount of memorization; here the women pretend that they have rigorously learned what is actually their native speech.

409 **well-disposed** healthy, constitutionally good – often used to mean sexually keen as well. George Puttenham writes of a 'bride shewing her self every waies well disposed and still supplying occasions of new lustes and love to her husband, by her obedience and amorous embracings and all other alluramentes' (41–2).

410 **got** begot

410–11 **too well-grown . . . own** Oliver suggests that he has slept with beggar-women in the past.

417 **straw-coloured one** i.e. a louse. Meriel hints at the proverb 'A louse is a beggar's companion' (Tilley, L471). Often, as here, the connection between man and louse was thought positive. Evans, in *MW*, 1.1.17–18, maintains that the louse 'is a familiar beast to man, and signifies love'. Hence the 'Jest of a louse and a flea', where a 'prentise spied a louse creeping upon the side of [Hobson's] gowne and tooke it off: . . . oh (qd. Maister Hobson) this is good lucke: . . . for this kind of vermine chiefly breedeth on mankind, and there-upon gave five shillings to his man . . . another of his Prentises . . . made as though he tooke a flea from the same . . . Maister Hobson . . . . said to him, what dost thou make mee a dogge? . . . and so [for] the five shillinges he lookd for he had given fiveteene stripes' (Johnson, *Hobson*, sig. D1ʳ).

420–1 **moved . . . moved** a 'whim'; the girls are asking whether Oliver is affected by feelings of compassion (*moved*); Oliver replies that he is physically stirred (*moved*).

405 rote] *Dodsley;* wrote *Q1*   409, 413 SDs] *Lawrence*

OLIVER   Moved? I am moved. No flesh and blood more moved.

MERIEL   Then pray, sir, your benevolence.

OLIVER   Benevolence? Which shall I be benevolent to, or which first? I am puzzled in the choice. Would   425
some sworn brother of mine were here to draw a cut with me.

RACHEL   Sir, noble sir –

OLIVER   First let me tell you, damsels, I am bound by a strong vow to kiss all of the woman sex I meet this   430
morning.

MERIEL   Beggars and all, sir?

OLIVER   All, all. Let not your coyness cross a gentleman's vow, I beseech you – *Kisses* [*them*].

RACHEL   You will tell now.   435

OLIVER   Tell, quotha! I could tell a thousand on those lips – and as many upon those. [*aside*] What life-restoring breaths they have! Milk from the cow steams not so sweetly. I must lay one of 'em aboard; both, if my tackling hold.   440

423–4 **benevolence . . . Benevolence** (financial) kindness . . . (physical) kindness or sex; *OED n.* 2 quotes Tyndale's translation of Corinthians, 7.3: 'Let the man geve unto the wyfe due benevolence.'

426 **sworn brother** man who has sworn to share fortunes with me. The phrase came from the medieval term *fraters jurati*; it was, however, used more generally to signify very close friends. Cf. *1H4*, 2.4.6–7: 'I am sworn brother to a leash of drawers'; or *MA*, 1.1.67–8: 'He hath every month a new sworn brother.'
draw a cut draw lots or draw straws; a way of deciding by a lottery using straws of different lengths. There may also be a play on *cut* and 'cunt'; Oliver is indifferent

about which woman to have first, seeing them as merely sexual objects.

433 **coyness** (1) shyness; (2) unwillingness
cross thwart

436 **quotha** said s/he. The word gives contemptuous force and is spoken after repeating words that someone else has said.
tell a 'whim' – Meriel had used the word in its sense of 'say'; Oliver repositions it in its sense of 'count'.

439 **lay . . . aboard** place one of them alongside; a nautical image from the practice of running a ship alongside an enemy's boat to board it and fight. There is also a *double entendre* in *lay*.

440 **tackling hold** ship's rigging remains up, with a *double entendre*

434 SD *Kisses*] *(Kiss) them*] *Lawrence*   437 SD] *Lawrence*

RACHEL, MERIEL   Sir, sir!

OLIVER [*aside*]   But how to bargain, now, will be the
doubt. They that beg so high as by the handfuls may
expect for price above the rate of good men's wives.

RACHEL   Now, will you, sir, be pleased?   445

OLIVER   With all my heart, sweetheart. And I am glad
thou knowest my mind. Here is twelvepence apiece
for you.

RACHEL, MERIEL   We thank you, sir.

OLIVER   That's but in earnest. I'll jest away the rest   450
with ye. Look here – all this. Come, you know my
meaning. Dost thou look about thee, sweet little one?
I like thy care. There's nobody coming. But we'll get
behind these bushes. I know you keep each other's
counsels – Must you be drawn to't? Then I'll pull.   455
Come away –

RACHEL, MERIEL   Ah, ah –

Enter SPRINGLOVE, VINCENT [*and*] HILLIARD.

VINCENT   Let's beat his brains out –

OLIVER   Come, leave your squealing.

RACHEL   Oh, you hurt my hand.   460

HILLIARD   – or cut the lecher's throat.

SPRINGLOVE   Would you be hanged? Stand back. Let
me alone.

443 **doubt** difficulty
  high excessively
444 **price . . . wives** ironic; he fears being
  charged more than for sleeping with the
  respectable wives of *good men*.
445 **pleased** agreeable
450 **in earnest** by way of 'earnest' (money
  paid as a foretaste of greater financial
  abundance)
451 **all this** Oliver may jingle his money, or
  gesture towards his groin, at this point.

453 **care** heedfulness
454–5 **keep . . . counsels** keep secrets for each
  other, as in *Ham*, 3.2.134–5: 'The players
  can not keep counsel – they'll tell all.'
455 **drawn** dragged; forced
457 The cries of the women parallel the cries
  of Springlove in 192 when the men are
  switched. All the beggar-aristocrats have
  now been shown screaming.
462–3 **Let me alone** 'Let me handle this
  myself.'

442 SD *Lawrence*   457 SD *and*] *Brome Online*

MERIEL   You shall not pull us so.

SPRINGLOVE   Oh, do not hurt 'em, master.   465

OLIVER   Hurt 'em? I meant 'em but too well. Shall I be
so prevented?

SPRINGLOVE   They be but young and simple. An if
they have offended, let not your worship's own hands
drag 'em to the law, or carry 'em to punishment.   470
Correct 'em not yourself. It is the beadle's office.

OLIVER   Do you talk, shake-rag? [*aside*] Heart, yond's
more of 'em. I shall be beggar-mauled if I stay. –
Thou sayest right, honest fellow. There's a tester for   474
thee.   *Exit, running.*

VINCENT   He is prevented and ashamed of his purpose.

SPRINGLOVE   Nor were we to take notice of his purpose
more than to prevent it.

HILLIARD   True, politic Springlove, 'twas better his own
fear quit us of him than our force.   480

RACHEL   Look you here, gentlemen, twelvepence
apiece.

MERIEL   Besides fair offers and large promises. What
ha' you got today, gentlemen?

VINCENT   More than, as we are gentlemen, we would   485
have taken.

---

471 **beadle's office** beadle's job. The beadle, an inferior parish officer, whipped whores as one of his tasks. Lear refers to this when he addresses an imaginary beadle: 'Thou, rascal beadle, hold thy bloody hand; / Why does thou lash that whore? . . . Thou hotly lusts to use her in that kind / For which thou whipp'st her' (*KL*, 4.6.156–9).

472 **shake-rag** ragged disreputable person (*OED n.*, citing this passage). John Wilkins describes a 'Shake-rag' as a beggar 'clothed (freq.) with torn vest' (*Essay*, sig. 3pʳ).

474 **tester** colloquial term for a sixpence, named after the 'teston' or shilling of Henry VIII in its debased and depreciated form. Elisha Coles describes a 'Teston' as 'an old silver coin formerly worth 12 pence, sinking by degrees to gilt brass and six pence' (sig. 2N2ʳ).

476 **prevented** forestalled

477–8 We are supposed to prevent his intention without acknowledging what it is.

477 **take notice of** acknowledge, remark upon

479 **politic** judicious; sensible

472 SD] *Lawrence*

HILLIARD   Yet we put it up in your service.

RACHEL, MERIEL   Ha, ha, ha! Switches and kicks. Ha, ha, ha! –

SPRINGLOVE   Talk not here of your gettings. We must   490
quit this quarter. The eager gentleman's repulse may
arm and return him with revenge upon us. We must
therefore leap hedge and ditch now, through the
briers and mires, till we scape out of this liberty to
our next rendezvous, where we shall meet the crew   495
and then 'hey toss' and laugh all night.

MERIEL [*to Rachel*]   As we did last night.

RACHEL [*to Meriel*]   Hold out, Meriel.

MERIEL (*to Springlove*)   Lead on, brave general.

VINCENT [*to Hilliard*]   What shall we do? They are in   500
heart still. Shall we go on?

HILLIARD [*to Vincent*]   There's no flinching back, you
see.

SPRINGLOVE   Besides, if you beg no better than you
begin, in this lofty fashion, you cannot scape the gaol   505
or the whip long.

VINCENT [*to Hilliard*]   To tell you true, 'tis not the least
of my purpose to work means for our discovery, to
be released out of our trade.

---

487 **put it up** put up with it; endure it

490 **gettings** gains; earnings

493–4 **leap ... mires** a version of a literary
formula for travellers in which the difficulties of the journey are presented in
rhyming or alliterative words. Cf. *MND*,
2.1.2–4: 'Over hill, over dale, / Thorough
bush, thorough briar / Over park, over
pale, / Thorough flood, thorough fire'.

494 **liberty** district

495 **rendezvous** meeting place

496 **'hey toss'** one of many exclamations of
joy used in the play, and another instance
of a formula starting with *hey* (see also

2.2.98n.). This particular exclamation
appears to signify a dance to which the
words were attached. Cf. 'Now could I
Caper through the Moon: – Hey Tosse –
Hang one Fiddle, we'll have a whole
Kennel: – Come you Jade – Dance'
(*Cheats*, 78).

497 The girls tossed (twisted and turned) in
hay the night before.

500–1 **in heart** in good spirits. See *TS*, 4.5.78:
'Well, Petruccio, this has put me in heart.'

502 **flinching** sneaking; slinking

507–8 **'tis ... purpose** it's my intention

508 **work means** find a way

497, 498, 500, 502 SDs] *Lawrence*   507 SD] *this edn*

Enter MARTIN *and* AMY *in poor habits.*

SPRINGLOVE   Stay, here come more passengers. Single   510
yourselves again and fall to your calling discreetly.

HILLIARD   I'll single no more. If you'll beg in full cry
I am for you.

MERIEL   Ay, that will be fine; let's charm all together.

SPRINGLOVE   Stay first and list a little.   515

[*Springlove, Hilliard, Vincent, Meriel and Rachel
walk aside.*]

MARTIN   Be of good cheer, sweetheart. We have scaped
hitherto, and I believe that all the search is now
retired and we may safely pass forwards.

AMY   I should be safe with thee. But that's a most lying
proverb that says 'where love is, there's no lack'.   520
I am faint and cannot travel further without meat,
and if you loved me you would get me some.

MARTIN   We'll venture at the next village to call for
some. The best is, we want no money.

AMY   We shall be taken then, I fear. I'll rather pine to   525
death.

MARTIN   Be not so fearful. Who can know us in these
clownish habits?

AMY   Our clothes, indeed, are poor enough to beg with.
Would I could beg, so it were of strangers that could   530
not know me, rather than buy of those that would
betray us.

510 **Stay** an imperative used as an injunction to pause or arrest one's course

510–11 **Single yourselves** separate yourselves from one another

512 **in full cry** in a pack, from the yelping of hounds in the chase

514 **charm** bewitch; enchant

515 **Stay** pause
list listen

518 **retired** withdrawn

520 **'where . . . lack'** proverbial (Dent, L485). Amy's choice of a proverb ending on *lack* may be significant as a comment on her prospective marriage.

524 **The best is** the best circumstance is. See *TGV*, 3.1.333: 'the best is, she hath no teeth to bite'.

528 **clownish** rustic; uncultivated

515 SD] *this edn*

MARTIN   And yonder be some that can teach us.

SPRINGLOVE   [*aside to Meriel, Rachel, Hilliard and Vincent*]   These are the young couple of runaway lovers disguised that the country is so laid for.   535
Observe and follow now. [*to Martin and Amy*] Now the Lord to come with ye, good loving master and maystress, your blessed charity to the poor, lame and sick, weak and comfortless, that will night and day –

MERIEL, RACHEL, HILLIARD, VINCENT   – duly and truly   540
pray for you. Duly and truly pray for you.

SPRINGLOVE   [*to Meriel, Rachel, Hilliard and Vincent*] Pray hold your peace and let me alone. [*to Martin and Amy*] Good young master and mistress, a little comfort amongst us all, and to bless you where'er you go, and –   545

MERIEL, RACHEL, HILLIARD, VINCENT   – duly and truly pray for you. Duly and truly –

SPRINGLOVE   [*to Meriel, Rachel, Hilliard and Vincent*]   Pray do not use me thus. [*to Martin and Amy*] Now sweet young master and mistress, to look upon your poor, that have no relief or succour,   550
no bread to put in our heads –

VINCENT   [*to Springlove*]   Wouldst thou put bread in thy brains?

All [*speak*] *together.*

---

535 **laid for** lying in wait for
538 **maystress** Springlove adopts a rustic accent.
544 **comfort** i.e. money
551 **bread . . . heads** Springlove must have intended to say that they have no bread for their stomachs; the interruptions of the others have confused him. Possibly

he comes up with *heads* because of its near rhyme with *bread*.
553 SD From Dodsley's 1744 edition onwards, the lines at 554–66 have regularly been bracketed together indicating that they are to be spoken at the same time. As only 554–62 are in italic in Q1 – indicating beggar speech – however, presumably only those lines are to be spoken concurrently.

---

534 SD] *Brome Online*   536 SD] *this edn*   540 – duly] *this edn;* Duly *Q1*   542 SD] *this edn*   542–3 SD] *this edn*   546 SP] *this edn;* All *Q1*   548 SD] *this edn*   548–9 SD] *Brome Online*   552 SD] *Brome Online*   553 SD *speak*] *Brome Online*

VINCENT   – no lands or livings –

SPRINGLOVE   – no house nor home, nor covering from   555
the cold, no health, no help but your sweet charity –

MERIEL   – no bands or shirts but lousy on our backs –

HILLIARD   – no smocks or petticoats to hide our
scratches –

RACHEL   – no shoes to our legs, or hose to our feet –   560

VINCENT   – no skin to our flesh, nor flesh to our bones
shortly –

HILLIARD [*aside*]   – if we follow the devil that taught us
to beg.

MERIEL, RACHEL, HILLIARD, VINCENT   – duly and truly   565
pray for you.

SPRINGLOVE [*aside to Meriel, Rachel, Hilliard and
Vincent*]   I'll run away from you if you beg a stroke
more. [*to Martin and Amy*] Good worshipful master
and misteress –

MARTIN   Good friend, forbear. Here is no master or   570
mistress. We are poor folks. Thou seest no worship

557 **bands** collars or ruffs of cambric or linen starched to stand up ('standing bands'), or worn flat ('falling bands'); they could be worn by men or women. Bands were very expensive. Cf. 'Hee is not a Gentleman, nor in the fashion, whose band of Italian cut-work now standeth him not at the least in three or foure pounds' (Peacham, 61).
shirts These are more expensive wear. Made of white linen or silk, early modern shirts had high necks and long sleeves, and were about three feet long. They might be embroidered or ornamented; fine shirts were intended to show through slashes in the doublet.
lousy louse-ridden
558 **smocks** innermost garments for women, serving as chemise and night-gown, and generally made of fine linen. They had a slit front opening and, often, embroidered or edged neck- and sleeve-bands; that beggars should wear smocks as well as other clothes was an outrageous idea.
petticoats undershirts or undergarments that might be worn by men or women; literally little or small coats. Though often hidden, they were decorated and could be exposed if the overskirt needed to be tucked up. Beggars would not have been expected to own petticoats.
560 **hose** clothing for the legs and loins
563–4 i.e. we won't have any of these goods if we keep following Springlove's method.
567 **stroke** coinage (*OED n.*[1] 4; Scottish usage)
570 **forbear** desist

554 SP] *this edn; not in Q1*   563 SD] *Dodsley*   565 SP] *this edn;* All *Q1*   567 SD] *this edn*   568 SD]
Brome Online   569 misteress] *this edn;* misteres *Q1*

upon our backs, I am sure. And for within, we want
as much as you, and would as willingly beg – if we
knew how – as well.

SPRINGLOVE   Alack, for pity. You may have enough.   575
And what I have is yours, if you'll accept it. [*Offers
food.*] 'Tis wholesome food from a good gentleman's
gate [*Amy takes food and eats.*] – Alas, good mistress
– much good do your heart. [*aside*] How savourly
she feeds!   580

MARTIN   What, do you mean to poison yourself?

AMY   Do you show love in grudging me?

MARTIN   Nay, if you think it hurts you not, fall to. I'll
not beguile you. [*Offers money.*] And here, mine
host, something towards your reckoning.   585

AMY [*aside*]   This beggar is an angel, sure!

SPRINGLOVE   Nothing by way of bargain, gentle master.
'Tis against order and will never thrive. But pray, sir,
your reward in charity.

---

572 **upon our backs** either figuratively,
meaning that no requirement for the term
worshipful is 'weighing upon us as a
burden' (see *OED* back *n.* 1 VI 23), or, as
Brome Online suggests, literally meaning
that there are no symbols of office in
the form of insignia or badges on our
clothing

577–8 **gentleman's gate** Beggars asked for
alms at gentlemens' gates. In Taylor's
'The Praise, Antiquity, and Commoditie
of Beggerie, Beggers, and Begging', a
lord is depicted with a 'Great store of
Beggers dayly at his Gate, / Which he did
feed, and much Compassionate. / (For
'tis within the power of mighty men, / To
make five hundred Beggers, and feed
Ten)' (*Works*, 98).

579 **How savourly** with what relish, keenness

581–2 a fulfilment of Oliver's prediction
(273–4) that Martin would grudge Amy
food

582 **grudging** begrudging

583 **fall to** begin eating

584 **beguile** deprive

584–5 **mine host** a phrase used for addressing the landlord of an inn

585 **reckoning** bill (US check)

587 **by ... bargain** as a transaction that
brings with it the obligation of some kind
of return

588 **order** beggars' rules

589–91 **charity ... charity** Springlove asks
for remuneration in love rather than
money; Martin, who can only understand
transactions financially, takes *charity* to
mean 'benevolence to the poor' and pays
him accordingly.

576–7 SD] *this edn*   578 SD] *this edn*   579 SD] *Lawrence*   584 SD] *this edn; after 585 Brome
Online*   586 SD] *this edn*

MARTIN [*Gives money to Springlove.*] Here, then, in 590
charity. [*aside*] This fellow would never make a
clerk.

SPRINGLOVE What! All this, master?

AMY What is it? Let me see't.

SPRINGLOVE 'Tis a whole silver threepence, mistress. 595

AMY [*to Martin*] For shame, ingrateful miser! [*Gives
money to Springlove.*] Here, friend, a golden crown
for thee.

SPRINGLOVE Bountiful goodness! Gold? If I thought a
dear year were coming, I would take a farm now. 600

AMY I have robbed thy partners of their shares, too.
There's a crown more for them. [*Gives money to
others.*]

MERIEL, RACHEL, HILLIARD, VINCENT Duly and truly
pray for you!

MARTIN [*aside to Amy*] What have you done? Less 605
would have served, and your bounty will betray us.

AMY [*aside to Martin*] Fie on your wretched policy!

SPRINGLOVE No, no, good master. I knew you all this
while, and my sweet mistress too. And now I'll tell
you. The search is every way; the country all laid for 610
you. 'Tis well you stayed here. Your habits, were
they but a little nearer our fashion, would secure you
with us. But are you married, master and mistress?

597 **a golden crown** a coin worth five
shillings
599–600 **a dear year** a damagingly expensive year when, because crops are poor,
farmers make good sales. Cf. 'what
covetous Farmer, but is glad of a deere
yeare? A dearth of Corne makes such
Cormorants Fat?' (Dekker, *Black*, 13–14),
and 'you have your Garners which have
corne of two or three yeares old, upon
hope still of a deare yeare' (Greene,
Quip, sig. F1ᵛ).
607 **policy** prudence
610 **laid** beset; filled with watches and guards
(*OED* lay *v.*[1] 18c)
611 **stayed** stopped

590 SD] *this edn; Offering money again* | *Brome Online* 591 SD] *Lawrence* 596 SD] *Brome
Online* 596–7 SD] *this edn* 602 SD] *this edn* 603 SP] *Lawrence; 4. Q1* 605 SD] *Brome Online
subst.* 607 SD] *Lawrence subst.*

Are you joined in matrimony? In heart I know you
are. And I will, if it please you, for your great bounty,   615
bring you to a curate that lacks no licence, nor has
any living to lose, that shall put you together.

MARTIN   Thou art a heavenly beggar!

SPRINGLOVE   But he is so scrupulous and severely
precise, that unless you, mistress, will affirm that   620
you are with child by the gentleman, or that you
have, at least, cleft or slept together, as he calls it, he
will not marry you. But if you have lain together,
then 'tis a case of necessity, and he holds himself
bound to do it.   625

MARTIN   You may say you have.

AMY   I would not have it so, nor make that lie against
myself for all the world.

SPRINGLOVE   (*aside*) That I like well, and her
exceedingly. – I'll do my best for you, however.   630

MARTIN   I'll do for thee that thou shalt never beg more.

SPRINGLOVE   That cannot be purchased scarce for the
price of your mistress. Will you walk, master? – We
use no compliments.   [*Exeunt all except Amy.*]

AMY

By enforced matches wards are not set free   635
So oft as sold into captivity,

616–17 **curate . . . lose** literally, an authorized clergyman without an assigned
parish as a benefice; but probably a
further use of 'whim'. Springlove may in
fact be referring to the Patrico, who *lacks
no licence* in that he has no licence to
lack; similarly he cannot lose his living
by performing marriages, as he has none.

619 **scrupulous** troubled with doubts or
scruples of conscience; over-nice or
meticulous in matters of right and wrong
(*OED adj.* 1a)

620 **precise** strict

622 **cleft** adhered or clung to

623 **lain together** had sexual intercourse
(*OED* lie *v.* 1f)

631 **do for** satisfy

634 **use no compliments** do not act on
ceremony

635 **wards** minors subject to guardians. The
Court of Wards, established in 1540,
ceased to function in 1645; its abolition
was confirmed in 1660. While it existed it
sold wealthy orphans who had been left

634 SD] *Lawrence*

Which made me, fearless, fly from one I hate
Into the hazard of a harder fate.   [*Exit.*]

4.1   *Enter* TALLBOY [*and*] OLIVER[*, carrying a letter*],
          with riding switches.

TALLBOY

  She's gone:
  Amy is gone.
  Ay me, she's gone,
  And has me left
  Of joy bereft   5
  To make my moan.
  Oh me, Amy!

OLIVER [*aside*]   What the devil ails the fellow, trow? –
Why! Why, Master Tallboy, my cousin Tallboy that
shouldst ha' been, art not ashamed to cry at this   10
growth? And for a thing that's better lost than found,
a wench?

TALLBOY   Cry! Who cries? Do I cry, or look with a
crying countenance? I scorn it, and scorn to think on
her but in just anger.   15

as 'wards of the crown' to guardians who
wished to pay for them. As the guardians
then had the legal right to choose whom
their wards should marry, a ward was
often forced to make a match into their
guardian's family.
638 hazard risk
4.1 Location: Oldrents' house
3   **Ay me** Tallboy's sigh echoes the name
'Amy'.

7   **Oh me, Amy** This line draws parallels
between sounds of sighing – 'oh me' and
'ah me' – and Tallboy, *me*, himself.
8   **trow** do you think?
10–11 **at this growth** when you are so well
grown (a reference to the name Tallboy,
and to the boy player, who was either
exceptionally tall or exceptionally short
– see List of Roles, 20n.).
11   **better ... found** proverbial (Dent, L454)
14   **countenance** appearance

638 SD] *Lawrence*   **4.1**] *(Actus Quartus. Scena Prima.)*   0.1 *and*] *Lawrence   carrying a letter*] *this edn*
2–7] *Dodsley & Reed; prose Q1*   8 SD] *this edn*

OLIVER   So, this is brave now, if 'twould hold.

TALLBOY   Nay, it shall hold. And so let her go, for
a scurvy what-d'ye-call-it; I know not what bad
enough to call her. But something of mine goes with
her, I am sure. She has cost me in gloves, ribbons,   20
scarves, rings and suchlike things, more than I am
able to speak of at this time. Oh –

OLIVER   Because thou canst not speak for crying. Fie,
Master Tallboy, again?

TALLBOY   I scorn it again, and any man that says I cry or   25
will cry again. And let her go again, and what she has
of mine let her keep, and hang herself and the rogue
that's with her. I have enough, and am heir of a well-
known estate, and that she knows. And therefore,
that she should slight me, and run away with a wages-   30
fellow, that is but a petty clerk and a serving-man –
there's the vexation of it. Oh, there's the grief and the
vexation of it. Oh! –

OLIVER [*aside*]   Now he will cry his eyes out! – You, sir.
This life have I had with you all our long journey,   35
which now is at an end here. This is Master Oldrents'
house, where perhaps we shall find old Hearty, the
uncle of that rogue Martin that is run away with your
sweetheart.

TALLBOY   Ay, 'tis too true, too true, too true. You need   40
not put me in mind on't. Oh – oh –

---

16   **brave** intrepid; stout-hearted
     hold continue
17   **let her go** dismiss her from thought
18   **scurvy** worthless; contemptible
19   **something of mine** At first it appears that
     Tallboy is saying that his love or heart
     goes with her. The next sentence makes
     clear, however, that he is talking about
     material goods.

25   **it** i.e. weeping
30   **run away** elope (*OED* run *v.* 2b cites this
     passage)
30–1   **wages-fellow** used contemptuously of
     one who receives wages (*OED* wage *n.* 4,
     citing this example)

34 SD] *Lawrence*

OLIVER   Hold your peace and mind me. Leave your
bawling, for fear I give you correction. This is the
house, I say, where it is most likely we shall hear of
your mistress and her companion. Make up your face   45
quickly. Here comes one of the servants, I suppose.

Enter RANDALL.

Shame not yourself forever and me for company.
Come, be confident.

TALLBOY   As confident as yourself or any man – but my
poor heart feels what lies here. Here! Ay, here it is.   50
Oh –

OLIVER   Good morrow, friend. This is Squire Oldrents'
house, I take it.

RANDALL   Pray, take it not, sir, before it be to be let. It
has been my master's and his ancestors' in that name   55
above these three hundred years, as our house
chronicle doth notify, and not yet to be let. But as a
friend, or stranger, in guestwise, you are welcome to
it, as all other gentlemen are, far and near, to my

---

42 **mind** pay attention to

43 **give you correction** chastise you physically, by hitting or flogging, etc. Once
again, Tallboy's childishness brings out
Oliver's instinctive violence.

45 **Make up** arrange (*OED* make *v.*[1] 10b,
citing this instance)

47 **for company** for company's sake, i.e. as
well

50 **here. Here! . . . here** Tallboy presumably
gestures emphatically at his heart, or
beats it – though the lines also suggest he
has trouble finding it. He might gesture
towards the wrong side of his body, or
to another body part altogether, before
'discovering' his heartbeat.

54 **take it not** a 'whim'. Oliver says he
believes (*I take it*) this to be Squire
Oldrents' house; Randall asks him not
to lease it (*take it*) before it has been
offered as a rental property.

56–7 **house chronicle** an account of the
history of the house, written from its
foundation, and updated by subsequent
owners. There may be a joke here. Such
chronicles were usually associated with
cathedrals and monasteries; private house-
holds did not tend to have such books.

58 **in guestwise** as a guest (*OED* guestwise
n. and *adv.* A, quoting this instance).
Cf. *MND*, 3.2.171–2: 'My heart to her
but as guest-wise, sojourn'd, / And now
to Helen is it home return'd'.

good master, as you will find anon when you see 60
him.

OLIVER   Thou speakest wittily and honestly. But I
prithee, good friend, let our nags be set up; they are
tied up at the post. You belong to the stable, do you
not?   65

RANDALL   Not so much as the stable belongs to me, sir.
I pass through many offices of the house, sir. I am the
running bailie of it.

OLIVER   We have rid hard, hoping to find the squire at
home at this early time in the morning.   70

RANDALL   You are deceived in that, sir. He has been out
these four hours. He is no snail, sir. You do not know
him, I perceive, since he has been new moulded. But
I'll tell you, because you are gentlemen.

OLIVER   Our horses, good friend –   75

RANDALL   My master is an ancient gentleman, and a
great housekeeper, and prayed for by all the poor in
the country. He keeps a guesthouse for all beggars,
far and near, costs him a hundred a year at least, and
is as well-beloved among the rich. But of late he fell   80

---

60 **anon** at once; instantly
63 **nags...up** i.e. horses or ponies be put
    in a stable. Thomas Ellwood writes about
    the occasion 'When I... had set up my
    Horse at an Inn' (21).
64 **tied...post** attached to the tethering post
67 **offices** positions of trust
68 **running bailie** i.e. temporary bailiff: he
    is standing in as steward managing the
    estate while Springlove is gone, as was
    arranged in 1.1.318–20.
69 **rid hard** ridden strenuously or fiercely
72 **no snail** (1) no sluggard; a gesture towards
    the proverb 'As slow as a snail' (Dent,
    S579); (2) no homebody (unlike snails,
    which are always in their 'house' or
    shell). Cf. *2 Honest Whore*, 3.3.51–2: 'I
    am a Snaile, sir, seldome leave my house,

if't please her to visit me, she shall be
welcome,'
73 **new moulded** shaped anew; reshaped.
    Randall is referring to Oldrents' change
    of mood from despair to hysterical mirth,
    and his associated change of character.
76 **ancient gentleman** gentleman of estab-
    lished lineage
77 **great housekeeper** hospitable house-
    holder; one who keeps or owns a large
    house. In *London Prodigal*, 'Shee hath
    refus'de seaven of the worshipfulst and
    worthyest hous-keepers this day in *Kent*'
    (sig. B1ᵛ).
78 **guesthouse** hospital, poorhouse (*OED*
    guest house *n.* 2b, citing this example).
    1.1.264–5, however, has already shown
    this guesthouse to be Oldrents' barn.

into a great melancholy, upon what I know not, for
he had then more cause to be merry than he has now.
Take that by the way.

OLIVER   But good friend, our horses!

RANDALL   For he had two daughters that knew well to   85
order a house and give entertainment to gentlemen.
They were his house-doves. But now they are flown,
and no man knows how, why or whither.

TALLBOY   My dove is flown too. Oh –

RANDALL   Was she your daughter, sir? She was a young   90
one then, by the beard you wear.

TALLBOY   What she was, she was, d'ye see? I scorn to
think on her – but I do – oh!

OLIVER   Pray hold your peace, or feign some mirth if
you can.   95

TALLBOY (*Sings.*)

> Let her go!
> Let her go!
> I care not if I have her,
> I have her, or no.

Ha, ha, ha – Oh, my heart will break – oh –   100

OLIVER   Pray think of our horses, sir.

RANDALL   This is right my master. When he had his
daughters, he was sad, and now they are gone, he is the
merriest man alive. Up at five o'clock in the morning

---

83 **by the way** incidentally
85–6 **to order a house** how to keep a house
in order
87 **house-doves** commonly applied to
people (especially women) who stay in
the house. Robert Greene writes, 'You
are provde such a house dove of late, or
rather so good a Huswife, that no man

may see you under a couple of Capons'
(*Menaphon*, sig. K3ʳ).
89 **My dove** i.e. Amy – but the term further
contributes to the play's idea that gentry
are caged birds who seek to fly away, as
Amy has done.
90–1 **young . . . wear** Tallboy has a youthful,
not very full, beard.
102 **right** i.e. just like

84 friend] *Dodsley & Reed;* fiend *Q1;* friends *Dodsley*   92+ d'ye] *this edn;* d'ee *Q1*   96–9] *this edn;*
prose Q1

and out till dinnertime. Out again at afternoon, and   105
so till suppertime. Skice out this-a-way and skice out
that-a-way – he's no snail, I assure you – and tantivy
all the country over, where hunting, hawking or any
sport is to be made, or good fellowship to be had, and
so merry upon all occasions that you would even   110
bless yourself if it were possible.

OLIVER   Our horses, I prithee.

RANDALL   And we, his servants, live as merrily under
him, and do all thrive. I myself was but a silly lad
when I came first, a poor turnspit boy. Gentlemen   115
kept no whirling jacks then to cozen poor people of
meat. And I have now, without boast, forty pounds in
my purse, and am the youngest of half a score in the
house, none younger than myself but one, and he is
the steward over all; his name is Master Springlove   120
(bless him, where'er he is); he has a world of means,
and we, the underlings, get well the better by him,

---

106 **Skice** move quickly; skip or frisk about
(*OED v.*¹, citing this instance). 'S.', an
unnamed contributor (almost certainly
George Steevens) to Dodsley & Reed,
10.397, however, speculates that the
word intended was 'skirr' – to pass
hastily – as in *Mac*, 5.3.35: 'Send out
more horses, skirr the country round.'

107 **tantivy** at full gallop; swiftly (*OED adv.*,
citing this example)

111 **bless yourself** sanctify yourself by
making the sign of the cross – perhaps
as a sign of Catholicism; perhaps because
Oldrents appears to be possessed, as a
1653 translation of Rabelais suggests:
'When they heard these words, some . . .
blest themselves with both hands, thinking . . . that he had been a devil disguised'
(158).

114 **silly** humble; insignificant

115 **turnspit boy** boy whose job was to turn
the spit on which meat was roasted in

front of the fire. Otherwise performed by
a dog (see 2.1.12n.), this was the
humblest of kitchen tasks. *Pierce
Penniless* describes 'poore Scullians,
that, from turning spit in the chimney
corner, are on the sodaine hoised up from
the Kitchin into the waiting Chamber'
(Nashe, 1.173).

116 **whirling jacks** automated turnspits,
which were either wound up like a clock
or actuated by the draught of heated
air up the chimney. Cf. 'It stood . . . like
a Germane clock, or an English, *Jack*
or *Turne-spit*, upon skrewes and vices'
(Dekker, *Seven*, 12–13).
    cozen cheat. Randall ludicrously main-
tains that it is mechanical turnspits, rather
than human turnspits, who steal meat.

118 **half a score** ten

121 **means** financial resources

122 **underlings** subordinates
    get well do well (financially)

besides the rewards many gentlemen give us that
fare well and lodge here sometimes.

OLIVER   Oh! We shall not forget you, friend, if you   125
remember our horses before they take harm.

RANDALL   No hurt, I warrant you. There's a lad walking
them.

OLIVER   Is not your master coming, think you?

RANDALL   He will not be long a-coming. He's no snail,   130
as I told you.

OLIVER   You told me so, indeed.

RANDALL   But of all the gentlemen that toss up the ball,
yea, and the sack too, commend me to old Master
Hearty, a decayed gentleman, lives most upon his   135
own mirth and my master's means, and much good
do him with it. He is the finest companion of all; he
does so hold my master up with stories, and songs,
and catches, and tother cup of sack and such tricks
and jigs you would admire. – He is with him now.   140

OLIVER   That Hearty is Martin's uncle. I am glad he is
here. Bear up, Tallboy. [*to Randall*] Now, friend,
pray let me ask you a question. Prithee stay.

RANDALL   Nay, marry, I dare not. Your yauds may take   144
cold, and never be good after it.   *Exit.*

OLIVER   I thought I should never have been rid of him.
But no sooner desired to stay, but he is gone. A pretty
humour!

---

125 **We ... forget you** i.e. 'we will reward
you financially'

133 **toss ... ball** a figurative proverb (see Dent,
T90a.11) that seems to have implied irre-
verent discourse in which the same words
or terms feature repeatedly. Cf. '[Courtiers]
do tosse lyke a tennes ball wythoute al feare
and reverence the name of oure Lord God
from mouth to mouth' (Gilby, sig. A8ᵛ).

134 **commend me to** let me recommend

138 **hold ... up** sustain

144–5 **Your ... it** Having ignored all pleas
to look after the horses while he is talking, Randall decides to go to them when
his conversation is actually required.

144 **yauds** mares, perhaps from the north-
country pronunciation of 'jade'. The term
is usually applied to old mares, or old and
worn-out horses (see *OED* yaud *n.* 1,
citing this example).

142 SD] *Brome Online*

Enter RANDALL.

RANDALL   Gentlemen, my master will be here e'en now,   149
doubt not, for he is no snail, as I told you.   *Exit.*

OLIVER   No snail's a great word with him. Prithee,
Tallboy, bear up.

Enter USHER.

Here comes another grey fellow.

USHER   Do you stand in the porch, gentlemen? The
house is open to you. Pray enter the hall. I am the   155
usher of it.

OLIVER   In good time, sir. We shall be bold here, then, to
attend your master's coming.

USHER   And he's upon coming, and when he comes he
comes apace. He is no snail, I assure you.   160

OLIVER   I was told so before, sir. No snail! Sure 'tis the
word of the house, and as ancient as the family.

USHER   This gentleman looks sadly, methinks.

TALLBOY   Who, I? Not I. Pray pardon my looks for that.
But my heart feels what's what. Ay me –   165

USHER   Pray walk to the buttery, gentlemen. My office
leads you thither.

OLIVER   Thanks, good Master Usher.

USHER   I have been usher these twenty years, sir. And
have got well by my place, for using strangers   170
respectfully.

149 **e'en now** at any minute
152 **bear up** keep your spirits up
152 SD USHER servant who has charge of the
   door and admits people
153 **grey** i.e. grey-haired
157 **be bold . . . to** venture to; presume so far
   as to
159 **upon** close on; almost

160 **apace** swiftly; quickly
162 **the family** i.e. the family's lineage; see 76n.
166 **buttery** place for storing liquor and other
   provisions
   My office the duties of my post
170 **got well** earned substantial financial
   reward (through tips)
   for by

166 buttery] *(buttry)*

OLIVER [*aside*]   He has given the hint, too.

USHER   Something has come in by the by, besides
standing wages, which is ever duly paid, thank a
good master and an honest steward, heaven bless   175
'em. We all thrive under 'em.

Enter BUTLER *with glasses and a napkin.*

Oh, here comes the butler.

BUTLER   You are welcome, gentlemen. Please ye draw
nearer my office and take a morning drink in a cup of
sack, if it please you.   180

OLIVER   In what please you, sir. We cannot deny the
courtesy of the house in the master's absence.

BUTLER   He'll come apace when he comes. He's no
snail, sir. [*He starts*] *going.*

OLIVER   Still 'tis the house-word. And all the servants   185
wear livery-beards.

BUTLER   Or perhaps you had rather drink white wine
and sugar. Please yourselves, gentlemen; here you

---

174 **standing** fixed, settled; not casual, fluctuating or occasional

179 **office** room used as a place of business for non-manual work

179–80 **morning . . . sack** The custom was to have a morning drink of beer, wine or spirits rather than to eat a breakfast. 'My diet', explains Charles Cotton, 'is always one Glass so soon as I am drest, and no more till Dinner' (25). Venner records that 'THE custome of drinking in the mornings fasting, a large draught of White wine, of Rhenish wine, or of Beere, hath almost with all men so farre prevailed, as that they judge it a principall meanes for the preservation of their health' (*Via Recta*, 193). Cf. *MW*, 2.2.136–9: 'Master Brook . . . hath sent your worship a morning's draught of sack.'

181 **In . . . you** i.e. I'm pleased by what pleases you.

185 **house-word** motto; significant phrase or short sentence associated with the house

186 **livery-beards** uniform beards, i.e. beards of the same kind

187–8 **white . . . sugar** Originally a sign of ostentation amongst the rich, sugar was added to red and white wine, both of which were drunk while young or 'hard'. When wine 'dranke somewhat harde', Greene recommended that 'Rose-water and Sugar' be added to improve it (*3 Coney-catching*, sig. D1ʳ); in *Miser*, Timothy sends for a 'Bottle of white Wine; I have Sugar in my pocket, the Rogues at Tavern's make us pay three pence a paper for it' (20).

172 SD] *Lawrence*   184 SD *He starts*] *this edn*

may taste all liquors. No gentleman's house in all
this county, or the next, so well stored; —— make us   190
thankful for it. And my master, for his hospitality to
gentlemen, his charity to the poor and his bounty to
his servants, has not his peer in the kingdom; ——
make us thankful for it. And 'tis as fortunate a house
for servants as ever was built upon fairy-ground.   195
I myself, that have served here man and boy these
four-and-forty years, have gotten together – besides
something, more than I will speak of, distributed
among my poor kindred – by my wages, my vails at
Christmas and otherwise, together with my rewards   200
of kind gentlemen that have found courteous
entertainment here –

OLIVER   There he is, too.

190, 193 —— **make us thankful** A dash usually represents a word cut from the text either at the point of printing or earlier. If a prompter or the Master of the Revels removed the word, the actor would have been able to fill the space with a gesture or a word of his choice; it remains possible, however, that the word was spoken onstage and only censored for printing purposes (see Stern, 255). As, however, the word that has been struck out is almost certainly 'God', this may in fact be a joke on Brome's part: the Butler's habitual repetition of this phrase – see also 206, 209 – defines him by a sentence he cannot say in its entirety. God is markedly absent from this play.

193 **peer** equal

194 **fortunate** The Butler appears to be saying that the house is favoured by good fortune (luck) – but as his subsequent sentiments go on to show, what he is

actually saying is that the house is the source of fortune (wealth).

195 **fairy-ground** ground that resembles fairyland, i.e. beautiful and unsubstantial; unreal (see *OED* faerie, faery *n.* (*a.*) 4, citing this example). The reference is part of the play's mock pastoral, and appears to equate the house with the idealized version of England suggested by *Faerie Queene*.

199 **vails** tips or gratuities. In the seventeenth and eighteenth centuries, servants were largely paid through gratuities, and the practice of giving them is frequently alluded to in the literature of the period. Cf. 'Out of the wages allowed by the citie with other veiles I could wel-nigh maintaine my family' (Oldenbarnavelt, sig. F3ᵛ).

200 **rewards** i.e. financial rewards; tips

203 Oliver is surprised that the Butler, like Randall (see 123–5), is asking so pointedly for *rewards*.

199 kindred] *Dodsley;* Kinred *Q1*

BUTLER – have, I say, gotten together, though in a
        dangerous time I speak it, a brace of hundred pounds; 205
        —— make me thankful for it. And for losses, I have
        had none. I have been butler these two and thirty
        years, and never lost the value of a silver spoon, nor
        ever broke a glass; —— make me thankful for it.
        White wine and sugar, say you, sir?   210
OLIVER Please yourself, sir.
BUTLER [*Points at Tallboy.*] This gentleman speaks not.
        Or had you rather take a drink of brown ale with a
        toast, or March beer with sugar and nutmeg? Or had
        you rather drink without sugar?   215
OLIVER Good sir, a cup of your household beer. I fear
        he will draw down to that at last.   *Exit Butler.*

204–5 **in . . . time** apparently a political reference. Since the 1620s, Charles I had been financing his deficit through 'forced loans' from his people. The Butler's possession of a substantial sum of money would have been particularly dangerous in 1641, when the play was performed, as the monarch was likely to requisition it for the army. That a butler could have had such a great sum of money is a joke in itself, possibly implying that Oldrents' household is generous in its rewards to the man who supplies them with drink.

205 **brace** pair

211 Oliver is indifferent about what he drinks.

213–14 **brown . . . toast** Hot toasted bread was commonly served in beer as a 'sop'. So Richard Head records, 'In Winter for morning draughts we furnished our Guests with *Gravesend* toasts . . . if we put any of them into drink before our Guests (as sometimes we were forced to do) we would be sure to warm the beer or ale before-hand, and in putting in the toast cry siz, although it were as cold as a stone' (75).

214 **March beer** an especially strong beer made with the best malt, prepared in March at the end of the brewing season. Gervase Markham explains, 'This March Beere would be brewd in the moneths of *March* or *Aprill*, and should (if it have right) have a whole yeere to ripen in: it will last two, three and foure yeeres if it lie coole and close, & endure the drawing to the last drop, though with never so much leasure' (246).

216 **household beer** beer brewed up in the house; a relatively weak concoction. William Harrison records, 'The bere that is . . . for the housholde . . . is usually not under a monethes age, eache one coveting to have ye same stale as he may so that it be not soure' (Holinshed, 95).

217 **draw . . . that** (1) get to that item in his list; (2) draw sufficiently much from the casks to reach that substandard layer of drink

212 SD] *this edn*

Enter BUTLER *with a silver can of sack.*

BUTLER   Here, gentlemen, is a cup of my master's small
beer, but it is good old canary, I assure you. And
here's to your welcome. [*Drinks. Gives glasses to*   220
Oliver, Tallboy and Usher.]

Enter COOK[*, taking a glass*].

COOK   And welcome, the cook says, gentlemen. Brother
butler, lay a napkin; I'll fetch a cut of the sirloin to
strengthen your patience till my master comes, who
will not now be long, for he's no snail, gentlemen.

OLIVER   I have often heard so. [*Takes a glass.*] And   225
here's to you, Master Cook. (*to Tallboy*) Prithee
speak, Master Tallboy, or force one laugh more, if
thou canst.

COOK   Sir, the cook drinks to you.

TALLBOY   Ha, ha, ha –   230

OLIVER   Well said.

TALLBOY   He is in the same livery-beard too.

COOK   But he is the oldest cook, and of the ancientest
house, and the best for housekeeping, in this county

---

217 SD2 *can* vessel for holding liquids

218–19 **small beer . . . canary** *small beer* was
weak beer, famously lacking in alcohol,
and typically served as a morning drink.
It was too watery to produce drunkenness
or significantly change the emotions.
In *Four Letters Confuted*, Thomas Nashe
refers to bad poetry as 'more spiritlesse
than smal beere' (Nashe, 1.302). As
Oldrents' small beer, however, is then
described as *canary* – an expensive
sweet wine from the Canary Islands – the
Butler is actually saying that what is
small beer to Oldrents is fine drink to
anyone else.

220 **here's to** the standard formula for
pledging a drink

221 **welcome** The term seems to be another
formula for pledging a drink.

222 **lay a napkin** Sometimes food was served
from a napkin directly. Thomas Deloney
writes that 'a faire napkin was laide upon
the little table in the Parlour, hard by the
fire side, whereon was set a good cold
Capon' (sig. I4ᵛ).

233 **he . . . cook** The Cook refers to himself
in self-justificatory language, having
heard Tallboy's critical observation about
his beard.

234 **housekeeping** hospitality; entertaining
visitors or guests with food and drink

220 SD1] *this edn*   SD2 *taking a glass*] *this edn*   225 SD] *this edn*   226 SD] *after 228 Q1 (To Talb)*

or the next. And though the master of it write but   235
'squire', I know no lord like him.

Enter CHAPLAIN.

And now he's come. Here comes the word before
him. The parson has ever the best stomach. I'll dish
away presently.   *Exit.*

BUTLER   Is our master come, Sir Domine?   240

CHAPLAIN   *Est ad manum. Non est ille testudo.*

OLIVER   He has the word, too, in Latin. Now bear up,
Tallboy.

CHAPLAIN   Give me a preparative of sack. It is a gentle
preparative before meat. [*Takes a glass.*] And so a   245
gentle touch of it to you, gentlemen.

OLIVER   It is a gentle offer, sir, and as gently to be taken.

---

236 **squire** Ranking next down from knight under the feudal system of military service and tenure, a squire was a principal landowner who was a gentleman but not part of the aristocracy.

237–8 **Here . . . him** either 'here comes word of his arrival, in front of the arrival itself' or 'here comes the parson' (the parson being the representative of the *word* of God)

238 **The parson . . . stomach** That churchmen of all kinds were gluttonous had been a commonplace since the Middle Ages. Hence Jonson names his gluttonous parson in *The Magnetic Lady* 'Parson Palate', while Nevergood, in *Hey for Honesty*, says that if he changes his faith he 'will turn fat Presbyter or Anabaptist' (30).

238–9 **dish away** serve up, put food into a dish

240 **Domine** Master; vocative case of Latin *dominus* ('lord'). The word was used as a respectful address to the clergy or members of learned professions.

241 'He is at hand. He is no snail.' This is 'dog Latin': the phrases are in English terminology, translated into Latin for humorous effect.

244–5 **preparative . . . preparative** preparation or incentive – in this case, a preparatory drink to encourage the appetite. Thomas Heywood explains that 'to drinke moderately sharpeneth the appothite, helpeth digestion, and prepareth the spirits to active mirth and alacritie' (*Philocothonista*, 49).

246 **touch** trace; smidgen
to you a formula for drinking a toast

247 **gentle . . . gently** kind . . . nobly

245 SD] *this edn*

Enter OLDRENTS *and* HEARTY.

OLDRENTS   About with it, my lads. And this is as it
should be. [*Butler offers glass.*] – Not till my turn,
sir, I. Though, I confess, I have had but three morning   250
draughts today.

OLIVER   Yet it appears you were abroad betimes, sir.

OLDRENTS   I am no snail, sir.

OLIVER   So your men told us, sir.

OLDRENTS   But where be my catchers? Come, a round.   255
And so let us drink.

[*Oldrents and Hearty take glasses.*]
The catch [is] sung, and they drink about.
The singers are all greybeards.

USHER, BUTLER, CHAPLAIN, HEARTY, OLDRENTS (*Sing.*)
A round, a round, a round, boys, a round.
Let mirth fly aloft, and sorrow be drowned.
Old sack, and old songs and a merry old crew

---

248 **About with it** 'Hand the drink around.'

250–1 **three morning draughts** i.e. an excessive amount

252 **betimes** early in the morning, as in *TN*, 2.3.1–2: 'Not to be abed after midnight is to be up betimes.'

255 **catchers** those who sing in a catch or round, each succeeding singer taking up or catching his part in turn (see *OED* catcher *n.* 3, citing this example)
round (1) a quantity of liquor served round a company, or a cup drunk in rotation by each person present; (2) a kind of song sung by two or more persons, each taking up the strain in turn. The song that follows contains the word *round*, continuing the 'whim'.

256.2 **drink about** drink in rotation

256.3 **grey-beards** old men. As the only people present onstage to be Oldrents' *catchers* are the Usher, Butler and Chaplain, and as we have already been told that the Usher is *grey* (153), and that Oldrents' servants have the same standard *livery-beards* (185, 232; and later Tallboy would like to be one of Oldrents' servants 'if I had but a grey beard', 369), presumably Oldrents' servants, together with Oldrents and Hearty, constitute the grey-bearded singers.

257–60 Music for this song, under the title 'A Round', by Mr William Lawes, is printed in Hilton (1667), no. 78 [misnumbered 79]. These words also feature as the burden or refrain of a freestanding lyric, 'A Way with all grief and give us

---

249 SD] *this edn; Butler offers him wine | Lawrence; Refusing the Butler's offer to serve him first | Brome Online*   256.1] *this edn*   256.2 is] *Brome Online*   257 SP] *Brome Online subst.*

Can charm away cares when the ground looks
    blue.   260

OLDRENTS Well said, old Hearty. And, gentlemen,
    welcome.

TALLBOY Ah – *He sighs.*

OLDRENTS Oh, mine ears! What was that? A sigh? And
    in my house? Look! Has it not split my walls? If not,   265
    make vent for it. Let it out; I shall be stifled else.

                                        Exit Chaplain.

OLIVER He hopes your pardon, sir, his cause considered.

OLDRENTS Cause? Can there be cause for sighing?

OLIVER He has lost his mistress, sir.

OLDRENTS Ha, ha, ha. Is that a cause? Do you hear me   270
    complain the loss of my two daughters?

OLIVER They are not lost, I hope, sir.

OLDRENTS No more can be his mistress. No woman can
    be lost. They may be mislaid a little, but found again,
    I warrant you.   275

TALLBOY Ah – *He sighs.*

OLDRENTS Od's my life! He sighs again, and means to
    blow me out of my house. To horse again! Here's no
    dwelling for me! Or stay; I'll cure him if I can. Give
    him more sack to drown his suspirations.   280

---

more sack', preceding Brome's *Weeding* in *Five New* (1659), sig. A1ᵛ, and presumably meant to be sung in it. As the successive singers take up the song, the word *round* will repeat such that the song itself becomes 'circular', its beginning and ending conjoining. See p. 268.

260 **looks blue** The phrase was proverbial, but usually one was said to drink until the ground looks blue, because vision is skewed after too much alcohol. Drinking to prevent the ground looking blue is probably a 'whim'. It refers to drinking in order to ease low spirits, as 'blue' meant 'depressed' or 'miserable' from at least 1550 (see *OED* blue *adj.* 3).

266 **vent** opening or slit

267 **cause** provocation

277 **Od's** God's

280 **suspirations** sighs; Hamlet inveighs against 'the windy suspiration of forced breath' (*Ham*, 1.2.79).

276 SD] *(Sigh.)*

205

*While Oldrents and Tallboy drink, Oliver takes
Hearty aside.*

OLIVER   Sir, I am chiefly to inform you of the disaster.

HEARTY   May it concern me?

OLIVER   Your nephew Martin has stolen my father's
ward, [*pointing at Tallboy*] that gentleman's bride
that should have been.   285

HEARTY   Indeed, sir.

OLIVER   'Tis most true – *He gives Hearty a letter.*

HEARTY   Another glass of sack! This gentleman brings
good news.

OLIVER   Sir, if you can prevent his danger –   290

HEARTY   Hang all preventions. Let 'em have their
destiny.

TALLBOY (*to Oldrents*)   Sir, I should have had her, 'tis
true – But she is gone, d'ye see? And let her go.

OLDRENTS   Well said. [*to Hearty*] He mends now.   295

TALLBOY   I am glad I am rid of her, d'ye see, before
I had more to do with her –

HEARTY [*to Oldrents*]   He mends apace. *Reads the letter.*

TALLBOY   – for should I have married her before she
had run away, d'ye see, and that she had run away,   300
d'ye see, after she had been married to me, d'ye see,
then I had been a married man without a wife, d'ye
see. Where now, she being run away before I am
married, d'ye see, I am no more married to her, d'ye
see, than she to me, d'ye see. And so long as I am   305
none of hers, d'ye see, nor she none of mine, d'ye
see, I ought to care as little for her, now she is run
away, d'ye see, as if she had stayed with me, d'ye
see.

---

281 **chiefly** especially; particularly   295 **mends** improves; regains health

283 SP] Dodsley; Old. *Q1*   284 SD] *this edn*   295 SD] *this edn*   298 SD1] *this edn*   SD2] *this edn;*
Hearty *reads the letter Q1*

OLDRENTS   Why, this is excellent! Come hither, Hearty.   310
TALLBOY   I perceive it now, and the reason of it, and
how, by consequence, d'ye see, I ought not to look
any further after her. (*Cries.*) But that she should
respect a poor base fellow, a clerk at the most and a
serving-man at best, before me, that am a rich man,   315
at the worst, and a gentleman, at least, makes me –
I know not what to say –
OLDRENTS   Worse than ever 'twas! Now he cries
outright.
TALLBOY   I know not what to say – what to say – oh –   320
HEARTY   Then I do, sir. The poor base fellow that you
speak of is my nephew; as good a gentleman as
yourself. I understand the business by your friend
here.
TALLBOY   I cry you mercy, sir.   325
OLDRENTS   You shall cry no mercy nor anything else
here, sir, nor for anything here, sir. This is no place to
cry in. Nor for any business. (*to Oliver*) You, sir, that
come on business –
OLIVER   It shall be none, sir.   330
OLDRENTS   My house is for no business but the belly-
business. You find not me so uncivil, sir, as to ask
you from whence you came, who you are, or what's
your business. I ask you no question. And can you be
so discourteous as to tell me, or my friend, anything   335
like business? If you come to be merry with me, you
are welcome. If you have any business, forget it; you
forget where you are else. And so to dinner.

---

316 **at least** The logic and balance of the
sentence requires 'at best': so *at least*,
though meaning 'at the very least', is
particularly jarring.

323 **understand . . . by** apprehend . . . from
325 **I . . . mercy** 'I beg your pardon.'
331–2 **belly-business** (1) food and drink
(known as belly-cheer); (2) laughter

328 SD] *after* that *Q1*

HEARTY   Sir, I pray let me only prevail with you but to
read this.   340

OLDRENTS   Spoil my stomach now, and I'll not eat this
fortnight. *He reads aside.*

HEARTY   While he reads, let me tell you, sir. That my
nephew Martin has stolen that gentleman's mistress,
it seems, is true. But I protest, as I am a gentleman,   345
I know nothing of the matter, nor where he or she is.
But, as I am the foresaid gentleman, I am glad on't
with all my heart. Ha, my boy Mat. Thou shalt restore
our house.

OLIVER *[Points at Tallboy.]*   Let him not hear, to grieve   350
him, sir.

HEARTY   Grieve him? What should he do with her?
Teach their children to cry?

TALLBOY   But I do hear you, though, and I scorn to cry
as much as you, d'ye see, or your nephew either,   355
d'ye see?

HEARTY   Now thou art a brave fellow. So, so, hold up
thy head, and thou shalt have a wife and a fine thing.

TALLBOY   Hang a wife, and pax o'your fine thing, d'ye
see? I scorn your fopperies, d'ye see?   360

OLDRENTS   And I do hear thee, my boy, and rejoice in
thy conversion. If thou canst but hold now.

TALLBOY   Yes, I can hold, sir. And I hold well with your
sack. I could live and die with it, as I am true Tallboy.

OLDRENTS   Now thou art a tall fellow, and shalt want   365
no sack.

---

348 **Mat** i.e. Martin
349 **restore our house** i.e. by marrying money
357–8 Hearty speaks to Tallboy as adults speak to children when offering bribes to stop them crying.

358 **a fine thing** (1) a lovely toy; (2) genitals
359 **pax** pox (*OED n.*² cites this instance)
360 **fopperies** follies
362 **hold** maintain or sustain (your mood)
365 **tall** brave or bold – a reference to his name

350 SD] *this edn*

TALLBOY   And, sir, I do honour you, d'ye see, and
should wish myself one of your household servants,
d'ye see, if I had but a grey beard, d'ye see? 'Hey',
as old Master Clack says.   370

OLDRENTS   Well, I have read the business here.

OLIVER   Call it not business, I beseech you, sir. We defy
all business.

TALLBOY   Ay, marry, do we, sir. D'ye see, sir? And
'a-hey', as old Master Clack says.   375

OLDRENTS   Gramercy, sack. Well, I have read the matter
here written by Master Clack. And do but bear up in
thy humour, I will wait upon thee home. *Knocking within*
Hark! They knock to the dresser. I have heard much
of this old, odd-ceited Justice Clack, and now I long   380
to see him. 'Tis but crossing the country two days
and a night's journey. We'll but dine, and away
presently. Bear up, I say, Master Tallboy.

TALLBOY   I will bear up, I warrant you, d'ye see, sir –   384
but here's a grudging still –   *Exeunt.*

369 **'Hey'** exclamation expressing exultation, incitement or surprise (see also 2.2.98n.)
372–3 Oliver quotes back at Oldrents his own anti-business sentiments of 328 and 331–2.
374 **marry** indeed; a term used to add emphasis to one's words
376 **Gramercy** thank you, from the Old French *grant merci*, 'great thanks'
378 **wait upon thee** accompany or escort you
379 **knock . . . dresser** Knocking on the dresser was a way of signalling that a meal was about to be served, as a dresser was the kitchen sideboard or table on which food was dressed or prepared, or

the dining-room or hall table from which dishes were served. Brome refers to the practice of knocking on the dresser in *Northern Lass*, too: 'All the unquietnesse will be in the Kitchin presently. If your meat stay for you. Gallants. (*Knock within.*) Twas time to speake. They knock at Dresser already. Will yee in?' (sig. M2ᵛ).
380 **odd-ceited** odd-conceited; eccentric (*OED* odd *adj.*, *n.*¹ and *adv.* C2 cites this usage)
385 **here's** Possibly Tallboy makes another attempt to find his heart at this word.
grudging reluctance

378 SD *Knocking*] *(Knock)*

4.2   *A great noise within of rude music, laughing,*
singing, etc.

Enter AMY, RACHEL [*and*] MERIEL.

AMY   Here's a wedding with a witness and a holiday
with a hoy! Let us out of the noise, as we love our
ears.

RACHEL   Yes, and here we may pursue our own discourse
and hear one another.   5

MERIEL   Concerning Springlove and yourself, Mistress
Amy.

AMY   Well, ladies, my confidence in you, that you are
the same that you have protested yourselves to
be, hath so far won upon me that I confess myself   10
well-affected both to the mind and person of that
Springlove. And, if he be, as fairly you pretend, a
gentleman, I shall easily dispense with fortune.

RACHEL, MERIEL   He is, upon our honours.

AMY   How well that high engagement suits your habits.   15

RACHEL   Our minds and blood are still the same.

AMY

I have passed no affiance to the other
That stole me from my guardian and the match
He would have forced me to, from which I would
Have fled with any, or without a guide.   20
Besides, his mind, more clownish than his habit,

4.2 Location: the beggars' camp
0   SD1.1 **rude** turbulent; boisterous
2   **a hoy** a call of 'hoy' (see *OED* hoy *int.*
and *n.²* B1, citing this example). Alternatively, as Q1's spelling suggests, the
word intended is in fact 'hoigh', meaning
a rush of excitement.
11 **well-affected** well-disposed
12 **fairly you pretend** you candidly allege

15 'How well that lofty pledge (*upon our
honours*, 14) suits your clothing' (ironic):
the words and clothes are at odds – the
one is courtly, but the other, beggarly.
17 **affiance** pledge of faith; formal marriage
troth or contract
the other i.e. Martin
21 **clownish** uncultivated – a comment
about the clothing that Martin and Amy
have chosen to wear. See 3.1.527–8.

4.2] *(Scena Secunda.)*   0 SD2 *and*] *Brome Online*   2 hoy] *(*hoigh*)*

Depraved by covetousness and cowardice,
Forced me into a way of misery:
To take relief from beggars.

MERIEL   From poor us.

AMY   And then, to offer to marry me under a hedge, as   25
the old couple were today, without book or ring, by
the chaplain of the beggars' regiment, your patrico,
only to save charges!

RACHEL   I have not seen the wretch these three hours.
Whither is he gone?   30

AMY   He told me, to fetch horse and fit raiment for us
and so to post me hence; but I think it was to leave
me on your hands.

MERIEL   He has taken some great distaste sure, for he is
damnable jealous.   35

RACHEL   Ay, didst thou mark what a wild look he cast
when Springlove tumbled her and kissed her on the
straw this morning, while the music played to the old
wedding-folks?

MERIEL   Yes, and then Springlove, to make him madder,   40
told him that he would be his proxy, and marry her
for him, and lie with her the first night with a naked
cudgel betwixt 'em, and make him a king of beggars.

25 **under a hedge** Beggars were said to choose hedges and woods for their weddings. Dekker writes of beggar marriages that 'Everie hedge being [a] Parish . . . the marrying of couples' takes place 'in a wood under a tree, or in the open field' (*Bellman*, sig. D4ʳ).

26 **without . . . ring** without a copy of the Book of Common Prayer or a wedding ring, the accoutrements of regular marriage

28 **charges** expense. Marriage cost a payment to the officiating minister. John Manningham, in his diary entry for 28 June 1602, wrote about a man who 'would needes be married', but 'the preist told him he would not marry him because he had not money sufficient to pay him his duty for that service' (42). Weddings also involved further additional outlay for a ring, clothes, a feast for friends and entertainments.

29 **the wretch** i.e. Martin

31 **fit raiment** suitable clothing

32 **post me hence** hurry away

34 **distaste** dislike; aversion

37 **tumbled her** rolled her about

41 **proxy** substitute

42–3 **lie . . . 'em** i.e. lie with her but without having sex. There may be an allusion to the practice of 'tarrying' or 'bundling', where couples before marriage could experiment in bed while keeping a bolster

AMY   I saw how it angered him. And I imagined then, and before, that there was more in Springlove than 45 downright beggar. But though he be never so good a gentleman, he shall observe fit time and distance till we are married.

RACHEL   Matrimony forbid else! [*aside*] She's taken. – But while we talk of a match towards, we are missed 50 within in the bride-barn among the revel-rout.

AMY   We have had all the sport they could make us in the past passages.

MERIEL   How cautious the old contracted couple were for portion and jointure! 55

RACHEL   What feoffees she, being an heir of fourscore and seven years stone-blind, had in trust for her estate.

AMY   And how carefully he secured all to himself, in case he outlived her, being but seven years older than 60 she. And what pains the lawyer of the rout here took about it.

---

between them to prevent activities getting out of hand. See also *Malfi*, 1.2.404–7, where the Duchess suggests to Antonio, 'We'll only lie and talk together . . . and if you please / Like the old tale in *Alexander and Ludowick*, / Lay a naked sword between us, keep us chaste.' Yet while a sword can be unsheathed, and so made *naked*, a *cudgel*, which has no sheath, cannot: *naked* is therefore used for suggestive purposes only.

47   **observe . . . distance** i.e. avoid making sexual advances

50   **towards** in preparation; imminent (*OED prep.* and *adv.* 8B, *predicative adv.* I 1)

51   **revel-rout** loud company of revellers – a variant of the term 'rebel-rout', a loud company of rebels

53   **passages** events; occurrences

55   **portion and jointure** Financial arrangements attendant on a marriage settlement: a *portion* was the dowry a woman brought to her husband in marriage; a *jointure* was the provision made by a husband for the support of his wife in the event of his death.

56–8   **feoffees . . . estate** Feoffees were people granted properties or fees in return for service (*OED* feoffee *n.* 2). The exclamation concerns what the old woman has put in place to prevent her property being given to her husband.

57   **stone-blind** completely blind (*OED adj.* (and *n.*) a)

49 SD] *Lawrence*

RACHEL   And then, how solemnly they were joined,
and admonished by our Parson Underhedge to live
together in the fear of the lash and give good example   65
to the younger reprobates: to beg within compass, to
escape the jaws of the justice, the clutch of the
constable, the hooks of the headborough and the
biting blows of the beadle. And, in so doing, they
should defy the devil and all his works, and after   70
their painful pilgrimage in this life, they should die
in the ditch of delight.

MERIEL   Oh, but poet Scribble's epithalamium:
          To the blind virgin of fourscore,
          And the lame bachelor of more: 75
          How Cupid gave her eyes to see,
          And Vulcan lent him legs,

---

64   **Parson Underhedge** i.e. the hedge-priest, the Patrico, who marries couples under hedges. See 25n.

64–72   **to live ... delight** a parody of the marriage service, which in the Book of Common Prayer of 1559 enjoins couples 'to lyve together after Goddes ordynaunce', after which each promises 'to have and to holde' the other 'from this day forwarde, for better, for worse, for rycher, for poorer, in syckenes, & in helth, to love and to cheryshe, tyll death us departe, accordynge to goddes holye ordinaunce' (BCP, sig. S7ᵛ).

65   **lash** whip; the standard punishment for rogues and beggars

66   **within compass** within the bounds of moderation. Sir John Davies remarks, 'in 200. yeares before (I speake much within compasse) no such Commission had bin executed' (266).

68   **hooks** seemingly a reference to *securis falcata*, a hooked axe that could be used

to prevent the arrested from escaping (also sometimes known as a bill or brown-bill)

headborough a parish officer identical in functions with the petty constable. Cf. *TS*, Ind.1.10–13: 'HOSTESS ... I must go fetch the headborough. SLY Third, or fourth, or fifth borough, I'll answer him by law.'

69   **biting ... beadle** See 3.1.471n.

71–2   **painful ... delight** the passage from life to afterlife conceived of in beggar terms

73   **epithalamium** nuptial song or poem written for a marriage, praising the bride and bridegroom and praying for their prosperity

76   **Cupid** in Roman mythology, the god of love, and son of Mercury and Venus, corresponding to the Greek Eros

77   **Vulcan** in Roman mythology, the lame god of fire and of metal-working, husband of Venus, corresponding to the Greek Hephaestus

How Venus caused their sport to be
Prepared with buttered eggs,
Yet, when she shall be seven years wed,   80
She shall be bold to say
She has as much her maidenhead
As on her wedding day.

RACHEL So may some wives that were married at
sixteen to lads of one-and-twenty.   85

AMY   But at the wedding feast, when the bride bridled it,
and her groom saddled it! There was the sport, in her
mumping, and his champing, the crew scrambling,
ourselves trembling; then the confusion of noises in
talking, laughing, scolding, singing, howling; with   90
their actions of snatching, scratching, tousing and
lousing themselves and one another –

---

78 **Venus** in Roman mythology, the goddess of beauty and love (especially sensual love), wife of Vulcan, corresponding to the Greek Aphrodite
sport amorous play

79 **buttered eggs** Butter and eggs were both regarded as aphrodisiacs. Eggs, thought to resemble semen, were said to invigorate or replace it; so a bandit in *Rebellion* calls for 'compound of Muskadine / And egges; for the truth is, I am a Gyant in my / Promises but in the act a Pigmy' (sig. G1ᵛ). Butter and eggs together are referred to in the ballad 'Westminster Frolic' (1670–96), where they are both said to be sexual restoratives and to represent the products of copulation itself: a wanton wife seduces a young man with 'When I'me in bed then come my Lad / the pleasure is so sweet; / We'l have a dish of butter'd Eggs / when we again do meet.'

81 **be bold** venture; take the liberty

86 **bridled** pun: (1) threw up the head and drew in the chin (as a horse does when reined in); (2) assumed a dignified or offended air or manner (*OED* bridle *v.* 3a); (3) 'played the bride'

87 **saddled** rode or bestrode (an animal). The suggestion is that the bride is a horse trying to throw the groom as he attempts to 'ride' her.

88 **mumping** chewing with or as with toothless gums; moving the jaws as if munching food. The term emphasizes the old woman's age and feebleness.
champing crushing and chewing by vigorous and noisy action of the jaws; probably a reference to elderly sexual desire. The old beggar may also be 'champing the bit' to get to his bride; in *Mad Couple*, an old man is accused as loving 'to champ upon the bit to please thy old coltish tooth still'; he enjoys 'the memory of the former sweets which now thou canst not relish' (sig. G1ʳ).
scrambling contending with each other, probably for a share of food

91 **tousing** pulling (a woman) about indelicately, or in horse-play; tousling

92 **lousing** delousing; tickling as though delousing

Enter SPRINGLOVE, VINCENT *and* HILLIARD.

But who comes here?

SPRINGLOVE   Oh, ladies, you have lost as much mirth as
would have filled up a week of holidays.   95

Springlove takes Amy aside, and courts her in a
gentle way.

VINCENT   I am come about again for the beggars' life
now.

RACHEL   You are. I am glad on't.

HILLIARD   There is no life but it.

VINCENT

With them there is no grievance or perplexity;   100
No fear of war or state disturbances;
No alteration in a commonwealth
Or innovation shakes a thought of theirs.

MERIEL

Of ours, you should say.

HILLIARD   Of ours, he means.
We have no fear of lessening our estates;   105

---

94 **lost** missed

95.1–2 **in a gentle way** (1) in a soft, gentle
fashion; (2) in a noble, gentlemanly
fashion

96 **I . . . for** 'I've come round to'

100 **no grievance** 'Grievance' had a particular parliamentary meaning at the
time: 'the submission of grievances by
parliament to the king in the form of
the petition of right had been a cause of
the 1629 dissolution and the instigation
of personal rule' (Sanders, *Caroline*, 65).
perplexity trouble; affliction

103 **innovation** political revolution, rebellion
or insurrection, here with the suggestion of
the pending Civil War between Parliament
and King. Cf. *1H4*, 5.1.76–8: 'poor dis-
contents, / Which gape and rub the elbow
at the news / Of hurly-burly innovation'.

103–4 **theirs . . . ours**   Vincent,   while
praising the beggars' life, forgets that he
is now one of them himself.

104–12 **Of ours, he means . . . fall** As
Martin Butler explains, this speech states
that the beggars live in a state of freedom from politics while also indicating that the free state is one of poverty:
'they have no fears and grudges about
unparliamentary taxation only because
they have no estates to lose in the first
place' (*Theatre*, 277–8). Jessica Dyson
points out: 'The reference to lending or
giving on command evokes the collection
of the Forced Loan and ship money, and
Hilliard's parenthetical "without taxation" highlights the potential illegitimacy
of such Crown demands' (236).

Nor any grudge with us, without taxation,
To lend or give, upon command, the whole
Strength of our wealth for public benefit;
While some that are held rich in their abundance –
Which is their misery, indeed – will see   110
Rather a general ruin upon all
Than give a scruple to prevent the fall.

VINCENT   'Tis only we that live.

RACHEL   I'm glad you are so taken with your calling.

MERIEL   We are no less, I assure you. We find the   115
sweetness of it now.

RACHEL   The mirth, the pleasure, the delights. No ladies
live such lives.

MERIEL   Some few, upon necessity, perhaps. But that's
not worth gramercy.   120

VINCENT [*aside to Hilliard*]   They will never be weary.

HILLIARD [*aside to Vincent*]   Whether we seem to like
or dislike, all's one to them.

VINCENT [*aside to Hilliard*]   We must do something to
be taken by and discovered; we shall never be   125
ourselves and get home again else.

Springlove and Amy come to the rest.

SPRINGLOVE [*to Amy*]   I am yours forever. [*to Rachel
and Meriel*] Well, ladies, you have missed rare sport,
but now the bride has missed you with her half-half

---

106 **Nor any grudge** nor does anyone
begrudgingly ask us
without taxation (1) without paying tax;
(2) without censure or reproof
109 **held ... abundance** said to be rich
because they have prosperity
111 **a general ... all** everything go to ruin
112 **scruple** small unit of weight or
measurement
116 **sweetness** delight

119 **upon necessity** i.e. through the power
of circumstance
120 **not worth** literally, not worth thank you,
i.e. not worth anything. See also 4.1.376n.
125 **taken** caught
128–9 **missed ... missed** failed to see
(because absent) . . . failed to see (because
blind)
129–30 **half-half eye** quarter eye – or two half
eyes: the old woman is, as we have already
learned (57), *stone*- (i.e. entirely) *blind*.

121, 122, 124 SDs] *Brome Online*   127 SD] *Lawrence*   127–8 SD] *Brome Online*

eye, and the bridegroom, with the help of his crutches,   130
is drawing her forth for a dance here in the opener
air. The house is now too hot for 'em.

[*Enter* SOLDIER, COURTIER, LAWYER, SCRIBBLE,
BRIDE *and* GROOM.]

Oh, here come the chief revellers. The soldier, the
courtier, the lawyer and the poet, who is Master of
their Revels, before the old couple in state. Attend,   135
and hear him speak as their inductor.

SCRIBBLE

Here, on this green, like king and queen,
For a short truce, we do produce
   Our old new-married pair.
Of dish and wallet, and of straw pallet,   140
With rags to show, from top to toe,
   She is the ancient heir.

He is the lord of bottle-gourd,
Of satchel great for bread and meat,
   And for small pence, a purse.   145
To all that give, 'Long may you live',
He loudly cries, but who denies
   Is sure to have his curse.

134–5 **Master . . . Revels** A Master of the Revels was a person appointed to organize censorship as well as revels – festivities such as dances and masques – in the Royal Household or the Inns of Court; here used ironically.

135 **in state** with great pomp and solemnity; with splendid or honorific trappings and insignia

136 **inductor** one who introduces or initiates

138 **short truce** temporary respite or intermission

140 **dish and wallet** Beggars carried a dish for alms of food or drink and a wallet for alms of money. Both are referred to in *How a Man May Choose*: 'if I bee turned a begging . . . Ile goe and set up my Trade, a dish to drink in that I have within, a wallet that Ile make of an old shirt . . .' (sig. I3^r-v).

143 **bottle-gourd** The fruit of *Lagenaria vulgaris*, dried and hollowed, was used for holding water.

144 **satchel** small bag with or without a strap to hang over the shoulders, often carried by beggars

132.1–2] *Haaker subst.*

VINCENT   Well said, field-poet. Phoebus, we see, inspires
    as well the beggar as the poet laureate.   150
SPRINGLOVE   And shines as warm under a hedge-bottom
    as on the tops of palaces.
SCRIBBLE   I have not done yet. Now this is to incite you
    to dance.

> Prepare yourselves, like fairy elves,   155
>   Now in a dance to show
> That you approve the God of love
>   Has many shafts to's bow

> With golden head, and some of lead,
>   But that which made these feel,   160
> By subtle craft, was sure a shaft
>   That headed was with steel.

> For they were old; no earth more cold;
>   Their hearts were flints entire;
> Whence the steel's stroke did sparks provoke   165
>   That set their bloods on fire.

> Now strike up, piper; and each lover here
> Be blithe and take his mistress by the goll.

149 **Phoebus** in Roman mythology, the god of the sun, and of poetry and music (see 3.1.101n.); he presided over the Muses, and was often seen as the genius or inspiration behind poetry.

150 **poet laureate** originally an eminent or distinguished poet, thought worthy of the laurel crown of the Muses. The title was, from Jonson onwards, given to a poet appointed as an officer of the Royal Household to write poetry for court and national occasions. Davenant had become poet laureate in 1638, and this passage may be a dig at him. See p. 28.

151 **shines ... warm** because Phoebus was also god of the sun

155 **fairy elves** Seemingly a variety of fairy, 'fairy elves' are usually associated with dancing in a ring. Henry Chettle, in 'The Shepheards Spring-Song', makes reference to dancing 'in ringlets, like to Fairie Elves' (sig. F4^r); and Arthur Golding describes Pan as being 'among the fayrye elves that dawnced round toogither' (137).

157–66 The conceit is that Cupid has arrows with shafts tipped with gold, lead and steel: as steel makes flints produce fire, so the steel-tipped shafts were able to provoke sparks in the flinty hearts of the cold elderly people.

157 **approve** acknowledge

160 **these** i.e. the old couple
    feel have their sensibilities excited (by one another)

161 **subtle craft** artful magic

168 **goll** hand: cf. *City Madam*, 4.1.21–2: 'All the gamsters are / Ambitious to shake

HILLIARD   That's no rhyme, poet.

SCRIBBLE   There's as good poetry in blank verse as   170
metre.   *Music.*

SPRINGLOVE   Come, hey! The dance, the dance! Nay,
we'll ha' the old couple in, as blind and lame as they
are.

BRIDE   What, will you so? [*Bride and Groom*] *dance.*   175

SPRINGLOVE   Well hobbled, bridegroom!

VINCENT   Well groped, bride!

HILLIARD   Hey, lusty! Hey, holiday!

SPRINGLOVE   Set 'em down; set 'em down. They ha'
done well.   180

GROOM   Aha! I am lustier than I was thirty years ago.

BRIDE   And I than I was threescore past. Ahem, ahem.

---

the golden golls / Of worshipfull Master *Luke*'. As Hilliard points out (169), a rhyme is expected and denied here. The unspoken word might be 'gear', which meant genitals: 'Chaude-colle' is described as 'Saltnesse, leacherousnesse, geereitch' in 1611 (Cotgrave, sig. Q4ᵛ). 'S.', an anonymous gentleman who supplied notes to Dodsley and Reed (*Old Plays 2*, 12.430), however, demurs: 'I believe that no wanton allusion was intended. This couplet does not necessarily join to the preceding song, and therefore might not be meant to rhyme. Had it been printed in the Roman type, as a speech, no one would have suspected obscenity to have been couched under it. The writers of this age were not very industrious either to exclude or palliate the grossness of their ideas; nor was this poet (the speaker) designed for a licentious character.'

170–1 **blank verse . . . metre** As, technically, blank verse contains metre (but lacks rhyme), Scribble is either anticipating ignorance in Hilliard or showing his own ignorance.

171 SD The music may be made by one of the fiddlers stipulated in 'The Persons of the Play' (see p. 89), or by the piper who has already played for some of the dances.

176 **hobbled** limped or clumsily danced

177 **groped** grasped or felt for (because she is blind), though perhaps with a suggestion of crude sexuality too

179 **Set 'em down** either (1) lower them (suggesting that the two old people have been picking one another up – or that they are sexually aroused); or (2) sit them down (suggesting that the two old people are becoming too tired, or too lusty, to go on)

182 **threescore past** sixty (years) ago
Ahem, ahem possibly a factitious clearing of the throat as a way of providing a mock 'nudge' (cf. the anonymous *Wit*: 'I hope there is no body heares mee: a hem, well I must cleere this same rough throate of mine', sig. C2ᵛ); possibly a way of indicating that the old lady is struggling for breath as a sign of her lack of health (cf. *Sparagus Garden*: 'Uh, uh, uh . . . A hem, a hem, I will out-live you both', sig. L3ᵛ).

175 SD *Bride and Groom*] *Lawrence subst.*

VINCENT   What a night here's towards!

HILLIARD   Sure they will kill one another.

SCRIBBLE   Each with a fear the tother will live longest.   185

SPRINGLOVE   Poet, thou hast spoken learnedly and acted
bravely. Thou art both poet and actor.

SCRIBBLE   So has been many famous men. And if here
were no worse, we might have a masque or a comedy
presented tonight in honour of the old couple.   190

VINCENT
Let us each man try his ability
Upon some subject now extempore.

SPRINGLOVE   Agreed. Give us a theme, and try our
action.

SCRIBBLE   I have already thought upon't. I want but   195
actors.

HILLIARD   What persons want you? What would you
present?

SCRIBBLE
I would present a commonwealth: Utopia,
With all her branches and consistencies.   200

RACHEL   I'll be Utopia. Who must be my branches?

---

183 **towards** approaching; in prospect

187 **bravely** capitally; well

188 **many famous men** Examples include Shakespeare, Jonson, Nathan Field and Thomas Heywood.

189 **masque** a form of courtly dramatic entertainment, often richly symbolic, in which music and dancing played a substantial part, costumes and stage machinery tended to be elaborate and the audience might be invited to contribute to the action or the dancing. The masque became a clearly defined genre during the reigns of James I and Charles I.

192 **extempore** composed, spoken, performed or acted at the moment, without premeditation, preparation or a written text

193 **theme** topic or subject to be extemporized around

199 **commonwealth** government or independent community operating by the common consent of the whole people
Utopia Originally written in Latin in 1516, Thomas More's *Utopia* was about an imaginary island ('Utopia' translates as both 'good place' and 'no place'); 'Utopia' came to represent any imaginary country or locality that had a revealing attitude to politics, laws, customs or conditions. As More's *Utopia* was also thought to comment on England itself, the idea of staging a Utopia play about a disintegrating country is socially telling.

200 **branches and consistencies** subdivisions and agreements

SCRIBBLE   The country, the city, the court and the camp,
    epitomized and personated by a gentleman, a
    merchant, a courtier and a soldier.
SOLDIER   I'll be your soldier. Am not I one? Ha!   205
COURTIER   And am not I a fashionable courtier?
SCRIBBLE   But who the citizen or merchant?
SPRINGLOVE   I.
VINCENT   And I your country gentleman.
HILLIARD   Or I.   210
SCRIBBLE   Yet to our moral I must add two persons,
    divinity and law.
LAWYER   Why, la you now! And am not I a lawyer?
SCRIBBLE   But where's divinity?
VINCENT   Marry, that I know not. One of us might do   215
    that, if either knew how to handle it.
SPRINGLOVE   Where's the old patrico, our priest, my
    ghostly father? He'll do it rarely.
1 BEGGAR   He was telling fortunes e'en now to country
    wenches. I'll fetch him –   *Exit.*
SPRINGLOVE   That patrico I wonder at. He has told me   221
    strange things in clouds.
AMY   And me somewhat that I may tell you hereafter.
SPRINGLOVE   That you shall be my bride?
AMY   I will not tell you now.   225
VINCENT   Well, but what must our speeches tend to?
    What must we do one with another?

203 **epitomized** characterized; summarized
208 **I** While the other characters identify
    with the jobs or rank they had before,
    Springlove identifies with what he will,
    presumably, become – a merchant and
    citizen.
211 **moral** morality play
213 **la you** exclamation used to introduce
    or accompany a conventional phrase or
    an address, or to call attention to an
    emphatic statement
218 **ghostly father** spiritual father; father
    confessor. The term was often used of
    priests, and is another of the play's
    gestures towards Catholicism.
219 SP Hitherto '1 Beggar' has been Scribble,
    but as Scribble needs to remain onstage to
    introduce his play, one of the other beggars
    – Bride, Groom, Soldier, Courtier or
    Lawyer – must go off to fetch the Patrico.
221 **told** foretold
226 **tend to** lead or incline towards

SCRIBBLE   I would have the country, the city and the
    court be at great variance for superiority. Then would
    I have divinity and law stretch their wide throats to   230
    appease and reconcile them. Then would I have the
    soldier cudgel them all together and overtop them
    all. Stay, yet I want another person.
HILLIARD   What must he be?
SCRIBBLE   A beggar.   235
VINCENT   Here's enough of us, I think. What must the
    beggar do?
SCRIBBLE   He must at last overcome the soldier and
    bring them all to Beggars' Hall. And this, well acted,
    will be for the honour of our calling.   240
ALL   A Scribble! A Scribble!
HILLIARD   Come, where's this patrico, that we may
    begin?

Enter PATRICO.

PATRICO
    Alack and welladay,
    This is no time to play.   245
    Our quarter is beset.

229 **at great variance** in great discord or
contention
230 **stretch ... throats** cry out loudly. Cf.
Isabella, in *MM*, 2.4.152–3: 'with an
outstretch'd throat I'll tell the world
aloud / What man thou art'.
232 **overtop** surmount and overpower
239 **Beggars' Hall** mock-grandiose term for
any barn in which beggars kept company
– so the opposite of court, as exemplified
in the poem 'The Prodigal Son': 'I lost
the Court, and found the Beggars hall'
(*Flamma*, 82). Daniel Heinsius dedicated
his book in praise of the louse to 'the
worshipful Masters and Warders of

Beggars Hall' (sig. B1ʳ); a popular song
of the time was 'The Map of Mock-begger
Hall with his Situation in the Spacious
Country, called, Anywhere' (1634). *Brome
online* suggests that the joking assumption behind this term 'is that beggars, like
grocers, barber-surgeons, glovers, or any
other city company, constitute a respectable guild of citizens with a meeting-hall
belonging to the company'.
240 **calling** vocation, i.e. to be a beggar
244 exclamations expressing sorrow or
lamentation
246 **quarter** residence
    beset surrounded

244–8] *this edn; Q1 lines* play. / Net. / Glee. /

We are all in the net.

Leave off your merry glee.

VINCENT

You begin scurvily.

SPRINGLOVE   Why, what's the matter?   250

BEGGARS (*within*)   Bing awast, bing awast! The queer
cove and the harman-beck!

Some BEGGARS *run over the stage.*

SPRINGLOVE   We are beset indeed. What shall we do?

VINCENT [*to Hilliard*]   I hope we shall be taken.

HILLIARD [*to Vincent*]   If the good hour be come,   255
welcome by the grace of good fortune.

Enter SENTWELL, CONSTABLE, Watch.
The [beggar] crew slip away.

SENTWELL   Beset the quarter round. Be sure that none
escape.

SPRINGLOVE   Lord to come with you, blessed master, to
a many distressed –   260

VINCENT, HILLIARD   – duly and truly pray for you.

RACHEL, MERIEL   Good your good worship, duly and
truly, *etc.*

---

247 **in the net** i.e. trapped like birds or fish

248 **glee** entertainment; sport

249 Vincent, picking up the Patrico's rhyme, critiques it while responding in it; he appears to think that this is the start to the extemporized play.
scurvily unsatisfactorily; rudely

251 **Bing awast!** *cant* Hurry away!

251–2 **queer cove** *cant* rogue

252 **harman-beck** *cant* constable

255 **good hour** fortunate or happy time – from the French '*à la bonne heure*'

256.1 **Watch** Literally 'those who watch', the watch patrolled and guarded the streets of a town, proclaimed the hour and accompanied the constable when necessary.

257 **Beset** encircle

263 *etc.* The speakers are to go on in the same vein, presumably repeating 'duly and truly pray for you' as at 3.1.540–1.

251 SP] *this edn; not in Q1*   254, 255 SDs] *Lawrence*   256.2 beggar] *this edn*

SENTWELL A many counterfeit rogues! So frolic and so
    lamentable all in a breath? You were acting a play   265
    but now. We'll act with you. Incorrigible vagabonds.
SPRINGLOVE Good master, 'tis a holiday with us. An
    heir was married here today.
SENTWELL Married! Not so, I hope. Where is she? 'Tis
    for an heir we seek.   270
SPRINGLOVE [*Draws forward Bride.*] Here she is,
    master. [*to the others*] Hide yourselves in the straw
    – the straw! Quickly, into the straw –
SENTWELL What tellest thou me of this? An old blind
    beggar-woman! We must find a young gentlewoman-   275
    heir among you. Where's all the rest of the crew?
CONSTABLE Slipped into the barn and the bushes by,
    but none can scape.
SENTWELL Look you to that, and to these here.
                          Exit with [Constable and] Watch.
SPRINGLOVE [*to the others*] Into the straw, I say!   280
VINCENT No, good Springlove. The ladies and we are
    agreed now to draw stakes and play this lousy game
    no further.
HILLIARD We will be taken and disclose ourselves. You
    see we shall be forced to it else. The cowardly clerk 285
    has done't to save himself.
SPRINGLOVE Do you fear no shame, ladies?
RACHEL Dost think it a shame to leave begging?
MERIEL Or that our father will turn us out to it again?

---

264 **counterfeit** disguised or pretend –
    because they suddenly seem unhappy
    when hitherto they have been joyously
    preparing a play
282 **draw stakes** withdraw what is staked as
    a wager (*OED* stake *n.*² 1d)
    lousy (1) dreadful; (2) louse-inducing

284 **disclose ourselves** reveal who we really
    are
285 **cowardly clerk** i.e. Martin, clerk to
    Justice Clack, who has revealed the
    beggars' whereabouts to save himself
    from them

271 SD] *this edn*   272 SD] *this edn*   279 SD *Constable and*] *this edn*   280 SD] *this edn*

SPRINGLOVE   Nay, since you are so resolute, know that I   290
myself begin to find this is no course for gentlemen.
This lady shall take me off it.

AMY   Make but your protestations good, and take me
yours. And for the gentleman that surprises us,
though he has all my uncle's trust, he shall do   295
anything for me to our advantage.

VINCENT   If, Springlove, thou couldst post now to thy
tiring-house and fetch all our clothes, we might get
off most neatly.

SPRINGLOVE   A horse and six hours' travel would do   300
that.

AMY   You shall be furnished, doubt not.

Enter SENTWELL, [CONSTABLE *and*] *Watch.*

SENTWELL   She's scaped or is invisible. [*to Springlove*]
You, sir, I take to be the chief rogue of this regiment.
[*to Constable*] Let him be whipped till he brings   305
forth the heir.

CONSTABLE   That is but till he stinks, sir. Come, sir,
strip, strip!

AMY   Unhand him, sir. What heir do you seek, Master
Sentwell?   310

---

294 **the gentleman . . . us** i.e. Sentwell

297 **post** hurry; make haste

298 **tiring-house** room for 'attiring' or dressing. The tiring-house was the place in which actors dressed and undressed; hence this is a metatheatrical joke. Within the narrative, the wish is that Springlove will go to the place where the clothes have been stored – presumably Oldrents' barn; in the world of the theatre, the wish is that the actor playing Springlove will fetch the clothes from backstage.

298–9 **get off** escape punishment

302 **furnished** supplied; i.e. she will supply Springlove with money later.

304 **regiment** organization

305–7 **whipped . . . stinks** i.e. beaten until he farts and excretes. This was a proverbial phrase; see Dent (B160.11), which quotes, among other examples, 'be[a]t me tyll I fart & shyt againe' (Plautus, sig. D3ᵛ). There is an additional pun on *heir* and 'air'.

302 SD CONSTABLE] *Lawrence and*] this edn   303, 305 SDs] *Brome Online*

SENTWELL [*aside*]   Precious, how did my haste oversee her? – Oh, Mistress Amy! Could I, or your uncle Justice Clack, a wiser man than I, ever ha' thought to have found you in such company?

AMY   Of me, sir, and my company, I have a story to   315
delight you, which, on our march towards your house, I will relate to you.

SENTWELL
And thither will I lead you as my guest.
But to the law surrender all the rest.   319
I'll make your peace.

AMY   We must fare all alike.   *Exeunt.*

5.1   [*Enter*] CLACK [*and*] MARTIN.

CLACK   I have forgiven you. Provided that my niece be safely taken and so to be brought home. Safely, I say; that is to say, unstained, unblemished, undishonoured; that is to say, with no more faults, criminal or accusative, than those she carried with her.   5

MARTIN   Sir, I believe –

CLACK   Nay, if we both speak together, how shall we hear one another? You believe her virtue is armour

---

311 **Precious** for 'God's precious blood' or 'God's precious body'
   oversee overlook
316 **march** steady, measured or deliberate walk
320 **make your peace** effect a reconciliation for you
   We ... alike i.e. we must all be treated in the same way (either all as guests or all under arrest as beggars).
5.1 Location: Justice Clack's house

4   **that ... say** Clack is a caricature of a man of law whose constant need to rephrase what he has just said is illustrated by his repeated use of 'that is to say'.
5   **accusative** accusatory or containing an accusation. Cf. 'Episcopacy and their Cathedrals (with whom it is now the *Accusative* age)' (Smectymnuus, 168).
8–9 **armour of proof** armour of tested power of resistance, i.e. impenetrable, resistant.

311 SD] *Brome Online*   **5.1**] (Actus Quintus)   0 SD *Enter*] *Dodsley*   *and*] *Brome Online*

of proof, without your council or your guard, and
therefore you left her in the hands of rogues and   10
vagabonds to make your own peace with me. You
have it. Provided, I say, as I said before, that she be
safe, that is to say, uncorrupted, undefiled, that is to
say – as I said before.
MARTIN   Mine intent, sir, and my only way –   15
CLACK   Nay, if we both speak together, how shall we
hear one another? As I said before. Your intent, and
your only way, you would ha' said, was to run away
with her, and that by her only instigation, to avoid
the tie of marriage with Master Tallboy; that is to say, 20
to shun the match that I had made for her; that is to
say, rather to disobey me than to displease herself.
Wherein, although she did not altogether transgress
the law, she did both offend and prejudice me – an
instrument, nay, I may say, a pillar thereof. And you,   25
in assisting her, furthering, and conveying her away,
did not only infringe the law in an unlawful departure
from your master, but in a higher point: that is to say,
top and top-gallows high. I would ha' found a jury
should ha' found it so.   30

Clack claims Martin believes Amy has
inviolable virginity.
11 **make . . . peace** effect . . . reconciliation
12, 17 **as . . . before** an example of 'the
premature cue' (Palfrey and Stern, ch. 6).
Clack three times gives out the same cue
of 'as I said before' to Martin, whose part
will have looked something like

———————— as I said before
Mine intent, sir, and my only way –

If Martin starts to respond each time he
hears the cue, that makes sense both of
Clack's 'Nay, if we both speak together,
how shall we hear one another?' and of
his 'Your intent, and your only way, you
would ha' said'.

19 **only** sole
25 **instrument . . . pillar** Clack corrects himself from saying that he is an agent of the
law, to saying that he is a mainstay of it.
28 **higher point** a 'whim': Clack segues from
higher point meaning point of greater
magnitude to *higher point* meaning the
highest part of a gallows.
29 **top and top-gallows** a parody of the
phrase 'top and topgallant' (short for
'topsail and topgallant sail'), which was
used to mean 'with all sail set, in full
array or career' (*OED* top *n.* 1 III 9c);
hence, here, fully set (on being hanged)
29–30 **I . . . so** Justice Clack declares that
he would have used his powers to find a
jury to hang Martin. He may be boasting

MARTIN   But sir, an't please you –

CLACK   Must we then both speak together? Have I not
borne with thee, to speak all thou pleasest in thy
defence? Have I not broke mine own rule, which is
to punish before I examine, and so to have the law   35
the surer o'my side? And dost thou still persist? Hold
your own peace or, as I am a Justice of the King's, I
will unsay what I said before, and set a 'Currat Lex'
at you, sirrah, that shall course you up the heavy hill.
[*Martin kneels.*] Oh, is your tongue fallen into your   40
leg now? Do not you know I have acquitted you?
Provided – as I said before. [*Martin rises.*] Go your
way in, and see that the gentlemen, who, I think,

about his powers of rhetoric, or suggesting that he would influence the outcome of the law case using threats or bribery.

35 **to punish . . . examine** a satirical commonplace that, though a criticism of current legal practice, had its roots in a saying of Rhadamanthus in Virgil's *Aeneid*, 6.567, '*Castigatque auditque dolos*', regularly translated as 'he punishes first and hears afterwards' (though the phrase probably actually means 'he punishes, and, for that purpose, hears the story of their crimes'). The practice was also known as 'Lydford Law' because of Lydford prison's poor reputation, as in, '*Lydford law*, by which they used to hang men first, and endite them afterwards' (Heylyn, 4).

36–7 **Hold . . . peace** Be quiet!

37 **Justice . . . King's** i.e. Justice of the King's Bench. Clack holds one of three judicial positions in the Court of King's Bench, a common law court that covered criminal matters and cases concerning the monarch.

38 **'Currat Lex'** Latin for 'let the law run (its course)'. Isaac Reed, in his 'additional notes' to *A Jovial Crew* (*Old Plays 2*, 12.430), suggests, 'Justice Clack is here probably made to allude to the print placed before the play of *Ignoramus*, published 1631; in which the principal character, which gives name to the drama, is represented with a label issuing out of his mouth, on which is written the words *currat rex*.'

39 **course . . . hill** send you to the gallows. Criminals were conveyed from Newgate and the Tower to the gallows at Tyburn by going up Holborn Hill, 'heavy' with grief in a cart; hence the nickname 'heavy hill' for Holborn. Cf. 'We wheel'd the top of th' heavy hill, call'd *Holborne*, / (Up which hath been full many a sinfull soule borne,)' (Taylor, *Travels*, 5).
course make you run

40–1 **tongue . . . leg** Martin has given up pleading with his tongue, so is kneeling instead. Cf. Sir Walter Terrill in *Satiromastix*, 3.2.36–9, who says, 'our very knees / Must humbly seeme to talke, and sute out speech; / For a true furnisht Cortyer hath such force, / Though his tonge faints, his very legs discourse'.

40, 42 SDs] *this edn*

were got in sack, christened in sack, nursed with
sack and fed up to grey hairs with only sack – see,   45
I say, that they want no sack.   [*Exit Martin.*]
My son Oliver, I thank him, has brought me a pair of
such guests –

Enter SENTWELL.

Oh, Master Sentwell! Good news?

SENTWELL   Of beggarly news, the best you have heard.   50

CLACK   That is to say, you have found my niece among
the beggars. That is to say –

SENTWELL   True, Sir Oliver, I found her –

CLACK   Now if we both speak together, who shall hear
one another?   55

SENTWELL   I thought your desire was to be informed.

CLACK   I can inform myself, sir, by your looks. I have
taken a hundred examinations i'my days, of felons
and other offenders, out of their very countenances,
and wrote 'em down verbatim to what they would   60
have said. I am sure it has served to hang some of
'em and whip the rest.

SENTWELL [*aside*]   Justice Clack still! He must talk all.
His clack must only go.

44   **got** begotten, conceived
     nursed reared; breastfed
51–2 **That . . . say** Another example of the
     premature cue. Sentwell's part will look
     something like this:

     ————————————That is to say –
     True, Sir Oliver, I found her –

     If Sentwell speaks as soon as he hears the
     cue, he will interrupt Clack, so bringing
     about the riposte, 'Now, if we both speak
     together, who shall hear one another?'
57   **I can . . . looks** Clack's refusal to be
     informed and insistence on guessing

creates links between him and Oldrents,
as Oldrents similarly had refused to read
the letter that would have informed him
of his daughters' disappearance (see
2.2.108–9).
60   **verbatim** 'word for word'; in the exact
     words (ironic)
63   **still** now as before
64   **clack** tongue; a contemptuous usage (see
     OED n. 8, citing this instance), named
     after the din made by senseless or continu-
     ous chatter
     go go on or be allowed to go on

44 christened] *(christned)*   46 SD] *Brome Online*   63 SD] *Lawrence*

CLACK   But to the point. You have found my niece. You   65
    have left her at your own house, not only to shift her
    out of her disguise, but out of her shame to come
    nearer me, until I send her pardon.
SENTWELL   Most true, sir. But the company she was in –
CLACK   Again! Do not I know the company? Beggars,   70
    rogues, vagabonds and hedge-birds.
SENTWELL   But do you know whom, or how many we
    have taken, and how the rest escaped?
CLACK   A needless knowledge. Why should we take
    more than herself? Or how could you take those that   75
    could escape?

Enter MARTIN.

MARTIN   Sir, the old gentlemen within sent me to wait
    upon you. Without you, they say, they need not my
    service.
CLACK   Tell 'em then, I'll wait on 'em presently.   80
                                              Exit Martin.
SENTWELL   But sir, we have taken with her such beggars,
    such rogues, such vagabonds and such hedge-birds,
    since you call 'em so, as you never knew or heard of,
    though now the countries swarm with 'em under
    every hedge, as if an innumerable army of 'em were   85
    lately disbanded without pay. Hedge-birds, said you?

66   **shift** change
71   **hedge-birds** literally, birds that live in or
    frequent hedges, and so a continuation
    of the play's bird imagery; figuratively,
    people born, brought up or accustomed to
    loiter under hedges – vagrants, vagabonds
    and beggars
77–8   **wait upon** accompany
84   **countries** rural districts, distant from
    cities and courts

85–6   **army ... pay** The King's northern
    army was, from early 1641, rioting for
    lack of pay. As Parliament lacked the
    money to pay military arrears, some of
    the army's soldiers were then disbanded;
    they often ended up begging in London.
    Ironically, the beggars are said to
    resemble the army rather than vice versa.

Hedge-ladybirds, hedge-cavaliers, hedge-soldier, hedge-lawyer, hedge-fiddlers, hedge-poet, hedge-players and a hedge-priest among 'em. Such we have taken for the principals. But to see how the multitude   90
scaped us was more sport than pity. How, upon a watchword given, they in the instant vanished by more several ways than there were legs among 'em; how the cripples leaped over pales and hedges; how the blind found their way through lakes and ditches;   95
how a doxy flew with two children at her back, and two more, perhaps, in her belly –

CLACK   A hedge-priest have you taken, say you?

SENTWELL   Yes, sir, an old patrico, an ancient prophet, to tell fortunes and cozen our poor country people of   100
their single money.

Enter OLIVER.

OLIVER   Sir, Master Oldrents, in that he enjoys not your company, begins to doubt of his welcome.

CLACK   Who led him into that doubt? I, or you that brought him hither?   105

OLIVER   Sir, his own desire and love to you brought him hither. I but showed him the way.

CLACK   You reason fairly. Tell him I come.

OLIVER   Pray, sir, be pleased to do so, for he says –

CLACK   Nay, if we both talk together –   110

OLIVER   – who shall hear one another?   *Exit.*

---

90 **principals** those first or highest in rank or importance
91 **more ... pity** more diversion than matter for sorrow
92 **watchword** password; here, a prearranged word used as a signal
93 **several** separate
94–5 **cripples ... blind** i.e. they are none of the things they pretend to be.

94 **pales** fences or enclosing barriers
101 **single money** single coins, hence small change
102 **enjoys not** does not have the pleasure of
103 **doubt of** call in question
104–5 i.e. they are not in fact welcome to Clack. See also 150–1.

CLACK   But are there players among the apprehended?

SENTWELL   Yes, sir. And they were contriving to act a
play among themselves, just as we surprised 'em and
spoiled their sport.   115

CLACK   Players! I'll pay them above all the rest.

SENTWELL   You shall do well in that, to put 'em in stock
to set up again.

CLACK   Yes, I'll put 'em in stocks, and set 'em up to the
whipping-post. They can act justices, can they? I'll   120
act a justice among 'em; that is to say, I will do
justice upon them; that is to say –

SENTWELL   Pray sir, be not severe; they act kings and
emperors as well as justices. And justice is blind,
they say: you may therefore be pleased to wink a   125
little. I find that you have merry old gentlemen in
your house that are come far to visit you. I'll
undertake that these players, with the help of their
poet, in a device which they have already studied,
and a pack of clothes which I shall supply 'em with,   130
shall give your guests much content and move
compassion in you towards the poor strolls.

---

116 **pay** (1) punish; take revenge on; (2)
reward with money

117–19 **put ... stock ... put ... stocks** (1)
provide them with stock to furnish a
business; (2) put them in the stocks
(a punishment). The 'whim' responds
to the two potential meanings of *pay* in
116.

120 **act justices** play at being judges

121 **act a justice** bring about judicial
proceedings

124 **justice is blind** proverbial (Dent,
J105.11)

125 **wink** close your eyes

128 **undertake** take upon myself; promise

129 **device** a fanciful invention, often a
dramatic one. Theseus, in *MND*, 5.1.48–
51, recalls '"The riot of the tipsy

Bacchanals" ... That is an old device,
and it was play'd / When I from Thebes
came last.'

already studied theatrical terminology
meaning 'learned off by heart in advance'.
As the play is to be *extempore* (4.2.192),
'study' will have taken no time at all.

130 **pack** bundle

132 **strolls** according to *OED* stroll *n.* 1,
which quotes this line, those who roam
or wander (stroll), though the word is
more likely to be a shortened form of
'strolling players'. *Spanish Gypsy*, 2.1.18–
19, has, 'We'll entertain no mounte-
banking stroll, / No piper, fiddler, tumbler
through small hoops', and later, 2.1.214–
15, 'You're / but a country company of
strolls.'

CLACK   But you know my way of justice – and that's a
sure way – is to punish 'em first and be compassionate
afterwards, as I find 'em upon their examination.   135

SENTWELL   But for your guests' sakes, who, I know, do
favour and affect the quality of actors very much,
permit 'em, sir. It will enlarge your entertainment
exceedingly.

CLACK   And perhaps save me the expense of a runlet   140
of sack the while. Well, sir, for that respect, and
upon your undertaking that they shall please, I will
prorogue my justice on the rogues. And so to my
merry gentlemen, whom I will prepare to see their
interlude against after-supper. But pray, Master   145
Sentwell, as you have found my niece, look to her,
and see her decently brought home.

SENTWELL   In her own best apparel. But you must
prorogue your displeasure to her too.

CLACK   I will do so, until my scarce-welcome guests be   150
gone.

Enter RANDALL.

RANDALL   Sir, my master sends you word, and plainly,
that without your company your entertainment
stinks. He has commanded me saddle his nags and

---

135 **as ... 'em** according to the way I find
them on investigation
137 **favour and affect** encourage and like
quality profession; occupation, especially that of an actor
138 **enlarge your entertainment** render your
hospitality more extensive
140 **runlet** the quantity of liquor, varying
between a pint or quart and three or four
gallons, contained in a particular cask
or vessel

141 **the while** during that time
for that respect in respect of that
142 **undertaking** pledge or promise
143 **prorogue** defer; postpone
145 **against** in time for; in anticipation of
after-supper the time after supper; the
time between supper and bedtime (*OED*
after-supper *n.* and *adj.* 1)
150 **scarce-welcome** (1) scarcely welcomed
yet; (2) not welcome
154 **stinks** is offensive; is abhorrent – from
smells foul

away tonight. If you come not at once, twice, thrice,   155
he's gone presently, before supper; he'll find an host
at an inn worth a hundred o'you.

CLACK   Good friend, I will now satisfy your master,
without telling him he has a saucy knave to his man.

RANDALL   Thank your worship.   *Exit Clack.*

SENTWELL   Do you hear, friend – you serve Master   161
Oldrents.

RANDALL   I could ha' told you that. And the best
housekeeper my master is of any gentleman in the
county he dwells in, and the best master to a man, as   165
I, the worst of twenty, can say for him, and would be
ashamed to say less.

SENTWELL   Your name is Randall.

RANDALL   Forgi' me! Are you so wise? You are too
young to be my godsire, and I hope not old enough to   170
be a witch. How know you that I am Randall? Were
you ever at my master's house i'Nottinghamshire, or
at Dunghillford, where I was born?

SENTWELL   No. But I have notes to know you by.

RANDALL   I was never twelve mile from thence i'my   175
life before this journey. God send me within ken of
our own kitchen smoke again.

---

155 **at once, twice, thrice** segues from
come . . . at once to the practice of count-
ing 'one, two, three' before leaving. It is
possible that the phrase 'once, twice,
thrice, gone!' was used, as later, in bargaining or conjuring.

156 **host** Inns, which were public houses that
also offered lodging, had landlords known
as 'hosts' who entertained for payment.

159 **saucy knave** insolent rogue
to his man for his servant

166 **worst of twenty** i.e. of Oldrents' twenty
servants, he is the worst.

170 **godsire** godfather

170–1 **old . . . witch** Witches were associated with infertility and hence with age;
see Botelho and Thane.

173 **Dunghillford** a comic name made from
'dunghill', a heap of dung or refuse, and
'ford', a shallow place in a river or other
water, which may be crossed by wading

174 **notes** signs or indications – characteristics
or distinguishing features – from which
something may be inferred

176 **ken** range of sight

160 SD] *after 159 Q1*

SENTWELL   Your master's steward's name is Springlove.

RANDALL   Master Springlove, an't please you. There is
not an honester gentleman between this and the head   180
of him. And my heart's with him, where'er he is.
Know you him too?

SENTWELL   Yes, and your master's daughters too.

RANDALL   Whau!

SENTWELL   And that they are all from home, your master   185
knows not where.

RANDALL   Whau, whau! Know you that too?

SENTWELL   Yes, and the two young gentlemen that are
with 'em, Master Vincent and Master Hilliard.

RANDALL   Whau, whau, again. You know 'em all, I   190
think. But know you where they all are?

SENTWELL   Even hereby, at my own house.

RANDALL   Whau! –

SENTWELL   And they, knowing that your master is here,
and Master Hearty too –   195

RANDALL   Whau, whau!

SENTWELL   And yourself too, they directed me to find
you, Randall, and bring you to 'em.

RANDALL   Whau, whau, whau, whau. – Why do we not
go, then?   200

SENTWELL   But secretly. Not a word to anybody.

RANDALL   Mum. – Will you go, then?

180–1 **this ... him** Randall will indicate
some part of his own body (probably his
head) with the word *this*. It is possible
that he reprises Tallboy's joke, and
struggles to locate his heart; see 4.1.50n.

184 **Whau!** Well! Why! (northern British
dialect), an exclamation that may derive
from 'whannow' or 'what now'.

185 **from** away from

192 **hereby** close by

202 **Mum** 'Hush!', 'Silence!', 'Not a word!';
also used to represent the inarticulate
sound made with closed lips as an indica-
tion of inability or unwillingness to
speak

Enter MARTIN.

MARTIN Oh, Master Oldrents' man. Pray let me entreat
you into the buttery.

RANDALL [*to Sentwell*] Will you go, master gentleman?   205

MARTIN Indeed it is my master's desire, and he
commanded me.

RANDALL Now, when it's suppertime, did he? To fill
my belly with thin drink to save his meat? It's the
manner in churls' houses. Will you go, master   210
gentleman?

MARTIN In troth, my master is so merry with yours
within –

RANDALL Shite o'your master. My master's steward's
a better man. I'll to him at this gentleman's house   215
and all the rest. Whau, whau!

SENTWELL [*to Randall*] Randall, you forget.

RANDALL Mum again, then. Why would you not go,
then?   [*Exeunt*] *Sentwell and Randall.*

MARTIN The man's as mad as his master. The strangest   220
strangers that ever came to our house.

Enter TALLBOY.

TALLBOY Well, Martin, for confessing thy fault, and
the means thou madest whereby she is taken, I am

---

203 **entreat** persuade; induce

209 **thin drink** another term for 'small beer':
beer of weak or inferior quality with a
low alcohol content. The idea that drinking spoils the appetite was commonplace.
In *Shoemaker's*, 5.4.8–9, Hodge explains
how the prentices 'have drunk so much
they can eate nothing'.

210 **churls'** niggards'; misers'

215 **to him** i.e. go to *My master's steward*,
Springlove

217 **you forget** i.e. you have forgotten that
you are meant to keep secret the pres-
ence of Springlove and others in the
house.

223 **means** intercession

205 SD] *this edn; Ignoring* MARTIN, *he speaks to* SENTWELL. | *Brome Online*   217 SD] *this edn; aside
to* RANDALL | *Brome Online*   219 SD *Exeunt*] Haaker; *Exit Q1*

friends with thee. But I shall never look upon her,
or thee, but with grief of mind, however I bear it
outwardly. Oh –   225

MARTIN You bear it very manfully, methinks.

TALLBOY Ay, you think so, and I know so – but what
I feel, I feel. Would one of us two had never both
seen one another. Oh –   230

MARTIN You speak very good sense, sir. But does my
master continue his merry humour with the old
gentlemen within?

TALLBOY Yes. Justice Clack's clack goes as merrily as
any.   235

MARTIN Well said, sir. Now you speak merrily, too. But
I could say somewhat that would still him. And for
your comfort, I'll tell you. Mistress Amy is fallen in
love with one of the beggars.

TALLBOY Then have I nothing else to do but to laugh at   240
thee as long as I live. Ha, ha, ha! – To let a beggar
cozen thee of her. Ha, ha, ha! A beggar! I shall die
merrily yet. Ha, ha, ha!

Enter CLACK, OLDRENTS, HEARTY [*and*] OLIVER.

CLACK A-hey, boys, a-hey! This is right; that is to say,
as I would have it; that is to say –   245

TALLBOY A beggar. Ha, ha, ha! –

MARTIN Ha, ha, ha! –

CLACK A-hey, boys, a-hey! They are as merry without
as we were within. A-hey, Master Oldrents and
Master Hearty! The virtue of your company turns all   250

---

225 **however** howsoever
229–30 **Would ... another** It is, of course,
    impossible for only one of *both* not to see
    the other.

237 **still** quiet
238 **comfort** pleasure, delight
244 **A-hey** lengthened form of 'hey', an
    exclamation expressing exultation, incite-
    ment, surprise, etc. See 2.2.98n.

243 SD *and*] *Brome Online*

237

to mirth and melody, with a [*singing*] 'hey trololly
lolly lolly'. Is't not so, Master Hearty?

OLDRENTS   Why, thus it should be. How was I deceived!
Now I see you are a good fellow.

OLIVER   He was never so before. If it be a lightening   255
before death, the best is, I am his heir.

TALLBOY, MARTIN   Ha, ha, ha! –

CLACK   Again, boys, again; that is to say, a-hey, boys,
a-hey! –

HEARTY   What is the motive of your mirth, nephew   260
Martin? Let us laugh with you.

OLDRENTS   Was that spoke like my friend, Hearty? Lack
we motives to laugh? Are not all things, anything,
everything to be laughed at? And if nothing were to
be seen, felt, heard or understood, we would laugh at   265
it too.

CLACK   You take the loss of your mistress merrily,
Master Tallboy.

TALLBOY   More merrily than you will take the finding
of her. Ha, ha, ha! – A beggar! Ha, ha, ha! –   270

CLACK   Can I be sad to find her, think you?

MARTIN   He thinks you will be displeased with her and
chide her.

CLACK   You are deceived, Master Tallboy; you are wide,
Master Tallboy, above half your length, Master   275

251–2 **'hey . . . lolly'** utterance, usually forming a musical phrase, expressive of gaiety
or joy. 'Coridon's Song', by John
Chalkhill, begins, 'Oh, the sweet contentment / The country man doth find! / high
trolollie loliloe, / high trolollie lee' (quoted
in Walton, 85–6). Clack may even be
singing a snatch of Hearty's song, 'There
was an old fellow at Waltham Cross',
which, in musical form, has a repeated
refrain of 'hey trolly lolly lolly lo'. See
2.2.99n. and p. 264.

254 **good fellow** convivialist
255–6 **lightening before death** defined in
OED lightening *n.*² b as 'the exhilaration
or revival of the spirits which is supposed
to occur in some instances just before
death'. Cf. *RJ*, 5.3.88–90: 'How oft, when
men are at the point of death, / Have they
been merry, which their keepers call / A
lightening before death.'
256 **the best is** the best thing is
274 **wide** i.e. wide of the mark; mistaken;
also a joke response to his name, Tallboy

251 SD] *Brome Online*

Tallboy. Law and justice shall sleep, and mirth and
good fellowship ride a circuit here tonight. A-hey,
Master Oldrents, a-hey, Master Hearty, and a-hey,
son Oliver, and a-hey, nephew Tallboy-that-should-
ha'-been, and a-hey, my clerk Martin, and a-hey for   280
the players! When come they? Son Oliver, see for
Master Sentwell, that is no readier with his new
company.

TALLBOY   Players! Let us go see, too. I never saw any
players.   [*Exeunt*] *Tallboy* [*and*] *Martin.*

OLIVER [*aside*]   This is the first fit that ever he had of   286
this disease. And if it be his last, I say, as I said
before, I am his heir.   *Exit.*

OLDRENTS   But is there a play to be expected and acted
by beggars?   290

CLACK   That is to say, by vagabonds; that is to say, by
strolling players. They are upon their purgation. If
they can present anything to please you, they may
escape the law; that is, a-hey! If not, tomorrow,
gentlemen, shall be acted abuses stripped and   295
whipped among 'em, with a-hey! Master Hearty, you
are not merry –

277 **ride a circuit** ride in a round. Richard
Vines refers to 'The destroying Angel,
that rode circuit that night' (4). The
circuit gone around, however, consisting
of mirth and good fellowship, is probably
a drinking one, i.e. this is a reference to a
round of drinks.

281 **see for** look for; try to find

287 **this disease** i.e. happiness or, perhaps,
drunkenness. The negative description
redounds on Oliver, who does not relish
joy, and on the play itself, which is
always insecure about merriment.

287–8 **as . . . before** Oliver repeats what he
said before about the extent to which he

would profit by the old man's death,
while using Clack's phrase. He means
this as a slur upon Clack; he is also
starting to turn into Clack in anticipation
of inheriting from him.

292 **upon their purgation** undergoing their
act of purification from the suspicion of
crime or guilt

295–6 **abuses . . . whipped** a reference to
George Wither's *Abuses Stripped, and
Whipped. Or Satirical Essays* (1613), a set
of satirical essays that use self-observation
as their basis for their moralizing remarks
on man. Clack's reference, however, picks
up on little more than the title.

285 SD *and*] *Dodsley*   286 SD] *Lawrence*

Enter SENTWELL.

‒ and a-hey, Master Sentwell, where are your
'dramatis personae', your 'prologus', and your 'actus
primus', ha? Ha' they given you the slip for fear of   300
the whip? A-hey!

SENTWELL   A word aside, an't please you ‒

Sentwell takes Clack aside, and gives him a paper.

OLDRENTS   I have not known a man in such a humour.

HEARTY   And of his own finding! He stole it, indeed, out
of his own bottles, rather than be robbed of his liquor.   305
Misers use to tipple themselves so.

OLDRENTS   He does so outdo us that we look like staid
men again, Hearty: fine sober things.

HEARTY   But how long will it last? He'll hang himself
tomorrow for the cost we have put him to.   310

OLDRENTS   I love a miser's feast dearly. To see how thin
and scattering the dishes stood, as if they feared
quarrelling.

HEARTY   And how the bottles, to scape breaking one
another, were brought up by one at once!   315

OLDRENTS   How one of the serving-men, untrained to
wait, spilled the white broth!

299–300 **'dramatis   personae'**... **'prologus'**... **'actus primus'** persons of the
drama ... prologue ... act one. Clack
is asking where the actors are, using
Latin terms that describe the layout of a
written (rather than performed) play:
dramatis personae, a list of characters,
precedes a play in a book; a *prologus*
comes after that, followed by *actus
primus*, the heading for the first act of a
play. The texts Clack refers to may be the
classical dramas that he read at school,
as, though a number of Latin terms are
used in early modern playtexts, *prologus*
is unusual ‒ Brome himself opts for
'prologue'.

304–5 **He ... liquor** i.e. Clack's good mood
is the result of the fact that he has been
obliged to drink large quantities of his
own alcohol in order to stop his guests
getting to it.

306 **tipple** intoxicate; make drunk

307 **staid** sedate; dignified, i.e. sober

311–12 **thin and scattering** few and widely
separated

315 **by one at once** one by one

316–17 **untrained to wait** not trained as a
waiter

317 **white broth** a thin white gravy or soup
in which chicken or fish have been
boiled. Its colour came from the ground
almonds and cream that it contained. One

HEARTY   And another, stumbling at the threshold, tumbled in his dish of rouncivals before him.

OLDRENTS   And most suitable to the niggardliness of his   320
feast, we shall now have an entertainment, or play, presented by beggars.

CLACK   Send 'em in, Master Sentwell.   *Exit Sentwell.*
Sit, gentlemen; the players are ready to enter. And here's a bill of their plays. You may take your choice.   325

OLDRENTS   Are they ready for them all in the same clothes? Read 'em, good Hearty.

HEARTY   First, here's *The Two Lost Daughters.*

OLDRENTS   Put me not in mind of the two lost daughters, I prithee. What's the next?   330

HEARTY   *The Vagrant Steward.*

OLDRENTS   Nor of a vagrant steward. Sure some abuse is meant me.

HEARTY   *The Old Squire and the Fortune-Teller.*

OLDRENTS   That comes nearer me. Away with it.   335

HEARTY   *The Beggar's Prophecy.*

OLDRENTS   All these titles may serve to one play of a story that I know too well. I'll see none of them.

HEARTY   Then here's *The Merry Beggars.*

OLDRENTS   Ay, that; and let 'em begin.   340

---

recipe recommends, 'Make reasonable good broth, with the crag-ends of Necks of Mutton and Veal . . . Beat a quarter of a pound of blanched Almonds with three or four spoonfuls of Cream, and, if you will, a little Rose water; then add some of your broth to it, so to draw out all their substance, mingling it with the rest of your broth' (*Closet*, 172).

319 **rouncivals** peas. The word is defined in Blount (1674) as 'a sort of great Peas, well known, and took name from *Ronceval*, a place at the foot of the *Pyrenean* Mountains, from whence they first came to us' (sig. 2n6ᵛ–7ʳ).

325 **bill . . . plays** paper or bill containing titles of all the plays they have on offer. Theseus is handed a similar 'brief' detailing the 'sports' he can 'Make choice of' in *MND*, 5.1.42–3.

326–7 **Are . . . clothes?** Clack is surprised that all the plays can be performed using the same clothes – which are also the clothes the beggars are already wearing. But, as every play is going to tell the same story, no alternative costumes are required.

328 *Two Lost Daughters* This, and every subsequent play-title, describes Oldrents' life.

335 **nearer** closer to

Enter TALLBOY *and* OLIVER.

TALLBOY   The players are coming in, and Mistress Amy
and your man Martin are to be actors among 'em.
CLACK   A-hey then for that, too. Some merry device, sure.
A flourish of shawms
Hark! The beggars' hoboys. Now they begin.
OLDRENTS   See, a most solemn prologue.   345

Enter Poet [SCRIBBLE] *for Prologue.*

To knight, to squire and to the gentles here,
We wish our play may with content appear.
We promise you no dainty wit of court,
Nor city pageantry nor country sport,
But a plain piece of action, short and sweet,   350
In story true. You'll know it when you see't.   [*Exit.*]
OLDRENTS   True stories and true jests do seldom thrive
on stages.
CLACK   They are best to please you with this, though, or
a-hey with a whip for them tomorrow!   355
OLDRENTS   Nay, rather than they shall suffer, I will be
pleased; let 'em play their worst.

343 SD *flourish of shawms* fanfare of
wooden double-reed wind instruments of
high pitch, with a compass of about two
octaves; their descendant is the oboe.
344 **hoboys** wooden double-reed wind instruments of high pitch, more courtly versions of shawms; see 343 SDn.
346 *gentles* a comic vulgarism for 'gentlefolks' (see *OED* gentle *adj.* and *n.* B *n.* b,
which cites this instance)
348 *dainty* fastidious; over-nice

349 *city pageantry* Entertainments, usually
run by the separate guilds, were held in
the London city streets to celebrate important civic occasions such as coronations
or the Lord Mayor's investitures. A
mixture of poetry, music and architec-
ture, they were co-written by playwrights,
musicans and designers.
351 *know . . . see't* possibly glancing towards
titles of plays that claimed to be true, like
Samuel Rowley's *When You See Me You
Know Me* (1605)

345 SD SCRIBBLE] *Brome Online* 351 SD] *Brome Online subst.*

A flourish. Enter PATRICO, *with* LAWYER *habited
like Oldrents.*

See our patrico among 'em.

HEARTY   That offered you a doxy in the barn.

PATRICO

Your children's fortunes I have told,   360
That they shall beg ere they be old,
And will you have a reason why?
'Tis justice in their destiny –

CLACK   Justice, ha! Are you meddling with justices
already?   365

PATRICO

Your grandfather, by crafty wile
Of bargaining, did much beguile
A thriftless heir of half the lands
That are descended to your hands;
And then, by law, not equity,   370
Forced him and his posterity
To woe and shameful beggary.

LAWYER   That was no fault of mine, nor of my children.

PATRICO

But our forefathers' debts and crimes,
Although forborne till future times,   375
Are not so paid. But what needs more:
I wish you happy in your store.   *Exit.*

357.1 *flourish* fanfare (of horns, trumpets, etc.), often used to announce the approach of a person of distinction

360–1 presumably a version of the lines that upset Oldrents just before *A Jovial Crew* begins and that Hearty summarizes at 1.1.48–51; here, however, the Patrico explains the meaning behind the prophecy.

363–4 *justice . . .* **Justice** a 'whim' playing with the senses of *justice* as (1) the quality of being (morally) just or righteous; (2) a judicial officer such as Clack himself

366 *crafty wile* sly trick; deceit

367 *beguile* cheat

368 *thriftless* without frugality or economy; improvident (*OED adj.* 3)

370 *by law, not equity* through legal 'justice' rather than through fairness

371 *posterity* descendants

375 *forborne* withheld; kept back (*OED* forbear *v.* 7)

377 *store* collective possessions; accumulated goods or money (*OED n.* 5a)

OLDRENTS   Dost note this, Hearty?

HEARTY   You said you would be pleased, let 'em play
their worst.   380

Lawyer walks sadly, beats his breast, etc. To
him enter SOLDIER *like Hearty and seems to comfort him.*

OLDRENTS [*aside*]   It begins my story, and by the same
fortune-teller that told me my daughters' fortunes,
almost in the same words. I know him now. And he
speaks in the play to one that personates me as near
as they can set him forth.   385

CLACK   How like you it, sir? You seem displeased. Shall
they be whipped yet? A-hey, if you say the word.

OLDRENTS   Oh, by no means, sir; I am pleased.

SOLDIER

Sad for the words of a base fortune-teller?
Believe him? Hang him! I'll trust none of 'em.   390
They have all whims and double-double meanings
In all they say.

OLDRENTS   Whom does he talk or look like now?

HEARTY   It is no matter whom. You are pleased, you say.

SOLDIER

Ha' you no sack i'th' house? Am not I here?   395
And never without a merry old song?

(*Sings.*) *Old sack, and old songs, and a merry old crew,*
Will fright away cares when the ground looks blue.

And can you think on gypsy fortune-tellers?

379 **You said . . . pleased** a reference to
Oldrents' promise at 356–7 that he will
be *pleased* rather than let the beggars be
whipped

397–8 a reprise of the song sung by Hearty
and the grey-beards at 4.1.257–60. However, the words are slightly different. The
original song had offered to *charm away*
cares with sack; now it will *fright* them
away – the action that drink will have is
more violent than palliative, suggesting
a darker mood than earlier.

381 SD] *Haaker*   397 SD *Sings.*] *(SING)*

LAWYER

I'll think as little of 'em as I can.   400

SOLDIER

Will you abroad then? But here comes your steward.

Enter SPRINGLOVE *to Lawyer.*

OLDRENTS   Bless me! Is not that Springlove?

HEARTY   Is that you that talks to him, or that coxcomb I,
    do you think? Pray let 'em play their play. The Justice
    will not hinder 'em, you see: he's asleep.   405

SPRINGLOVE

Here are the keys of all my charge, sir, and
My humble suit is that you will be pleased
To let me walk upon my known occasions this
    summer.

LAWYER

Fie! Canst not yet leave off those vagancies?
But I will strive no more to alter nature.   410
I will not hinder thee, nor bid thee go.

OLDRENTS   My own very words at his departure.

HEARTY   No matter. Pray attend.

LAWYER

Come, friend, I'll take your counsel.

Exeunt Lawyer [*and*] *Soldier.*

403 Hearty asks whether the player who resembles Oldrents or the player who resembles himself is talking to Springlove. He can, of course, see who is talking to Springlove; but he has begun to feel hostile towards his fictional self.
    coxcomb fool or simpleton; see also 2.1.63n.
406 *charge* responsibilities. The word had specific monetary connotations; *Wise Woman* refers to 'Having . . . a charge of money about me' (sig. C3ᵛ).

408 *my known occasions* my known (and, equally, mine own) particular (personal) needs or requirements (*OED* occasion *n.* 9b)
409 *vagancies* wanderings or strollings (*OED* vagancy *n.*, citing this example)
412 Oldrents had indeed said, 'I have no voice to bid you go or stay', but he had also determined to leave the outcome to 'time and Providence' (1.1.235, 237).

414 SD *and*] *Dodsley*

SPRINGLOVE

I've striven with myself to alter nature in me   415
For my good master's sake, but all in vain;
For beggars, cuckoo-like, fly out again
In their own notes and season.

          Enter RACHEL, MERIEL, VINCENT [*and*] HILLIARD.

RACHEL

Our father's sadness will not suffer us
To live in's house.
MERIEL   *And we must have a progress.*   420
VINCENT

Th'assurance of your loves hath engaged us –
HILLIARD

– to wait on you in any course.
RACHEL

Suppose we'll go a-begging?
VINCENT, HILLIARD   *We are for you.*
SPRINGLOVE

And that must be your course, and suddenly,
To cure your father's sadness, who is told   425
It is your destiny – which you may quit
By making it a trick of youth and wit.
I'll set you in the way.
VINCENT, HILLIARD, RACHEL, MERIEL   *But how? But how?*
(All talk aside.)

---

417 **cuckoo-like** The cuckoo's restless need   418 **notes** affairs; circumstances
to change habitat is compared to that of   421 **engaged** bound; committed
the beggars. The choice of a bird with   422 **wait on** minister to the comfort of
negative associations, and the fact that   **course** method of proceeding
Springlove is compelled rather than   423 **for** in support of; in favour of
excited by his inner beggar, signals the   424 **suddenly** without delay; immediately
change that is about to take place.   426 **quit** requite; cancel

418 SD *and*] *Brome Online*   428 SP] *this edn;* All 4. *Q1*

OLDRENTS

My daughters and their sweethearts too. I see
The scope of their design, and the whole drift   430
Of all their action now, with joy and comfort.

HEARTY   But take no notice yet. See a whim more of it.
But the mad rogue that acted me I must make drunk
anon.

SPRINGLOVE

Now! Are you all resolved?

VINCENT, HILLIARD, RACHEL, MERIEL   *Agreed, agreed!*   435

SPRINGLOVE

You beg to absolve your fortune, not for need.

> *Exeunt [Springlove, Vincent, Hilliard, Rachel*
> *and Meriel].*

OLDRENTS   I must commend their act in that. Pray thee,
let's call 'em and end the matter here. The purpose of
their play is but to work my friendship or their peace
with me, and they have it.   440

HEARTY   But see a little more, sir.

Enter RANDALL.

OLDRENTS   My man Randall too! Has he a part with
'em?

RANDALL [*aside*]   They were well set a-work when they
made me a player. What is that I must say? And how   445
must I act now? Oh! That I must be steward for the
beggars in Master Steward's absence, and tell my
master he's gone to measure land for him to purchase.

---

436 *absolve your fortune* discharge your fate
439 **work** bring about
444 **set a-work** set at work (*OED* a-work
    adj.)

448 **measure land** (1) ascertain the dimen-
    sions of the land (as a surveyor; see
    2.2.61); (2) travel or traverse the land (as
    a beggar)

435 SP] *this edn*   436 SD *Springlove . . . Meriel*] *this edn*   444 SD] *this edn*   a-work] *this edn*; a work *Q1*;
to work *Dodsley*

OLDRENTS   You, sir! Leave the work you can do no
   better – [*aside*] I can forbear no longer – and call the   450
   actors back again to me.

RANDALL   With all my heart, and glad my part is so
   soon done.   *Exit.*

Enter PATRICO.

PATRICO
   Since you will then break off our play,
   Something in earnest I must say,   455
   But let affected rhyming go.
   I'll be no more a patrico.
   My name is Wrought-on. – Start not! But, if you
   Desire to hear what's worth your best attention
   More privately, you may draw nearer me.   460
     Oldrents goes to him.

HEARTY
   Hear no more fortunes.

OLDRENTS   You shall give me leave.

PATRICO
   I am grandson to that unhappy Wrought-on
   Whom your grandfather, craftily, wrought out
   Of his estate. By which, all his posterity
   Were, since, exposed to beggary. I do not charge   465
   You with the least offence in this. But now
   Come nearer me, for I must whisper to you.
     (*Patrico takes Oldrents aside.*)

---

455 **in earnest** serious
457 **a patrico** As the Patrico readies himself
   to speak his actual name, he ceases to use
   'Patrico' for his name, instead using it as
   a description of his type or job.
458 **Wrought-on** 'Wrought' is an old-
   fashioned past tense for 'work'. To be

wrought or worked on means to be
prevailed upon, induced or persuaded.
Start not! Do not flinch!
459 **best** fullest
461 **give me leave** permit me
463 **wrought** tricked; manipulated
465–6 **charge . . . offence** blame you for the
   least fault

450 SD] *this edn*

I had a sister who, among the race
Of beggars, was the fairest. Fair she was
In gentle blood and gesture to her beauty,   470
Which could not be so clouded with base clothing
But she attracted love from worthy persons,
Which, for her meanness, they expressed in pity
For the most part. But some assaulted her
With amorous, though loose, desires, which she   475
Had virtue to withstand. Only one gentleman –
Whether it were by her affection or
His fate, to send his blood a-begging with her,
I question not – by her, in heat of youth,
Did get a son, who now must call you father.   480

OLDRENTS   Me?

PATRICO

You! Attend me, sir. Your bounty then
Disposed your purse to her, in which, besides
Much money – I conceive by your neglect –
Was thrown this holy relic. Do you know it?   485

OLDRENTS

The Agnus Dei that my mother gave me
Upon her deathbed! Oh, the loss of it

---

470 **gentle ... gesture** i.e. in well-bred blood-line and bearing
to in addition to

473 **for her meanness** (1) because of her lack of wealth; (2) because of her lowly status

478 **his blood ... with her** (1) his emotions pleading with her; (2) his bloodline going begging in her company

483 **Disposed ... to** bestowed ... on

484 **I ... neglect** 'I imagine through your negligence'

485 **holy relic** The terminology ensures that this will be understood as a Catholic token. Jeffrey Knapp writes, 'Daringly, Brome reconciles the wanderers of the play at the same time as he resurrects England's Catholic past ... Selecting the rogues' "patrico" ... as the character who preserves and then reveals the Agnus Dei, Brome implies that the larger "strife" in English society can be turned into "a comedy" not with the restoration of Catholicism but rather with a shared wandering from the precise sectarianism that has divided one otherwise "civil Christian" from another' (77–8).

486 **Agnus Dei** literally 'Lamb of God'. An 'Agnus Dei' was a disc of white wax, with the image of a lamb (representing Jesus) supporting the banner of the Cross impressed on it, which had been blessed by the Pope.

Was my sore grief, and now, with joy, it is
Restored by miracle! Does your sister live?

PATRICO

No, sir. She died within a few days after   490
Her son was born, and left him to my care,
On whom I, to this day, have had an eye
In all his wanderings.

OLDRENTS   Then the young man lives!

Enter SPRINGLOVE, VINCENT, HILLIARD,
RACHEL [*and*] MERIEL.

PATRICO

Here with the rest of your fair children, sir.

OLDRENTS

My joy begins to be too great within me!   495
My blessing, and a welcome to you all.
Be one another's, and you all are mine.

VINCENT, HILLIARD   We are agreed on that.

RACHEL   Long since. We only stood till you shook off
your sadness.   500

MERIEL   For which we were fain to go a-begging, sir.

OLDRENTS   Now I can read the justice of my fate, and
yours –

CLACK [*awakening*]   Ha! Justice? Are they handling of
justice?   505

492 **I . . . eye** 'I have watched over all this
time'. Yet Springlove also has a blood
relationship with, and hence aspects of
the personality of, the Patrico (his *I*, echoed
in *eye*). The beggar and the landowner
are united and perhaps reconciled by the
way in which Springlove combines the two.
493 **wanderings** wand'rings
497 **Be one another's** Oldrents enjoins his
daughters and their lovers to marry one
another.

499 **stood** waited (*OED* stand *v.* 16a)
501 **fain** eager, glad
502 **read** make out, discover or expound
the meaning or significance of (a riddle,
dream, omen, etc. (*OED v.* 2a)
502–4 **justice . . . Justice** As Oldrents realizes
that actual *justice* has occurred, Clack
wonders whether legal judges such as
himself are being mocked onstage.

493 wanderings] *(*wandrings*)*   493.2 and] *Brome Online*   504 SD] *Brome Online subst.*

OLDRENTS — but more applaud great Providence in both.

CLACK [*to Hearty*] Are they jeering of justices? I watched for that.

HEARTY [*to Clack*] Ay, so me thought. No, sir. The play 510 is done.

Enter SENTWELL, AMY, OLIVER [*and*] MARTIN.

SENTWELL [*to Clack*] See sir, your niece presented to you.
Springlove takes Amy [to Clack].

CLACK What, with a speech by one of the players? Speak, sir, and be not daunted. I am favourable. 515

SPRINGLOVE Then, by your favour, sir, this maiden is my wife.

CLACK Sure you are out o'your part. That is to say, you must begin again.

SPRINGLOVE She's mine by solemn contract, sir. 520

CLACK You will not tell me that. Are not you my niece?

AMY I dare not, sir, deny't; we are contracted.

CLACK Nay, if we both speak together, how shall we hear one another?

---

509 **watched** stayed awake

515 **favourable** inclined to be well-disposed

518 **you ... part** You have misremembered your actor's script (*part*). Cf. *Cor*, 5.3.41: 'I have forgot my part and I am out.' Clack affects to believe that the play is still taking place.

520 **solemn contract** formal betrothal. There were two forms of contract a couple could make: *de praesenti* (a mutual promise or contract of immediate matrimony) and *de futuro* (a mutual promise or covenant of marriage to be solemnized at a later date). The couple must have made a *de praesenti* contract, which had almost the force of marriage, in that it was indissoluble. It could be made by a simple exchange of promises: 'I do take thee to my wife'; 'I do take thee to my husband' (see *Spousals*, 8).

523–4 As there are no 'premature cues' or unfinished sentences here, no one is actually speaking at the same time as Clack. As it seems, Clack does not know what to say, so falls back on his old platitudes, though they are irrelevant.

508, 510 SDs] *Brome Online* 511 SD *and*] *Brome Online* 512 SD] *Lawrence* 513 SD *to Clack*] *Brome Online*

MARTIN   I must disprove the contract.   525

TALLBOY   That is my part to speak.

SENTWELL   None can disprove it. I am witness to it.

CLACK   Nay, if we all speak – as I said before.

OLDRENTS   Hear me for all, then. Here are no beggars (you are but one, Patrico), no rogues, nor players, but 530 a select company to fill this house with mirth. These are my daughters; these their husbands; and this that shall marry your niece, a gentleman, my son. I will instantly estate him in a thousand pound a year to entertain his wife, and to their heirs forever. Do you 535 hear me now?

CLACK   Now I do hear you. And I must hear you. That is to say, it is a match. That is to say – as I said before.

TALLBOY   And must I hear it too. Oh –

OLDRENTS   Yes, though you whine your eyes out.   540

HEARTY   Nephew Martin, still the child with a suckbottle of sack. [*to Tallboy*] Peace, lamb, and I'll find a wife for thee.

---

525 **disprove** disallow authoritatively; invalidate

526 Tallboy claims he should have the role which contains the words 'I must disprove the contract', a convoluted way of saying that he, as primary jilt, should be the one to refute Springlove's claim.

527 **witness** Sentwell has been witness at the marriage (a *de praesenti* marriage required two witnesses).

530 **you . . . one** you are the only one – a particularly ironic statement in that the Patrico is of gentle blood and is a beggar only because Oldrents' family made him one

532 **husbands** The men are not in fact husbands yet but have agreed that they will be (498); however, it is possible that they have also made *de praesenti* contracts with Oldrents' daughters.

534 **estate him** furnish him with an estate or property

541 **still the child** quiet or nurse the child – another reference to Tallboy's youthfulness

suckbottle infant's feeding-bottle (*OED n.* 1, citing this line); such 'bottles' were sometimes made of a cow's horn pierced at the tip, and sometimes of glass or silver; they had a piece of pierced leather or a cow's teat attached to the tapering end or spout. The term 'suck bottle' or 'sucking bottle' was, however, regularly used, as here, to mean a bottle of alcohol to which its owner was unduly attached. In Davenant's *Tempest*, Trinculo describes his drink-bottle as 'a sucking-Bottle for young *Trincalo*' (39).

542 **lamb** a term of endearment; Hearty is treating the weeping Tallboy like a child,

542 SD] *Brome Online*

OLDRENTS

Now, Patrico, if you can quit your function
To live a moderate gentleman, I'll give you   545
A competent annuity for your life.

PATRICO   I'll be, withal, your faithful beadsman, and
spend my whole life in prayers for you and yours.

CLACK   And now, Clerk Martin, give all the beggars my
free pass without all manner of correction! That is to   550
say, with a-hey, get 'em gone.

OLIVER [*to Vincent*]   Are not you the gentleman that
challenged me in right of your friend here?

VINCENT   Your inspection's good, sir.

RACHEL [*to Oliver*]   And you the gentleman, I take it,   555
that would have made beggar-sport with us, two at
once.

MERIEL   For twelvepence apiece, sir.

OLIVER   I hope we all are friends.

making his promise of finding a wife for
him ironic.

544 **quit your function** leave your trade

546 **competent** suitable; sufficient for comfortable living

547 **withal** additionally
beadsman an almsman who was paid for
praying on his rosary or 'beads' for the
soul or spiritual welfare of another person
– often, as here, his benefactor. This
appears to be a further Catholic reference,
though Protestant beadsmen did also
exist.

550 **free pass** a licence exempting the beggars
from vagrancy laws, and thus enabling
them to pass freely back to their parishes.
Yet 'the pass suggests the poor laws . . .

were . . . taking over the functions once
performed by the hospitable landowner' (Sullivan, 191). Without the pass,
beggars would be defined as 'rogues' and
'correction' would follow. Rogues, according to John Cowell, wander 'from place
to place without pasport' and, if caught,
are 'for the first offence, . . . called a
Roag of the first degree, and punished by
whipping, and boring through the grissell
of the right eare with a hot yron an inch
in compas: & for the second offence, . . .
called a Roag of the second degree, and
put to death as a felon, if [they] be aboue
18. yeares ould' (sig. 3m2ᵛ).

553 **in right of** on behalf of

554 **inspection** perception

552 SD] *Lawrence*   555 SD] *Brome Online*

SPRINGLOVE

[*to Oldrents*] Now on my duty, sir, I'll beg no more   560
But your continual love and daily blessing.

OLDRENTS   Except it be at court, boy, where if ever I
come, it shall be to beg the next fool-royal's place
that falls.   [*Exeunt all but Springlove.*]

SPRINGLOVE

A begging epilogue yet would not be,   565
Methinks, improper to this comedy.

EPILOGUE.

Though we are, now, no beggars of the crew,
We count it not a shame to beg of you.
The justice, here, has given his pass free
To all the rest unpunished; only we
Are under censure, till we do obtain   5

---

560 **beg** a 'whim' on two meanings of *beg*: 'be a beggar' and 'crave'

562 **at court** Brome's notion that people suing for preferment at court were beggars continues his critique of courtier-playwrights like Davenant and Suckling. As it was also the theme of his play *The Court Beggar*, acted at the Phoenix/Cockpit *c.* 1640, he may be making a direct reference to his earlier drama.

563 **fool-royal's** belonging to a great fool; *royal* here is an intensifier, denoting something on a grand scale. The only court place Oldrents would beg for is that of a jester or clown who professionally counterfeits folly for the entertainment of others (see *OED* fool *n.*[1] and *adj.* 2a, citing this line). He refers to the fact that he has been the dupe throughout this play – while simultaneously making clear that only such fools as he has been hitherto would beg for places at court. The great fools or dupes aimed at in this line may

still be Davenant and/or Suckling. See p. 28.

564 **falls** becomes vacant – but the use of falling also indicates how quickly court perferment wanes

565 **begging** The final 'whim' of the play confounds *begging* = being a beggar with *begging* = pleading.

EPILOGUE. The speaker of this epilogue appears, from the preceding lines, to be Springlove.

2   **We . . . shame** 'We do not esteem it shameful'

3–4 **justice . . . unpunished** See 5.1.549–50.

5–6 **under censure . . . beg again** It was the purpose of an epilogue to ask approval from a potentially censorious audience; if the audience did not 'pass' the play, it would be 'damned' and not performed again. If this epilogue were spoken at the last performance before the closure of the theatres, it would have been particularly poignant.

560 SD] *Brome Online*   564 SD] *this edn*   **EPILOGUE.**] *Q1*

Your suffrages that we may beg again,
And often, in the course we took today,
Which was intended for your mirth: a play
Not without action and a little wit,   9
Therefore we beg your pass for us and it.   [*Exit.*]

FINIS

6   **suffrages** support; approval
10 **beg your pass** (1) ask you to give us
    a beggars' pass (the official licence that
    allows the poor to beg); (2) ask you to
    approve, rather than condemn (the play
    and its actors – a typical epilogue request)

Epil.10 SD] *this edn*

APPENDIX 1
Songs

The contradiction between what is sometimes a disturbing story and the six upbeat songs it contains (two catches or rounds about drinking, a further drinking song, two beggars' cant songs and a song of the popular 'Come away' variety) partly explains critics' mixed opinions about *A Jovial Crew* as a whole: music gives a happy, abandoned, drunken atmosphere throughout, despite the nature of the story (Ingram, 500). Some of the play's contradictions are expressed or created, then, through dramatic use of music.

It is also music that unites the beggars and aristocrats: both groups entertain one another through their devil-may-care songs. Yet the words or ditties of beggar and aristocrat alike concern the search for happiness rather than happiness itself; both repeatedly express the hope that drink (and by extension music) will palliate sorrow, and repeatedly name the unhappiness they claim not to feel – 'No sorrow, no sorrow, no sorrow, no sorrow' (1.1.357); 'Let . . . sorrow be drowned' (4.1.258). Music and singing, like drinking, in this way become a means of breaking down social barriers while also, of course, reinforcing them. The drinking song 'A round, a round' is sung by the gentry (4.1.257) and then by the beggars (5.1.397–8) – with one crucial word changed: the 'sack' that the gentry hoped would 'charm' sorrow away is, in the words of the beggars, to 'fright' it away instead – the violence of the term suggesting that grief is not so easily removed. Song content is sometimes bleaker than at first appears.

The 'ditties' (the words to the songs) from *A Jovial Crew* circulated as texts in their own right after the drama itself was published, and perhaps before. Several of them were separately printed, sometimes as poems in books of poetry, sometimes individually as ballads and sometimes as jokes.

Though the music, surviving separately for three of the songs, post-dates publication of the play, it is likely to be original: each piece of music is traceable to a composer contemporary with Brome – William Lawes (1602–45), John Hilton (1599–1657) and John Goodgroome (*c.* 1625–1704). At least one, and probably more, of the songs was famous enough for its tune to be used for other lyrics. 'The ballad of the cloak: or, The Cloaks knavery' is to be sung '*To the tune of, From hunger and cold: or, Packington's pound*' (1680).

The suggestion, then, is that words and tunes became popular both separately and together. Possibly during the interregnum the songs, representing the kind of indulgence that Puritans were anxious to eradicate, were read or sung out of nostalgia for past pleasures now lost – including that of theatrical performance itself.

FIRST SONG, 'FROM HUNGER AND COLD', 1.1.351–8, 361–8

The melody to this lyric was first published as no. 64 in John Wilson's *Select Airs* (1659), where the title given to the piece, 'The Jovial Begger', creates a direct link between the lyric and the play (see Fig. 7). Tune and words, in the form of 'A Glee' (a song usually for three or more singers, consisting of separate but interwoven tunes) are provided in John Playford's *Musical Companion* (1672), 96, where the composer is said to be 'J. G.' (probably John Goodgroome). In a British Library music manuscript, MS Harley 3991, fol. 145^{r-v}, the composer is also identified as 'J. G.'.

The words alone are separately published in J. P.'s *Antidote* (1669), 133. They follow as the 'Second Part' of what is there called 'The Beggars Song', the first part of which begins, 'Cast your caps and cares away'. 'Cast your Caps', however, is actually a separate song found in Beaumont and Fletcher's play *Beggars' Bush*. Interestingly, then, singing beggars from two different plays have their texts fused in *Antidote*: in song form, Brome's beggars have come to seem standard all-purpose theatrical types, no longer individualized by play.

The text from the play

From hunger and cold who lives more free,
    Or who more richly clad than we?
Our bellies are full; our flesh is warm;
    And against pride our rags are a charm.
Enough is our feast, and for tomorrow
    Let rich men care: we feel no sorrow.
      No sorrow, no sorrow, no sorrow, no sorrow.
    Let rich men care: we feel no sorrow.

Each city, each town and every village
    Affords us either an alms or pillage
And, if the weather be cold and raw,
    Then in a barn we tumble in straw;
If warm and fair, by yea-cock and nay-cock,
    The fields will afford us a hedge or a haycock.
      A haycock, a haycock, a haycock, a haycock,
    The fields will afford us a hedge or a haycock.

Analysis

This song is ironic throughout. The music is in G minor, a key traditionally associated with sorrow: the joy the song claims to express is ironically undercut by its own sound. In the first verse, rhythm ensures heavy stress on 'richly' and, later, 'rich', so that the beggars' preoccupation with what they putatively despise is musically emphasized; likewise 'charm' is stressed, bringing out the ironic nature of the word in context – rags are a charm or talisman against pride, because they are the reverse

The Jovial Begger.

Rom Hunger and Cold who liveth more free, and who so richly choathed as we? Our Bellies are full, and our Flesh it is Warm, and againlt Pride our Rags is a Charm: Enough is a Feast to Morrow, Let rich men take care, we feel no Sorow.

7 'The Jovial Begger', from John Wilson, *Select Airs and Dialogues* (1659), no. 64. There appear to be printers' errors in the bass line, and in the last line, where words and underlay seem to be defective.

of charming wear. The final line is repeated, a variant of the repetition of 'No sorrow, no sorrow, no sorrow, no sorrow' in the playtext: the effect is the same. The beggars are protesting too much, and appear to be singing a melancholy song about not being melancholy – one of the themes of the play.

The second verse, too, is ironic: verbal and musical lines end in 'pillage', 'raw' and the negative 'nay-cock', so that the harshness of beggar life is again highlighted. Nevertheless, the fact that the last four lines conclude in 'cock', the last line then being musically repeated, suggests that, whether they are cold and, as the text tellingly puts it, taking a 'tumble' in straw, or warm and sleeping in a hedge, nature offers the beggars sexual compensations for the harshness of their life – another theme of the play.

SECOND SONG: 'COME, COME AWAY: THE SPRING', 1.1.499–518

Music for these words has never been published, and though a piece of music in Playford's *Wit* (1719; 4.142) has been said to reflect the source for the tune (Haaker, 34), it is in fact music for a song first introduced into the play in 1708, 'Courtiers, Courtiers, think it no scorn'. As 'Courtiers, Courtiers' is a line shorter than 'Come, come away', there is no reason to think that the same tune was applied to both sets of words.

The text from the play

Come, come away: the spring,
By every bird that can but sing
Or chirp a note, doth now invite
Us forth to taste of his delight.
In field, in grove, on hill, in dale,
But above all the nightingale,
Who in her sweetness strives t'outdo
The loudness of the hoarse cuckoo.

'Cuckoo', cries he; 'Jug Jug Jug', sings she
From bush to bush, from tree to tree;
Why in one place then tarry we?

Come away; why do we stay?
We have no debt or rent to pay,
No bargains or accounts to make,
Nor land or lease to let or take,
Or if we had, should that remore us,
When all the world's our own before us?
And where we pass and make resort,
It is our kingdom and our court.

Cuckoo cries he, *etc.*

Analysis

Though no tune is extant for this song, many 'Come away' laments of the period were composed by William Lawes, who wrote music for this play's 'A round, a round' (see p. 267); he may have been responsible both for this lost melody and for other music for the play that does not survive. 'Come' or 'Come away' songs, like 'Come away, come away death' in *Twelfth Night* (2.4.51ff.), were generally laments, often pastoral or Orphic in nature. They also tend to be, as here, used as exit songs in a play, so are valedictory in tone. This particular song, then, is likely, like the first song, to have had lamentational music for its joyful words, adding further to the play's theme of irony through music.

The song, like others of its kind, compares two omens of spring – the nightingale, whose plaintive lament ('Jug jug jug') was said to recall the cry of Philomela, raped by King Tereus, and the sound of the cuckoo ('Cuckoo'), which was said to mock married men with the threat of cuckoldry. Thus, though the text insists that the sound of the rival birds gives 'delight', in each instance the words highlight the threatened or threatening sexuality that, in spring, obliges beggars to wander. Spring and sex are at root connected, and both lead to travel, but the words suggest that neither is entirely joyful. This extends to the second verse, which states a different reason for travelling: money does not keep the beggars rooted to one spot – though the verse itself then questions that premise ('Or if we had'), perhaps because the beggars in this play are bound to Oldrents financially or, in the case of Springlove, by blood (a connection that may, too, be underlined by the reference to 'let' and 'rent').

THIRD SONG: 'THERE WAS AN OLD FELLOW AT WALTHAM CROSS', 2.2.96–101

This song, composed by John Hilton, is found with the title 'A Catch within a Catch' in Hilton's 1652 collection *Catch that Catch Can*, no. 31 (see Fig. 8). The words are also found under the title 'A Catch' in N. D.'s *Antidote* (1661), no. 67, and again as '6 Catch' in J. P.'s *Antidote* (1669), no. 164.

The text from the play

There was an old fellow at Waltham Cross,
Who merrily sung when he lived by the loss.
He never was heard to sigh with 'hey ho',
But sent it out with a 'hey trolly lo'.
He cheered up his heart when his goods went to wrack,
With a 'hem boy, hem' and a cup of old sack.

Analysis

Music

A catch or round was a short composition normally for three or more singers, each of whom sang the same melody successively – the second singer began the first line as the first went on to the second line, and so on. This song, however, is called 'A Catch within a Catch' because of a pun (or, as Brome might have put it, a 'whim'): the song contains three mini 'catches' (meaning musical rounds), provided by the refrain 'hey trolly lolly', each instance of which is surrounded by 'catches' or 'pitfalls' provided by the rests in the music. One singer would sing the verse; the others would join in sequentially once they heard the refrain – yet they were likely to miscount or stumble over the rests leading up to it. The consequence would be that the singers would make false entries, perhaps coming in with the previous singers, or simply at the wrong time. The result, which would

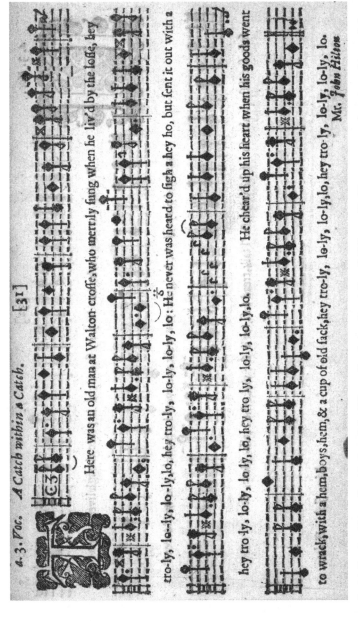

8 'A Catch within a Catch', from John Hilton, *Catch that Catch Can* (1652), no. 31. There appear to be printers' errors in bars 5–9.

be intensified if the tune is made to go ever faster, would be to make the singers themselves sound drunk.

In the play, Hearty sings the song: however, if the song was sung with the musical structure of Hilton's setting, Oldrents will have joined in the 'catch' or refrain. The song may also have been reprised at some other point in performance. Certainly Clack appears to know the tune (he sings 'hey trololly lolly lolly' at 5.1.251–2), perhaps because, in the fiction, Oldrents and Hearty have sung it with him while drinking, but perhaps because onstage the three sang it a further time in some performances.

Verbally, the song balances 'hey ho', a sad sigh, with 'hey trolly lo', a happy exclamation, which is reflected in a striking switch of tonality between the minor and major third. The attempt to show that one is essentially the same as the other is reinforced by this catch, for the first phrase will be overspoken, or corrected, by the second. The result, however, as with other songs, is that it is unclear whether unhappiness is being solved by happiness or vice versa; as the subject of the song is a ruined man, its theme is a sad one.

FOURTH SONG: 'HERE, SAFE IN OUR SKIPPER', 2.2.179–94

A Jovial Crew provides the only source for these lyrics; music for them is unknown.

The text from the play

Here, safe in our skipper, let's cly off our peck
And bowse in defiance o'th' harman-beck.
Here's pannum, and lap and good poplars of yarrum
To fill up the crib and to comfort the quarrom.
Now bowse a round health to the go-well and
    come-well
Of Cicely Bumtrinket that lies in the strummel.

Now bowse a round health to the go-well and
   come-well
Of Cicely Bumtrinket that lies in the strummel.

Here's ruffpeck, and casson and all of the best,
And scraps of the dainties of gentry cove's feast.
Here's grunter and bleater, with tib-of-the-butt'ry,
And margery-prater, all dressed without slutt'ry.
For all this bene cribbing and peck let us then
Bowse a health to the gentry cove of the ken.
Now bowse a round health to the go-well and
   come-well
Of Cicely Bumtrinket that lies in the strummel.

Analysis

This ditty, sung by the beggars as part of their celebration of a
new birth, recommends drinking as a defiance of the 'harman-
beck' or constable: drinking is itself an act of rebellion, and this
song is a celebration of transgressive behaviour. The first verse
celebrates food, drink and lastly the nursing mother; the second
verse expands on the source of the food – it is scraps from the
feast of a gentleman, or 'gentry cove', presumably Oldrents.
As a result of this realization, the song drinks a health first to
the gentleman and only secondly to the young mother who is
putatively its subject. It thus proleptically links Oldrents and
his beneficence to the theme of beggar-women and their births.
The name of the woman, Cicely Bumtrinket, depicts her nature
as merely a function of her sexuality; it is probably for the same
reason that the term 'slutt'ry' is also present in the second verse.

FIFTH SONG: 'THIS IS BENE BOWSE',
2.2.272 – 80

The music for the words is not extant. Words to the same song
are printed in Head (1671), 131–2, where the text reads exactly

as in *A Jovial Crew*, but extends to a third verse provided below.

The text from the play

This is bene bowse, this is bene bowse,
 Too little is my skew.
I bowse no lage, but a whole gage
 Of this I'll bowse to you.

This bowse is better than rombowse,
 It sets the gan a-giggling;
The autem mort finds better sport
 In bowsing than in niggling.

This is bene bowse, *etc.*

Additional verse from Head's English Rogue

Tis better than Peckidge, Plannam,
 Than Yarum, Loure, or Lage;
Then lift the same up to thy Nab,
 And Bowse off a whole Gage.
This is bene bowse, this is bene bowse,
 Too little is my skew.
I bowse no lage, but a whole gage
 Of this I'll bowse to you.

Analysis

A canting drinking song, sung to Oldrents by the Patrico's wife or Autem Mort, the ditty is not about water ('lage') or wine ('rombowse'), so presumably is a celebration of beer or, given the drunkenness exhibited, spirits. Either way, the giggling brought about by the drink is said to provide better sport than sex does – a telling comment for the wife of a man whose job is largely marrying couples. The additional verse, which may have been sung in the play – the '*etc.*' could ask for a repetition

of the chorus or indicate that more verses are to be sung –
praises drink above all forms of food.

SIXTH SONG: 'A ROUND, A ROUND, A ROUND, BOYS, A ROUND', 4.1.257–60; 5.1.397–8

This song is found in John Hilton's *Catch that Catch Can*
(1667) as no. 78 [misnumbered 79] (see Fig. 9); it was composed
by the famous William Lawes, musician-in-ordinary to the
King, who was well known for his elegant catches. Further
words for it can be found in the text for a song preceding
Brome's *The Weeding of the Covent Garden*, opening 'A Way
with all grief and give us more sack'; they are provided below.

The text from the play

The grey-beards' version
> A round, a round, a round, boys, a round.
> Let mirth fly aloft, and sorrow be drowned.
> Old sack, and old songs and a merry old crew
> Can charm away cares when the ground looks blue.

The Soldier's version
> Old sack, and old songs, and a merry old crew,
> Will fright away cares when the ground looks blue.

Longer text in Brome's Weeding, *sig. A2^v*

A Way with all grief and give us more sack.
'Tis that which we love, let love have no lack.
Nor sorrow, nor care can crosse our delights,
Nor witches, nor goblins, nor Buttery sprights,
Tho' the candles burne dimme while we can do thus,
We'll scorn to flie them: but we'll make them flie us.

267

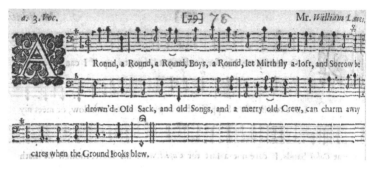

9   'A Round', from John Hilton, *Catch that Catch Can* (1667), no. 78 (misnumbered 79)

> Old Sack, and old Songs, and a merry old crew
> Will fright away Sprights, when the ground looks blew.

Analysis

Sung by 'grey-beards' or old men, part of the comedy of this song is its incongruity, though it also serves to link the grey-beards with the beggars and their drinking songs. That link is intensified later in the play when the song is reprised by the Soldier, the beggar who pretends to be Oldrents' friend Hearty.

In this self-referential song, the words 'A round, a round' both instruct the drinkers to pass 'around' the cup and inform the listeners that the song is 'a round' or catch. For this reason, the music to the song may actually differ from that for the longer version as it appears in *Weeding*. In this *Jovial Crew* version, the three singers take up the song successively, the words 'round' repeating so that the song itself becomes 'circular', its beginning and ending conjoining, an emphasis reinforced by the rhyming of 'round' and 'drowned', which marks the moment at the end of the first line when the second (and subsequently) third voices enter the catch, illustrated by the sign over the stave.

The second stress in the song is on 'old': sack, songs and the crew are described by this repeated adjective. The inanely cheerful melody provides a musical representation of drinking; this song, too, was probably intended to be sung with increasing speed. Yet the final words of the song are ironic. To drink until the ground looks blue was a proverbial phrase, meaning to drink until one's vision is skewed after too much alcohol (the word 'blue' is on a comically low note). See *Friar Bacon*, 'The Smith of the Towne his Liquor so tooke, / that he was perswaded the ground look'd blue' (sig. F3ʳ); Heywood's *Hierarchy*, 'he . . . dranke so long untill the ground lookt blew' (134); and Ford's *Lady's Trial*: 'We drinke till all looke blew, / Dance sing and roare, / Never give ore' (sig. h1ᵛ). In this way the song seems at first to parody a popular ballad form of the time in which members of jovial crews are enjoined to pay for their drink and prove themselves 'true blew' by doing so, as in William Blunden's 'Hang Pinching, or The Good Fellowes Observation, mongst a Jovial Crew, of them that Hate Flinching, but is Always True Blew' (1636). Yet drinking to *prevent* the ground looking blue seems to refer to drinking in order to ease low spirits, as 'blue' meant 'depressed' or 'miserable' from at least 1550 (see *OED* blue *adj.* and *n.* 4a). As ever, the singers are not as happy as they seem. That sack will in the first instance charm away cares and in the second fright them away suggests that the 'charm' may not have worked, or that more violence is necessary. In the version from *Weeding*, the sack will ward off bad spirits in dark evenings – but, again, the sense is not that the spirits are figments of the imagination, but that, with Dutch courage from drinking, the merry old crew can stand their ground in the face of the enemy.

APPENDIX 2
Rogue literature and cant

A Jovial Crew is a late example of what has come to be known as 'rogue literature', literature about the early modern underworld that supposedly uncovered the realities of vagabond life. These books, which explained rogues' scams and tricks as well as their language ('cant'), were hugely popular: through them readers felt initiated into an alien culture and able to partake in the glamour and secrecy of another world that was on their very doorsteps.

In fact, however, rogue literature seems to have had a heritage somewhat separate from the lives of actual beggars. Thomas Harman, in his influential *Caveat . . . for Common Cursitors* (1567), claimed to have his information directly from the vagrants he had met in his role as justice of the peace or had interviewed – but much of what he says is translated from the anonymous German pamphlet *Liber Vagatorum* (*c*. 1512). His suggestion that beggars were organized into hierarchies seems actually to have been made in order to give a structural logic to his book, which is divided by gradation of beggar. There is, in fact, little evidence for actual 'fraternities' of vagabonds in early modern England (Sharpe, 143).

Other pamphlets followed on from Harman, taking up his precepts and largely imitating him. In his series of coney-catching pamphlets, Robert Greene claimed to have knowledge from having infiltrated rogue society, yet he provides information that seems to originate in Harman, combined with material from John Awdelay's *The Fraternity of Vagabonds as Well of Ruffling Vagabonds, as of Beggarly, as well of Women as of Men, and as Well of Girls, as of Boys, with their Proper Names and Qualities* (1565), Gilbert Walker's *A Manifest Detection of the Most Vile and Detestable use of Diceplay* (1555), Andrew

Boorde's *The First Book of the Introduction of Knowledge* (1555) and Robert Copland's *The Highway to the Spital House* (1536). Collectively, these pamphlets conflated beggars, thieves and gypsies, and implied that all vagabonds were tricksters. They taught the application of the word 'rogue' to people who were often simply destitute (Woodbridge, *Vagrancy*, 3–4).

Rogue literature maintained and preserved cant, the language of vagabonds, in particular. It was through rogue literature – and particularly plays – that cant was taught to the general populace; much of it was eventually assimilated into slang as a result. Hence many current slang words have their origin in cant. 'Cove', the cant for man, was popular 1920s slang; 'booze' still means alcoholic drink; 'dude', which is cant for clothes, becomes the USA's 'dude' for man and 'duds' for clothes; 'peck', for food, survives in England as 'peckish' meaning hungry; 'ruffian' has lost its sense of devil, but is still employed for rowdy behaviour; 'niggle', though it has lost its sense of sex, is adopted for persist or fuss; 'queer', which originally meant bad, has become odd.

The following is a list of the cant found in *A Jovial Crew*. Descriptions of the words are taken from Harman's *Caveat*, which provides the earliest written account of cant terminology, Dekker's *Lantern and Candlelight* (1609), which also appears to have been one of Brome's sources, and Samuel Rid's *Martin Markall* (1610), which refines the definitions of Harman and Dekker. One last set of descriptions is taken from a rogue pamphlet published after *A Jovial Crew*, Richard Head's *English Rogue* (1671), which enlarges upon earlier cant literature. Head's work seems to reflect, or to have been influenced by *A Jovial Crew*, a song of which it borrows and perhaps enlarges (see pp. 265–6). When the explanations they offer are substantially the same, these definitions are combined.

271

CANT DEFINITIONS

Autem Mort **Harman**, sig. E4ᵛ, maried wemen, as there
be but a fewe. For Autem in their Language
is a Churche, so she is a wyfe maried at ye
Churche, and they be as chaste as a Cowe
I have, yt goeth to Bull every moone, with
what Bull she careth not. These walke most
times from their housbands companye a
moneth & more to gether, being asociate
with another as honest as her selfe. These
wyll pylfar clothes of hedges, some of them
go with children of x or xii yeares of age,
yf tyme and place serve for their purpose
they wyll send them into some house at the
window to steale and robbe . . . & wyll go
wt wallets on their shoulders, and slates at
their backs.
Dekker, sig. C2ʳ, **Rid**, sig. E2ʳ, a married
woman
Head, 138, another sort of these she-devils,
and differs onely from a walking Mort in
that she is married, for Autem in the Canting
tongue signifies a Church, although that be
a place she seldom comes at. They commonly
walk with their Wallets on their shoulders, and
Slates or sheets at their backs, and will pilfer
any thing that lies carelessly about houses.

beggar-nigglers *see* niggling
bene **Harman**, sig. G3ʳ, **Dekker**, sig. C2ʳ, **Rid**,
sig. E2ʳ, good
bing awast **Harman**, sig. G3ᵛ, **Dekker**, sig. C2ʳ, **Rid**,
sig. E2ʳ, go you hence
bleater **Harman**, sig. G3ʳ, 'a bleting chet' a calfe or
sheepe

bowse	**Harman**, sig. G3ʳ, **Dekker**, sig. C2ʳ, drinke
to bowse	**Harman**, sig. G3ᵛ, to drynke
bowsing ken	**Harman**, sig. G3ʳ, **Dekker**, sig. C1ʳ, **Rid**, sig. E2ʳ, an Ale house
to cant	**Harman**, sig. G3ᵛ, **Dekker**, sig. C1ʳ, to speake
casson	**Harman**, sig. G3ʳ, **Dekker**, sig. C1ʳ, cheese
clapperdudgeons	**Harman**, sig. C4ʳ⁻ᵛ, these go with patched clokes, & have their Morts with them, which they cal wives and if he goe to one house to aske his almes, his wife shal go to another, for what they get, as bread, cheese, malte, and woll, they sel the same for redy money, for so they get more, and if they went together, although they be thus devided in the daie, yet they mete jompe at night.
	Head, 134, go alwayes with their *Morts* at their heels, and draw people the more to pitty them, with Sperewort or Arsnick raise blisters on their legs, which they can cure again at their pleasure. When they come into the streets of a Town or Country village, they divide themselves, and beg one on one side of the street, and the other on the other side; the purchase which they thus get. They sell to poor Tradsmen, or other labouring people, and with the money are merry at the Bowsing-ken.
cly off	*not directly defined, but clearly* seize from; take from; get from
	Harman, sig. G4ᵛ, we . . . cly the Jarke
	Dekker, sig. C2ʳ, The Ruffin cly the nab of the Harman beck.
to couch a hogshead	**Harman**, sig. G3ᵛ, **Dekker**, sig. C2ʳ, to ly downe & slepe, **Rid**, sig. E2ᵛ, to lie downe

273

and sleepe: this phrase is like an Alminacke that is out of date: now the duch word to *slope* is with them used, to sleepe, and *liggen* to lie downe.

cove   **Dekker**, sig. C1ʳ, **Rid**, sig. E2ʳ, a Man, a Fellow, &c.

darkmans   **Harman**, sig. G3ʳ, **Dekker**, sig. C1ʳ, **Rid**, sig. E2ᵛ, the night

dell   **Harman**, sig. F4ʳ, A Dell is a yonge wench, able for generation, and not yet knowen or broken by the upright man. These go abroad yong, either by the death of their parentes, and no bodye to looke unto them, or els by some sharpe mystres that they serve to runne awaye oute of service, eyther shee is naturallye borne one, and then shee is a wylde Dell, these are broken verye younge, when they have beene lyen well by the upright man, then they be Doxes, & no Dels. These wyld Dels being traded up wt their monstreus mothers, must of necessyty be as evil or wursse then their parents.

Head, 137–8, Dells are young wenches that have not lost their maiden-head, but being once deflowred, (which commonly is when they are very young) they then change the name of Dell into Doxy, even as maids when they come to be married, loose that appellation, and are called women.

doxy   **Harman**, sig. F3ʳ⁻ᵛ, These Doxes be broken & spoyled of their maydenhead by the upright men, and then they have their name of doxes and not afore. And afterward she is common and indifferent for any that wyll use her, as *homo* is a commen name to all men. Such as be fayre and somewhat handsome, kepe company with the walkinge Mortes, and are redye alwayes for the upright men, and are chiefly maynteyned by them, for others shalbe spoyled for their sakes, the other inferior sort wyll resorte to noble mens places, and gentlemens houses standing at the gate, eyther lurkinge on the backsyde about backehouses, eyther in hedge rowes or some other thycket, expectynge their praye, whiche is for the uncomely company of some courteous gest of whom they be refreshed with meate and some monye, where exchaunge is made ware for ware: this bread and meate they use to carye in their greate hosen, so that these beastly brybinge breeches, serve manye tymes for bawdye purposes.

Head, 138, Doxyes are such as have been deflowred by the Upright-man, and are after common to any of the Brotherhood. They will if they see convenient for a small piece of money prostitute their bodies to any that will deal with them, and do too often murther those Infants which are so gotten. They have one special badge to be known by, for most of them go working of laces and shirt-strings, or such like stuff, onely to give colour to their idle wandring.

gage	**Harman**, sig. G3ʳ, **Dekker**, sig. C2ᵛ, **Rid**, sig. E2ᵛ, a quart pot
gan	**Dekker**, sig. G2ᵛ, **Rid**, sig. E2ᵛ, A mouth
gentry cove	**Harman**, sig. C4ᵛ, **Dekker**, sig. C1ʳ, a noble or gentleman
glaziers	**Harman**, sig. G2ᵛ, **Dekker**, sig. C2ʳ, **Rid**, sig. E2ᵛ, eyes

grunter	**Harman**, sig. G3^r, **Dekker**, sig. C1^r, 'a grunting chet' a pyg
harman-beck	**Harman**, sig. G3^r, **Dekker**, sig. C2^v, **Rid**, sig. E3^r, the Counstable
ken	**Dekker**, sig. C2^v, **Rid**, sig. E3^r, a house
lage	**Harman**, sig. G3^r, **Dekker**, sig. C2^v, water **Rid**, sig. E3^r, water or pisse
lap	**Harman**, sig. G3^r, **Dekker**, sig. C2^v, butter, mylke, or whey
margery-prater	**Harman**, sig. G3^r, **Dekker**, sig. C2^v, a hen
maund	**Harman**, sig. G3^v, to aske or requier
maunder	beggar; *see* maund
maunding	**Dekker**, sig. C2^v, asking, **Rid**, sig. E3^r, begging
niggling	**Dekker**, sig. C2^v, companying with a woman **Rid**, sig. E3^r, company keeping with a woman: this word is not used now, but *wapping*
pannum	**Harman**, sig. G3^r, bread
Patrico	**Harman**, sig. C2^r, Now also there is a Patrico and not a Patriarch, which in their language is a priest yt should make mariages tyll death dyd departe, but they have none suche I am well assured, for I put you out of doubte that not one amongest a hundreth of them are maried, for they take lechery for no synne, but naturall fellowshyp and good lykinge love. **Dekker**, sig. C2^v, **Rid**, sig. E3^v, a priest **Head**, 136, The Patrico is their Priest, every hedge is his Parish, and every wandring Rogue and Whore is his Parishioners. His service is onely marrying of couples, by bidding them go together and multiply, and fill the world with a generation of vagabonds.

peck	**Harman**, sig. G3^r, **Dekker**, sig. C2^v, meate **Rid**, sig. E3^r, meate, pecke is not meate but peckage, peck is taken to eate or byte; as the Buffa peckes me by the stampes, the dogge bites me by the shinnes.
poplars	**Harman**, sig. G3^r, porrage **Dekker**, sig. C2^v, Pottage
prat	**Harman**, sig. G2^v, **Dekker**, sig. C2^v, **Rid**, sig. E3^r, a buttocke
quarrom	**Harman**, sig. G2^v, **Dekker**, sig. C2^v, a body
queer cove	bad man *(from* queer = bad *and* cove = man; *see above)*; a rogue
queer cuffin	**Harman**, sig. G3^r, ye justicer of peace **Dekker**, sig. C1^r, a Churl is called, a Quier Cuffin; Quier signifies naught, and Cuffin . . . a man: and in Canting they terme a Justice of peace (because he punisheth them belike) by no other name then by Quier cuffin, that is to say a Churle, or a naughty man.
rombowse	**Harman**, sig. G3^v, **Dekker**, sig. C2^v, wyne **Rid**, sig. E3^v, wine: this word is always taken in the best sense, to shew a thing extraordinary or excellent.
ruffin	**Dekker**, sig. C3^r, **Rid**, sig. E3^v, the Divell
ruffpeck	**Harman**, sig. G3^r, **Dekker**, sig. C2^v, **Rid**, sig. E3^v, Bacon
skew	**Harman**, sig. G3^r, **Dekker**, sig. C3^r, a cuppe **Rid**, sig. E3^v, a Cuppe or Glasse, a Dish or any thing to drinke in
skipper	**Harman**, sig. G3^r, **Dekker**, sig. C3^r, **Rid**, sig. E3^v, a barne
Solomon	**Harman**, sig. G3^r, a altar or masse **Rid**, sig. E4^r, the masse: now when many doe presse the poore rogues so earnestly

to sweare by the Salomon, doe not blame them though they refuse it; for although you know not what it meanes, yet they very well know.

Head, 140, He will not . . . falsifie his oath, if he swear by his *Solomon* (which is the *Mass*) though you hang him.

stampers **Harman**, sig. G3ʳ, **Dekker**, sig. C3ʳ, shooes

strummel **Harman**, sig. G3ʳ, **Dekker**, sig. C3ʳ, **Rid**, sig. E4ʳ, strawe

tib-of-the-butt'ry **Harman**, sig. G3ʳ, **Dekker**, sig. C2ᵛ, a Goose

tour **Harman,** sig. G3ᵛ, to see

upright-man **Harman**, sig. B3ʳ, These unrewly rascales in their roilyng, disperce them selves into severall companyes, as occation servethe, sometyme more and somtime lesse. As yf they repayre to a poore husbandmans house, he wyll go a lone or one with him, and stoutely demaund his charity, either shewing how he hath served in the warres, and their maymed, eyther that he seketh service, & sayth he would be glad to take payn for his lyvinge, although he meaneth nothinge lesse. Yf he be offered any meate or drynke, he utterly refuseth scornefully, and wyl naught but money, and yf he espye yong pyggs or pultry, he well noteth the place and then the next nyght or shortly after hee wyll be sure to have some of them.

Head, 133, the chief of all the Ragged Regiment, he walks like a Commander with a short Truncheon in his hand . . . pretends himself to be a decayed Souldier, and claimes a share in all the Booties which any other inferior *Rogue* do get; he hath all the *Morts* and *Doxies* at his back, and can command them from any other of the Gang at his pleasure. By this description you see there is a great deal of difference betwixt an *Upright man* and an *honest man.*

walking morts **Harman**, sig. E4^v, These walkinge Mortes be not maryed, these for their unhappye yeres doth go as a Autem Morte, and wyll saye their husbands died eyther at Newhaven Ireland, or in some service of the Prince. These make laces upon staves & purses that they cary in their hands and whyte vallance for beddes. Manye of these hathe had, and have chyldren: when these get ought, either with begging bychery or brybery, as money or apparell, they are quickly shaken out of all by the upright men, that they are in a marvelous feare to cary any thing aboute them that is of some value.

Head, 138, one that hath encreased the World with Lullaby-cheats or young Children, yet was never married, they are very dangerous Queans to meet withal, being cunning in dessembling, and without all fear of God and good laws, and are kept in awe onely by the Upright-man, who oftentimes rifle them of all that they have.

yarrum **Harman**, sig. G3^r, **Dekker**, sig. C3^r, mylke **Rid**, sig. E4^r, pottage or milke

APPENDIX 3
Criticism and Brome's background

Before anything had been heard about Richard Brome as a writer, his relationship with the great playwright Ben Jonson was common knowledge. The earliest published references to Brome are not to him in his own right, but to his position as Jonson's servant: Brome is mentioned in *Bartholomew Fair* (1614) as Jonson's 'man, Master *Brome*, behind the arras' (Ind.6–7). His servile relationship with Jonson shaped his notions about himself. In 1647 he described himself as one of the 'Old Serving-creatures', though explaining that he now served 'the Muses' ('To the memory'), but even this idea came from a poem Ben Jonson had written in 1632 addressed to Brome, calling him 'My Old Faithful Servant, And (by His Continued Virtue) My Loving Friend The Author' ('To my . . . Servant').

After his death, Brome was repeatedly described as Jonson's servant made good. The posthumously published *Five New Plays* (1659) presented *The Weeding of the Covent Garden* as being by 'An Ingenious Servant, and Imitator of his Master, that famously Renowned Poet *Ben. Johnson*' (sig. A1ʳ). In 1675 Edward Phillips called Brome 'a Servant suitable to such a Master': 'whatever Instructions he might have from his Master Johnson, he certainly by his own natural parts improved to a great heighth, and at last became not many parasangues [units of length] inferior to him in fame' (*Theatrum*, 157); Gerard Langbaine wrote, in 1691, that Brome, 'tho' of mean Extraction (being Servant to the fam'd *Ben Johnson*) Writ himself into much credit' (35). This has come to affect, latterly, critical opinion of Brome's work. He has been presented as one of the 'common men' (Shaw, 32) and of 'mean origin' (Kaufmann, 20), both assumptions arising from modern ideas about social class; his writing is consequently said to have had a meekness that 'verges on servility' (Bayne, 224), and his 'view of the world' has been described as 'that of a groom' (Symonds, 304–5).

When and for how long Brome actually was a servant is not clear; it is also unknown whether he was a domestic servant or a theatre functionary. The question is further confused by the fact that Jonson claimed to have given Brome an apprenticeship as a playwright. Is this another way of describing Brome's job as servant, or did Brome progress from servant to apprentice? Jonson's own choice of vocabulary in this matter is pointed. Swapping the term 'servant' for 'apprentice' may have been Jonson's way of promoting Brome's talent – but if so, he made sure that, either way, he remained firmly Brome's 'master':

> I had you for a servant once, Dick Brome . . .
> Now you are got into a nearer room
> Of fellowship, professing my old arts.
> And you do do them well, with good applause
> Which you have justly gainèd from the stage,
> By observation of those comic laws
> Which I, your master, first did teach this age.
> You learned it well; and for it served your time
> A prenticeship, which few do nowadays.
>
> ('To my . . . Servant', 1–10)

Even if Brome progressed to 'apprentice', that role is difficult to define. There was, of course, no formal 'apprenticeship' for playwrights, as writing for the theatre was not a respectable 'trade' and consequently had no guild. Yet Brome genuinely does seem to have learned the art of playwriting under Jonson. When Brome analysed the Duke of Newcastle's play *The Variety* and declared that 'By God 'twas good', he traced this phrase to 'knowing Jonson', who had applied the same formula to his writing ('To my Lord of Newcastle'). He likewise boasted that his *City Wit* was granted 'the seal of *Ben*' (*City Wit*, sig. A2ʳ).

Towards the end of Jonson's life, audiences started preferring Brome's writing to Jonson's. Jonson compared the failure of his own play *New Inn* to Brome's many successes, writing bitterly that 'Broomes sweepings doe as well / . . . as his Masters Meale' ('Ode to Himself'), a taunt that reduced Brome to servant once more, and found servitude inherent within Brome's very name, which was pronounced 'broom'. Thomas Randolph concurred, commenting to Jonson that 'what *Broome* swept from thee' had now taken over (72).

Brome's role as apprentice playwright – as much as his role as servant – to Jonson, has shaped his reputation. John Hall's commendatory epistle to *A Jovial Crew* (see p. 76), having already presented Brome as a servant, congratulates him for having been 'by great Jonson . . . made free o'th' trade' (14); Brome himself defensively divides his fellow playwrights into those who are 'Traders in Poetry' or 'Prentices, or free' ('Upon . . . Humphry Mill'). Whether as apprentice or servant, Brome is equally seen as indebted to Jonson, rather than as an original in his own right. Alexander Brome, publishing *Five New Plays* in 1659, defended his namesake so weakly that he emphasized Brome's subjection:

> there are a sort . . . who think they lessen this *Author's* worth when they speak the relation he had to *Ben. Johnson.* We very thankfully embrace the Objection, and desire they would name any other Master that could better teach a man to write a good Play.
>
> (sig. A4ʳ)

Others suggested that Brome was simply Jonson all over again: 'Jonson's alive!' reads the start of a panegyric to Brome's *Antipodes*: 'stay, and let me tell you, where he is, / He sojournes in his *Brome's* Antipodes' (sig. A3ʳ). Recent critics have assimilated this notion too, repeatedly seeing Brome as a minor writer so highly imitative of Jonson as to be without a style of his own. Clifford Leech said Brome was 'always a minor writer' but that 'he had nevertheless a sharp comic skill that carried over Jonson's methods into a theatrically more realised age'. Only in 2004 did Matthew Steggle reframe the nature of the Brome/Jonson relationship, seeing it as not 'mere passive reproduction, but part of the forging of a distinctively new, distinctively Caroline theatre' (Steggle, *Brome*, 4).

Brome's literary relationship with Jonson made him part of the group called, at the invitation of Jonson, 'sons of Ben'. These were writers 'adopted' by Jonson, who traced aspects of their literary mastery to the inspirational writing of their 'father'. Included in this crowd were William Cartwright (1611–43), William Cavendish (1592–1676), William Davenant (1616–68), John Fletcher (1579–1625), Henry Glapthorne (1610–*c.* 1643), Peter Hausted (*c.* 1605–44), Thomas Killigrew (1612–83), Shackerley Marmion (1603–35), Jasper Mayne (1604–72), Thomas Nabbes (1605–41) and Thomas Randolph (1605–35). Brome, however, as a former servant, was in a unique position. He had shared time and quite possibly domestic space with his master, so in some respects he was closer to Jonson than other members of the group; as 'son', however, he may have felt socially unequal to his 'father' and 'brothers'. This tension led to awkwardnesses not just in the relationship between Brome and Jonson, but in the relationship between Brome and the other 'sons' – a tension that was, too, to shape Brome's self-presentation and hence what critics have come to think of him.

Brome was particularly threatened by the 'sons' well connected enough not to have, like him, to write for money. These included amateur academic writers, or, as Shirley's *Witty Fair One* (performed at the Cockpit/Phoenix in 1628) explained, 'Schollers . . . come from *Oxford* and *Cambridge* . . . with Dorsers [baskets] full of lamentable Tragedies and ridiculous Comedies', who would 'take no money' for their plays when they gave them to the professional theatre (sig. G2ʳ). One such writer was Cartwright, whose *Royal Slave* (1636) had music composed by Henry Lawes and sets built by Inigo Jones; it was performed at Christ Church, Oxford, to such acclaim that Charles I declared it 'the best that ever was acted' and demanded a repetition at Hampton Court (Evelyn, 1.854). The attacks on Cartwright's published *Comedies* in the paratext to *A Jovial Crew* may reflect bitterness at Cartwright's stage successes.

A second, sometimes overlapping group, was made up of court writers, including Davenant and Suckling (see p. 28). They likewise gave plays free to companies, or worse, as Brome acidly put it, '*To purchace fame give money with their Play*': that is, they sometimes paid professional theatres to mount their dramas (*Court Beggar*, sig. N4ᵛ).

The plays of both groups, amateur and court writers, were generally put on first at court and then transferred to the common playhouses, replete with court costumes, court scenery and court approval – as was the case with Suckling's *Aglaura* (see pp. 28–9). Lodowick Carlell's *Deserving Favourite* transferred to Blackfriars after performance at Whitehall in 1629, for instance; while Mayne's *City Match* (1639), going to Blackfriars after being produced at court, boasts that its author's 'unbought Muse did never fear / An Empty second day or a thinne share; / But can make th'Actors, though you come not twice, / No Loosers, since we act now at the Kings price' (sig. B1ʳ).

Theatres, lacking in money, enthusiastically took up the free plays even though, as Brome saw it, the amateurs were writing 'Lesse for your pleasure than their own delight' (*Court Beggar*, sig. N4ᵛ):

> The Court, and Inns of Court,
> Of late bring forth more wit, then all the Tavernes,
> Which makes me pity Play-Rights; they were poore
> Before, even to a Proverb; Now their trade

Must needs go down, when so many set up.

('Praeludium', thought to be by Brome, to *Careless*
Shepherdess, 6)

Hence Brome's defence of writing for money. In his prologue
to *Damoiselle* he does not *'claime / Lawrell, but Money . . .*
his maine intent / Is his owne welfare, and your merriment'
(sig. A2ʳ); in *Novella*, his epilogue's main concern is that
'his promis'd Pay / May chance to faile, if you dislike the Play'
(sig. N2ʳ).

Throughout his oeuvre, Brome mounted attacks on indulgent,
'wealthy' courtier staging that, according to him, relied on
'Scene magnificent and language high' rather than 'sportive,
merry *Wit*' (*Antipodes*, sig. A3ᵛ). Repeating the same phraseology, Brome regularly deplored what he entitled 'poetry' –
pretentious writing – in favour of 'wit': his *Northern Lass*
presents 'A strayne of Wit that is not *Poetrie*' (sig. A4ᵛ), and
Lovesick Court offers 'A little wit, lesse learning, no Poetry'
(89). When *A Jovial Crew* makes its 'poet' the man denigrated
by the name 'Scribble', 'poetry' as an art is being queried.

Misunderstanding the direction of Brome's attack, critics
have taken Brome at his word and decided he is not a poetic
writer. T. S. Eliot, for instance, was bemused that Swinburne
had given a whole essay over to Brome: 'If . . . Swinburne's
interest was in poetry, why devote an essay to Brome?' (Eliot,
21). In fact, though Brome deplored 'poetry', he relished what
he termed 'poesie' or 'verse'. He praised Marmion because
his *Cupid and Psyche* was so fine that 'thou some Iron hearts
of men / Hast made in Love with Poesie' ('To . . . Shackerley
Marmion'); he wrote to Humphry Mill about his own need
to get up in the night and compose poetic lines, driven by
the muse who could 'turne the whole world out of prose'
('Upon . . . Humphry Mill'). He hoped, he said in *Sparagus*
Garden, to find the kind of reader who would be able to 'scan
his Verse, and weigh his Prose', for the relationship between

285

both was also crucial to his writing (sig. A4^r). As his plays move with precision between prose, blank verse and songs, Brome is using language in as nuanced a fashion as any of the other playwrights of the period; what Brome called 'poetry' was not verse *per se*, but what he saw as overblown pretentious writing that threatened the future of professional playwrights.

Critical opinion of Brome saying that he is servile, the eternal apprentice, a minor imitator of Ben Jonson and not a poet has, as Steggle points out, conflated Brome's biography with the man himself – for which Brome is partly responsible (Steggle, *Brome*, 4). As this edition hopes to show, Brome had a nuanced vocabulary that needs to be properly understood. There is more to Brome than his background.

ABBREVIATIONS AND REFERENCES

Quotations from *A Jovial Crew* are keyed to this edition. Works by Shakespeare are cited from the most recent Arden editions. All other works are cited from early modern editions. Biblical citations are from the Authorized Version. *OED* references are to *OED²* online, accessed before January 2012. Place of publication is London unless otherwise noted.

ABBREVIATIONS
ABBREVIATIONS USED IN NOTES

*	precedes commentary notes involving readings altered from the base text
conj.	conjectured
n.	commentary note
n.s.	new series
SD	stage direction
SP	speech prefix
this edn	a reading adopted or proposed for the first time in this edition

SHORT TITLES FOR WORKS BY BROME

Antipodes	*The Antipodes* (1640), STC 3818
City Wit	*The City Witt*, in *Five New* (1653)
Court Beggar	*The Court Beggar*, in *Five New* (1653)
Damoiselle	*The Damoiselle*, in *Five New* (1653)
English Moor	*The English Moor*, in *Five New* (1659)
Five New (1653)	Richard Brome, *Five New Playes* (1653), Wing B4870, B4866, B4868
Five New (1659)	Richard Brome, *Five Newe Playes* (1659), Wing B4872
Late Lancashire Witches	[with Thomas Heywood,] *Late Lancashire Witches* (1634), STC 13373
Lovesick Court	*The Love-sick Court*, in *Five New* (1659)
Mad Couple	*A Mad Couple Well Matched*, in *Five New* (1653)
Northern Lass	*The Northern Lasse* (1632), STC 3819
Novella	*The Novella*, in *Five New* (1653)
Queen's Exchange	*The Queenes Exchange* (1657), Wing B4882
Sparagus Garden	*The Sparagus Garden* (1640), STC 3820

'To . . . Hastings, Deceased'	Richard Brome, 'To the Memory of the Right Noble, and most Hopeful, Henry Lord Hastings, Deceased', in R[ichard] B[rome] (ed.), *Lachrymae Musarum* (1649), Wing B4876, 74–5
'To my Lord of Newcastle'	'To my LORD of *Newcastle,* on his *PLAY* called *THE VARIETY.* He having commanded to give him my true opinion of it', preceding *Weeding,* in *Five New* (1659), sig. A4^r
'To . . . Shackerley Marmion'	'To his worthy friend Master *Shackerley Marmion,* upon his *Poem* of *Cupid* and *Psyche*', in Shackerley Marmion, *A Morall Poem, intituled the Legend of Cupid and Psyche* (1638), STC 17444a, sig. A3^r
'To the memory'	'To the memory of the deceased but ever-living *Authour* in these his *Poems,* Mr. JOHN FLETCHER', in Francis Beaumont and John Fletcher, *Comedies and Tragedies* (1647), Wing B1581, sig. g1^r
'Upon *Aglaura*'	'Upon AGLAURA printed in Folio', preceding *Weeding,* in *Five New* (1659), sig. A2^{r-v}
'Upon . . . Humphry Mill'	'Upon the Deserving Author, Master Humphry Mill, and his *Nights Search*', in Humphry Mill, *The Nights Search* (1640), STC 17921, sig. B3^v
Weeding	*The Weeding of the Covent Garden,* in *Five New* (1659)

WORKS BY AND PARTLY BY SHAKESPEARE

AC	*Antony and Cleopatra*
AYL	*As You Like It*
Cor	*Coriolanus*
Ham	*Hamlet*
1H4	*King Henry IV, Part 1*
2H4	*King Henry IV, Part 2*
1H6	*King Henry VI, Part 1*
JC	*Julius Caesar*
KL	*King Lear*
Lucrece	*The Rape of Lucrece*
MA	*Much Ado About Nothing*
Mac	*Macbeth*
MM	*Measure for Measure*
MND	*A Midsummer Night's Dream*
MV	*The Merchant of Venice*
MW	*The Merry Wives of Windsor*
Oth	*Othello*
RJ	*Romeo and Juliet*
Tem	*The Tempest*

TGV	*The Two Gentlemen of Verona*
Tim	*Timon of Athens*
TN	*Twelfth Night*
TNK	*The Two Noble Kinsmen*
TS	*The Taming of the Shrew*

REFERENCES

EDITIONS OF *A JOVIAL CREW* COLLATED

Q1	*A Joviall Crew: or, The Merry Beggars*, First Quarto (1652), Wing B4873
Q2	*A Joviall Crew: or, The Merry Beggars*, Second Quarto (1661), Wing B4874
Brome Online	Eleanor Lowe (Original Text), Helen Ostovich (Modern Text) and Richard Cave (General) (eds), *A Jovial Crew*, in *Richard Brome Online*, (http://www.hrionline.ac.uk/brome)
Dodsley	Robert Dodsley (ed.), *A Jovial Crew*, in *Old Plays*, vol. 6
Dodsley & Reed	Robert Dodsley and Isaac Reed (eds), *A Jovial Crew*, in *Old Plays 2*, vol. 10
Haaker	Ann Haaker (ed.), *A Jovial Crew*, Regents Renaissance Drama (1968)
Lawrence	Robert G. Lawrence (ed.), *A Jovial Crew*, in *Jacobean and Caroline Comedies* (1973)

OTHER WORKS CITED

Acteon	Robert Cox, *Acteon and Diana . . . John Swabber the Seaman* (1656), Wing C6710
Advertisements	Henry, Earl of Monmouth, trans. Traiano Boccalini, *I Ragguagli di Parnasso, or, Advertisements from Parnassus in Two Centuries* (1656), Wing B3380
Aeneid	Virgil, *Aeneid*, in *P. Vergili Maronis, Opera*, ed. R. A. B. Mynors (Oxford, 1969)
Aglaura	John Suckling, *Aglaura* (1638), STC 23420
Allen	Herbert F. Allen, *A Study of the Comedies of Richard Brome* (Stanford, Calif., 1912)
All for Money	Thomas Lupton, *A Moral and Pitieful Comedie, intituled, All for Money* (1578), STC 16949
Andrews	Clarence Edward Andrews, *Richard Brome* (New York, 1913)
Atheist's Tragedy	Cyril Tourneur, *The Atheist's Tragedie* (1611), STC 24146

Aubrey   John Aubrey, *Remaines of Gentilisme and Judaisme* (1686–7), ed. James Britten (1881)

Baker, *Biographia*   David Erskine Baker, *Biographia Dramatica*, 2 vols (1782)

Baker, *Companion*   David Erskine Baker, *The Companion to the Playhouse*, 2 vols (1764)

Bartholomew Fair   Ben Jonson, *Bartholomew Fair*, STC 14754, ed. John Creaser, in Jonson, *Works*, vol. 4

Bate   John Bate, *The Mysteries of Nature and Art* (1635), STC 1578

Bawcutt   N. W. Bawcutt, *The Control and Censorship of Caroline Drama* (Oxford, 1996)

Bayne   Ronald Bayne, 'Lesser Jacobean and Caroline dramatists', in A. W. Ward and A. R. Waller (eds), *The Cambridge History of English Literature*, 15 vols (Cambridge, 1910), 6.210–40

BCP   The Booke of Common Prayer (1559), STC 2295.01

Beaumont and Fletcher   *The Dramatic Works in the Beaumont and Fletcher Canon*, gen. ed. Fredson Bowers, 10 vols (Cambridge, 1966–96)

Bentley   Gerald Eades Bentley, *The Jacobean and Caroline Stage*, 7 vols (Oxford, 1941–68)

Berry   Herbert Berry, 'The Phoenix', in Glynne Wickham, Herbert Berry and William Ingram (eds), *English Professional Theatre* (Cambridge, 2000), 622–37

Bevan   Jonquil Bevan, 'Stage influences in *The Compleat Angler*', *RES*, 34 (1983), 452–7

Bitot   Michel Bitot, '"Alteration in a Commonwealth": disturbing voices in Caroline drama', *Cahiers Élisabethains: Late Medieval and Renaissance Studies*, 47 (1995), 79–86

Blount (1656)   Thomas Blount, *Glossographia: or a Dictionary* (1656), Wing B3334

Blount (1674)   Thomas Blount, *Glossographia, or, a Dictionary* (1674), Wing B3337

Bondman   Philip Massinger, *The Bond-man* (1624), STC 17632, in Massinger

Bonduca   [John Fletcher,] *Bonduca*, Wing B1581, ed. Cyrus Hoy, in Beaumont and Fletcher, vol. 4

Boorde   Andrew Boorde, *A Compendyous Regyment or a Dyetary of Healthe* (1547), STC 3380

Botelho and Thane   Lynn Botelho and Pat Thane (eds), *Women and Ageing in British Society since 1500* (Harlow, 2001)

Breton   Nicholas Breton, *Machivells Dogge* (1617), STC 3664.5

Brome, *Songs*   Alexander Brome, *Songs and other Poems* (1661), Wing B4852

Burton   Robert Burton, *The Anatomy of Melancholy* (1621), STC 4159

Butler, 'Brome'   Martin Butler, 'Richard Brome', in *A Dictionary of National Biography*, http://www.oxforddnb.com/view/article/3503?docPos=1, accessed 29 December 2011

Butler, *Theatre*   Martin Butler, *Theatre and Crisis* (Cambridge, 1984)

Camden   William Camden, *Britain* (1610), STC 4509

Careless Shepherdess   Thomas Goffe, *The Careles Shepherdess* (1656), Wing G1005

Carroll   William C. Carroll, *Fat King, Lean Beggar* (Ithaca, NY, 1996)

Cartwright, *Comedies*   William Cartwright, *Comedies, Tragi-comedies, with Other Poems* (1651), Wing C709

Cave *et al.*   Richard Cave, Brian Woolland, Helen Ostovich and Elizabeth Schafer, '*A Jovial Crew*, Critical introduction', in *Brome Online*, accessed 28 December 2011

Cheats   John Wilson, *The Cheats* (1664), Wing W2916

Chettle   Henry Chettle, *Englands Mourning Garment* (1603), STC 5122

Chiang   Hsiao-chen Chiang, 'Representations of vagabonds in Richard Brome's *The Jovial Crew*: a Menippean satire', in Alexander C. Y. Huang, I-chun Wang and Mary Theis (eds), *Class, Boundary and Social Discourse in the Renaissance* (Taiwan, 2007), 120–33

City Madam   Philip Massinger, *City-madam* (1658), Wing M1046, in Massinger

City Match   Jasper Mayne, *Citye Match* (1639), Wing M1467

Clark   Ira Clark, *Professional Playwrights: Massinger, Ford, Shirley, & Brome* (Lexington, Ky., 1992)

Closet   *The Closet of Eminently Learned Sir Kenelme Digbie Kt.* (1669), Wing D1427

Coles   Elisha Coles, *An English Dictionary* (1676), Wing C5070

Collins   Eleanor Clare Collins, 'Richard Brome and the Salisbury Court contract', in *Brome Online*, accessed 29 December, 2011

Colvil   Samuel Colvil, *Mock Poem, or, Whiggs Supplication* (1681), Wing C5426

Coryate   Thomas Coryate, *Coryats Crudities* (1611), STC 5808

Cotgrave   Randle Cotgrave, *A Dictionary of the French and English Tongues* (1611), STC 5830

Cotton   Charles Cotton, *The Compleat Angler. Being Instructions how to Angle for a Trout or Grayling in a Clear Stream* (1676), Wing C6381

Covent Garden   Thomas Nabbes, *Covent Garden* (1638), STC 18339

Cowell   John Cowell, *The Interpreter: or Booke Containing the Signification of Words* (1607), STC 5900

Cressy, 'Adamites'   David Cressy, 'The Adamites exposed', in *Agnes Bowker's Cat: Travesties and Transgressions in Tudor and Stuart England* (Oxford, 2000), ch. 15

Cressy, *England*   David Cressy, *England on Edge: Crisis and Revolution, 1640–1642* (Oxford, 2006)

Crowther   J. W. Crowther, 'The literary history of Brome's *A Joviall Crew*', *Studies in English Renaissance Literature*, 22, ed. Waldo F. McNeir (Baton Rouge, La., 1962), 132–48

Danchin   Pierre Danchin (ed.), *The Prologues and Epilogues of the Restoration: 1660–1700*, 4 parts (Nancy, 1981–5)

Davenant, *Tempest*   William Davenant, *The Tempest* (1670), Wing S2944

Davenant, *Works*   William Davenant, *The Works* (1673), Wing D320

Davies   Sir John Davies, *A Discoverie of the True Causes why Ireland was Never Entirely Subdued* (1612), STC 6348

Dekker, *Bellman*   Thomas Dekker, *The Belman of London* (1608), STC 6482

Dekker, *Black*   Thomas Dekker, *Black Rod* (1630), STC 6492.5

Dekker, *Dramatic Works*   *The Dramatic Works of Thomas Dekker*, ed. Fredson Bowers, 4 vols (Cambridge, 1964)

Dekker, *Lantern*   Thomas Dekker, *Lanthorn and Candlelight* (1609), STC 6486

Dekker, *O Per Se O*   Thomas Dekker, *O Per Se O* (1612), STC 6487

Dekker, *Penny Wise*   Thomas Dekker, *Penny-Wise, Pound Foolish* (1631), STC 6516

Dekker, *Rod*   Thomas Dekker, *A Rod for Runaways* (1625), STC 6520, 6520.4

Dekker, *Seven*   Thomas Dekker, *The Seven Deadly Sinnes of London* (1606), STC 6522

Deloney   Thomas Deloney, *The Pleasant Historie of John Winchcomb in his Yonguer Yeares called Jack of Newbery* (1626), STC 6560

Dent   R. W. Dent, *Proverbial Language in English Drama Exclusive of Shakespeare, 1495–1616* (Berkeley, Calif., 1984)

Dibdin	Charles Dibdin, *A Complete History of the English Stage*, 5 vols (1800)
Downes	John Downes, *Roscius Anglicanus* (1708)
Drayton	Michael Drayton, *Poly-Olbion* (1612), STC 7226
D'Urfey	Thomas D'Urfey, *Pendragon* (1698), Wing P1142
Dyson	Jessica Dyson, 'Staging Legal Authority: Ideas of Law in Caroline Drama' (Sheffield, 2007, dissertation)
Eliot	T. S. Eliot, *The Sacred Wood* (1928)
Ellwood	Thomas Ellwood, *The History of the Life of Thomas Ellwood* (1714)
Elyot	Sir Thomas Elyot, *The Dictionary* (1538), STC 7659
Evans	Robert C. Evans, 'Richard Brome's death', *Notes and Queries*, 234 (1989), 351
Evelyn	John Evelyn, *The Diary*, ed. E. S. de Beer, 6 vols (Oxford, 1955)
Fables	Sir Roger L'Estrange, *Fables of Aesop* (1692), Wing A706
Faerie Queene	Edmund Spenser, *The Faerie Queene* (1590), STC 23081
Farley-Hills	David Farley-Hills, *The Comic in Renaissance Comedy* (1981)
Flamma	R. W., *Flamma Sine Fumo* (1662), Wing W1076
Florio (1598)	John Florio, *World of Words* (1598), STC 11098
Florio (1611)	John Florio, *Queen Anna's New World of Words* (1611), STC 11099
Freehafer	John Freehafer, 'Brome, Suckling, and Davenant's theatre project of 1639', *Texas Studies in Literature and Language*, 10 (1968), 367–83
Friar Bacon	*The Famous Historie of Fryer Bacon . . . with the Lives and Deaths of the Two Conjurors, Bungye and Vandermast* (1627), STC 1183
Gaby	Rosemary Gaby, 'Of vagabonds and commonwealths: *Beggars' Bush*, *A Jovial Crew*, and *The Sisters*', *Studies in English Literature, 1500–1900*, 34 (1994), 401–24
Gage	Thomas Gage, *The English-American* (1648), Wing G109
Gamester	James Shirley, *The Gamester* (1637), STC 22443
Gilby	Anthony Gilby, *Commentarye upon the Prophet Mycha* (1551), STC 11887, 11886
Golding	Arthur Golding, trans., *The. xv. bookes of P. Ovidius Naso, entytuled Metamorphosis* (1567), STC 18956
Goodman	Cyndia Clegg Goodman, 'Mirth and Sense: A Critical Study of Richard Brome's Dramatic Art' (UCLA, 1976, dissertation)

Graham Elspeth Graham, 'Reading, writing, and riding horses in early modern England', in Erica Fudge (ed.), *Renaissance Beasts* (Urbana and Chicago, Ill., 2004), 116–37

Greene, *Menaphon* Robert Greene, *Menaphon* (1589), STC 12272

Greene, *Quip* Robert Greene, *A Quip for an Upstart Courtier* (1592), STC 12300

Greene, *2 Coney-catching* Robert Greene, *The Second Part of Conny-catching* (1591), STC 12281

Greene, *3 Coney-catching* Robert Greene, *The Third and Last Part of Conny-catching* (1592), STC 12283.5

Greg, *Bibliography* W. W. Greg, *A Bibliography of English Drama*, 4 vols (1939)

Greg, 'Theatrical' W. W. Greg, 'Theatrical repertories of 1662', *Gentleman's Magazine*, 31 (1906), 69–72

Gurr Andrew Gurr, *The Shakespearean Stage*, 3rd edn (Cambridge, 1992)

Haaker, 'Plague' Ann Haaker, 'The plague, the theatre, and the poet', *Renaissance Drama*, n.s. 1 (1968), 283–306

Hagthorpe John Hagthorpe, *Divine Meditations* (1622), STC 12602

Harman Thomas Harman, *A Caveat or Warning for Common Cursitors Vulgarly called Vagabonds* (1567), STC 12787

Haynes Jonathan Haynes, 'Representing the underworld: "The Alchemist"', *Studies in Philology*, 86 (1989), 18–41

Head Richard Head, *The English Rogue Continued* (1671), Wing H1249

Heinsius Daniel Heinsius, *Laus Pediculi* (1634), STC 13038

Heir Thomas May, *The Heire* (1622), STC 17713

Hembry Phyllis May Hembry, *The English Spa, 1560–1815: A Social History* (1990)

Herbert George Herbert, *The Temple* (1633), STC 13183

Hercules Buffoon John Lacy, *Sir Hercules Buffoon* (1684), Wing L147

Hey for Honesty Thomas Randolph, *A Pleasant Comedie, entituled Hey for Honesty* (1651), Wing A3685

Heylyn Peter Heylyn, *A briefe relation of the death and sufferings of the Most Reverend and renowned prelate, the L. Archbishop of Canterbury* (1644), Wing H1685

Heywood, *Dialogue* John Heywood, *A Dialogue Conteinyng the Number in Effect of all the Proverbes in the Englishe Tongue* (1546), STC 13291

Heywood, *Hierarchy*	Thomas Heywood, *The Hierarchie of the Blessed Angells* (1635), STC 13327
Heywood, *Philocothonista*	Thomas Heywood, *Philocothonista* (1635), STC 13356
Heywood, *Royal King*	Thomas Heywood, *The Royall King, and the Loyall Subject* (1637), STC 13364
Hilton (1652)	John Hilton, *Catch that Catch Can* (1652), Wing H2036
Hilton (1667)	John Hilton, *Catch that Catch Can, or The Musical Companion* (1667), Wing H2039
Holinshed	Raphael Holinshed, *The firste [laste] volume of the Chronicles of England, Scotlande, and Irelande* (1577), STC 13568b
2 Honest Whore	Thomas Dekker, *The Second Part of The Honest Whore* (1630), STC 6506, in Dekker, *Dramatic Works*, vol. 2
Hopton	Richard Hopton, *Pistols at Dawn* (2007)
How a Man May Choose	Thomas Heywood, *A Pleasant Conceited Comedie, wherein is shewed, How a Man May Chuse a Good Wife from a Bad* (1602), STC 5594
Humour out of Breath	John Day, *Humour out of Breath* (1608), STC 6411
Hyde Park	James Shirley, *Hide-Parke* (1637), STC 22446
If It Be Not Good	Thomas Dekker, *If it be not good, the Divel is in it* (1612), STC 6507, in Dekker, *Dramatic Works*, vol. 3
Ingram	R. W. Ingram, 'Operatic tendencies in Stuart drama', *Musical Quarterly*, 44 (1958), 489–502
Jeffreys	Stephen Jeffreys, *A Jovial Crew by Richard Brome* (1992)
Jeronimo	[Thomas Kyd,] *The First Part of Jeronimo* (1605), STC 15085
Jew's Tragedy	William Hemings, *The Jewes Tragedy* (1662), Wing H1425
Johnson, *Hobson*	Richard Johnson, *The Pleasant Conceites Of Old Hobson* (1607), STC 14688
Johnson, *Moore-fields*	Richard Johnson, *The Pleasant Walkes of Moore-fields* (1607), STC 14690
Jonson, *Masque of Augurs*	Ben Jonson, *Masque of Augurs* (1622), ed. Martin Butler, in Jonson, *Works*, vol. 5
Jonson 'Ode to Himself'	'Ode to Himself', *Ben: Jonson's Execration against Vulcan* (1640), STC 14771, sig. f2^r
Jonson, 'To my . . . Servant'	Ben Jonson, 'To My Old Faithful Servant, And (by His Continued Virtue) My Loving Friend The Author of this Work, Master Richard Brome', ed. Colin Burrow, in Jonson, *Works*, vol. 6

295

Jonson, 'To the . . . Belovèd'	Ben Jonson, 'To the Memory of my Belovèd, The Author, Master William Shakespeare', ed. Colin Burrow, in Jonson, *Works*, vol. 5
Jonson, *Works*	*The Cambridge Edition of the Works of Ben Jonson*, ed. David Bevington, Martin Butler and Ian Donaldson, 7 vols (Cambridge, 2012)
Jordan	Thomas Jordan, *Divine Raptures* (1646), Wing J1028
J. P., *Antidote*	J. P., *An Antidote Against Melancholy made up in Pills. Compounded of Witty Ballads, Jovial Songs, and Merry Catches* (1669), Wing D66B
J. T.	J. T., *The Hunting of the Pox* (1619), STC 23624.7
Kaufmann	R. J. Kaufmann, *Richard Brome, Caroline Playwright* (New York, 1961)
Kaufman-Osborn	Timothy Vance Kaufman-Osborn, *From Noose to Needle* (Ann Arbor, Mich., 2002)
Kent	Joan Kent, *The English Village Constable, 1580–1642* (Oxford, 1986)
Kephart	Carolyn Kephart, 'An unnoticed forerunner of "The Beggar's Opera"', *Music and Letters*, 61 (1980), 266–71
King Leir	*The True Chronicle History of King Leir* (1605), STC 15343
Knapp	Jeffrey Knapp, *Shakespeare's Tribe: Church, Nation, and Theater in Renaissance England* (Chicago, Ill., 2002)
Knave	John Day, *The Knave in Graine, New Vampt* (1640), STC 6174
Lady's Trial	John Ford, *The Ladies Triall* (1639), STC 11161
Lamb	Charles Lamb, *The Life, Letters and Writings*, ed. Percy Fitzgerald, 6 vols (1897)
Langbaine	Gerard Langbaine, *An Account of the English Dramatick Poets* (1691), Wing L373
Laud	William Laud, *The History of the Troubles and Tryal of the Most Reverend Father in God and Blessed Martyr, William Laud . . . wrote by Himself during his Imprisonment in the Tower* (1695), Wing L586, vol. 1
Leech	Clifford Leech, 'Review of *Richard Brome, Caroline Playwright* by R. J. Kaufmann', *MLR*, 58 (1963), 97–8
Leggatt	Alexander Leggatt, *Introduction to English Renaissance Comedy* (Manchester, 1999)
London Prodigal	*The London Prodigall* (1605), STC 22333
Love and Eloquence	Edward Phillips, *The Mysteries of Love & Eloquence* (1658), Wing P2066

Malfi	John Webster, *The Tragedy of the Dutchesse of Malfy* (1623), STC 25176, ed. Leah S. Marcus, Arden Early Modern Drama (2009)
Manningham	John Manningham, *Diary*, ed. John Bruce (1868)
Markham	Gervase Markham, *The English house-Wife* (1631), STC 17353
Marriott	John Marriott, *The Other Empire: Metropolis, India and Progress in the Colonial Imagination* (Manchester, 2003)
Martial	*Martial Epigrams*, ed. and trans. D. R. Shackleton Bailey, Loeb Classical Library, 3 vols (Cambridge, Mass., 1993)
Massinger	*The Plays and Poems of Philip Massinger*, ed. Philip Edwards and Colin Gibson, 5 vols (Oxford, 1986)
May	Thomas May, *Selected Epigrams of Martial* (1629), STC 17494
Middleton	*The Collected Works of Thomas Middleton*, gen. eds. Gary Taylor and John Lavagnino (Oxford, 2007)
Miser	Thomas Shadwell, *A Comedy Called The Miser* (1672), Wing S2837, S2861A, S2861
MLR	*Modern Language Review*
Mr Anthony	Roger Boyle, Earl of Orrery, *Mr Anthony* (1690), Wing O487
Nashe	*The Works of Thomas Nashe*, ed. Ronald B. McKerrow, 5 vols (Oxford, 1958)
N. D.	N. D., *An Antidote against Melancholy* (1661), Wing D66A
New and General	*A New and General Biographical Dictionary*, 8 vols (1795)
New Inn	Ben Jonson, *The New Inn* (1631), ed. Julie Sanders, in Jonson, *Works*, vol. 6
Noble Gentleman	Francis Beaumont and John Fletcher, *The Noble Gentleman*, Wing B1581, ed. Cyrus Hoy, in Beaumont and Fletcher, vol. 3
OED	*Oxford English Dictionary*: OED Online. Oxford University Press. www.oed.com
Oldenbarnevelt	Johan van Oldenbarnevelt, *Barnevels Apology: or Holland Mysterie* (1618), STC 18800
Old Fortunatus	Thomas Dekker, *The Pleasant Comedie of Old Fortunatus* (1600), STC 6517, in Dekker, *Dramatic Works*, vol. 1
Old Law	[Thomas Middleton, William Rowley and Thomas Heywood,] *The Excellent Comedy called, The Old Law* (1656), Wing M1048, ed. Jeffrey Masten, in Middleton

Old Plays	Robert Dodsley (ed.), *A Select Collection of Old Plays*, 12 vols (1744)
Old Plays 2	Robert Dodsley and Isaac Reed (eds), *A Select Collection of Old Plays*, 12 vols (1780)
Orrell, *Human*	John Orrell, *The Human Stage: English Theatre Design, 1567–1642* (Cambridge, 1988)
Orrell, 'Inigo'	John Orrell, 'Inigo Jones at the Cockpit', *Shakespeare Survey 30* (1977), 157–68
Pabisch	Marie Pabisch, *Picaresque Dramas of the 17th and 18th Centuries* (Berlin, 1910)
Palfrey and Stern	Simon Palfrey and Tiffany Stern, *Shakespeare in Parts* (Oxford, 2007)
Parrott and Ball	Thomas Marc Parrott and Robert Hamilton Ball, *A Short View of Elizabethan Drama* (New York, 1943)
Peacham	Henry Peacham, *The Truth of Our Times* (1638), STC 19517
Peacock	E. Peacock, 'The inventories made for Sir William and Sir Thomas Fairfax in the sixteenth and seventeenth centuries', *Archaeologia*, 48 (1884), 121–56
Pepys	Samuel Pepys, *The Diary*, ed. Robert Latham and William Matthews, 11 vols (London, 1970–83)
Perkins	William Perkins, *A Discourse of the Damned Art of Witchcraft* (1608), STC 19697
Pettie	George Pettie, *A Petite Pallace* (1576), STC 19819
PG	Peter Gilliver, private communication
Phillips, *Theatrum*	Edward Phillips, *Theatrum Poetarum* (1675), Wing P2075
Phillips, *Wit*	John Phillips *et al.*, *Wit and Drollery* (1661), Wing W3132
Philocothonista	Thomas Heywood, *Philocothonista, or, The Drunkard, Opened, Dissected, and Anatomized* (1635), STC 13356
Phoenix	Thomas Middleton, *The Phoenix* (1607), STC 17892, ed. Lawrence Danson and Ivo Kamps, in Middleton
Pimlico	*Pymlico* (1609), STC 19936
Plautus	Titus Maccius Plautus, *A New Enterlued for Chyldren to Playe, Named Jacke Jugeler* (1565), STC 14837a
Playford, *English*	John Playford, *The English Dancing Master* (1651), Wing P2477
Playford, *Musical*	John Playford, *The Musical Companion in Two Books* (1672), Wing P2490
Playford, *Wit*	Henry Playford, *Wit and Mirth: or Pills to Purge Melancholy: being a Collection of the best Merry Ballads and Songs, Old and New*, 5 vols (1719)

Polito and Windle   Mary Polito and Jean-Sébastien Windle, '"You see the times are dangerous": the political and theatrical situation of *The Humorous Magistrate*', *Early Theatre*, 12.1 (2009), 93–118

Price   Curtis A. Price, 'Restoration stage fiddlers and their music', *Early Music*, 7 (1979), 315–22

Puttenham   George Puttenham, *The Arte of English Poesie* (1589), STC 20519.5

Quarles   Francis Quarles, *Sions Sonnets* (1625), STC 2783

Rabelais   François Rabelais, *The First [second] Book of the Works of Mr. Francis Rabelais . . . faithfully translated into English*, [trans. Sir Thomas Urquhart and John Hall,] (1653), Wing R105

Randolph   Thomas Randolph, 'An answer to Mr *Ben Johnson*'s Ode', in *Poems with the Muses Looking-glasse* (1638), STC 20694

Rebellion   Thomas Rawlins, *The Rebellion* (1640), STC 20770

RES   *Review of English Studies*

Rich Closet   A. M., *A Rich Closet of Physical Secrets* (1652), Wing M7

Rid   Samuel Rid, *Martin Mark-all, Beadle of Bridewell* (1610), STC 21028.5

Ripa   Caesar Ripa, *Iconologia; or, Moral Emblems* (1709)

Rollo   [John Fletcher, Philip Massinger, Ben Jonson and George Chapman,] *The Tragoedy of Rollo Duke of Normandy* [also known as *The Bloody Brother*] (1640), STC 11065

RSC   Royal Shakespeare Company

Ruscelli   Girolamo Ruscelli, *The Secretes of the Reverende Maister Alexis of Piemount* (1558), STC 293

Rymer   Thomas Rymer, *Foedera, Conventiones, Literae and Cujuscunque Generis Acta Publica* (1735)

Sanders, *Caroline*   Julie Sanders, *Caroline Drama: The Plays of Massinger, Ford, Shirley and Brome* (Plymouth, 1999)

Sanders, 'Commonwealths'   Julie Sanders, 'Beggars' commonwealths and the pre-Civil War stage: Suckling's "The Goblins," Brome's "A Jovial Crew," and Shirley's "The Sisters"', *MLR*, 97 (2002), 1–14

Satiromastix   Thomas Dekker, *Satiro-mastix* (1602), STC 6521, in Dekker, *Dramatic Works*, vol. 1

Schnapper   Edith B. Schnapper (ed.), *British Union-Catalogue of Early Music*, 2 vols (London, 1957)

School of Compliment   James Shirley, *The Schoole of Complement* (1631), STC 22457

Scornful Lady	Francis Beaumont and John Fletcher, *The Scornful Ladie* (1616), STC 1686, ed. Cyrus Hoy, in Beaumont and Fletcher, vol. 2
Scott	Sir Walter Scott, *The Antiquary* (1816)
Sharpe	J. A. Sharpe, *Crime in Early Modern England: 1550–1750* (1984)
Shaw	Catherine M. Shaw, *Richard Brome* (Boston, 1980)
Sheppard	Samuel Sheppard, *The Joviall Crew, or, the Devill turn'd Ranter* (1651), Wing S3166
Shiells	Robert Shiells, *The Lives of the Poets of Great Britain and Ireland, to the Time of Dean Swift* (1753)
Shoemaker's	Thomas Dekker, *The Shomakers Holiday* (1600), STC 6523, in Dekker, *Dramatic Works*, vol. 1
Skelton	John Skelton, *Here after Foloweth Certayne Bokes* (1545), STC 22598
Smectymnuus	Smectymnuus, *A vindication of the answer to the humble remonstrance* (1641), Wing M798, M798A
Soncini	Sara Soncini, 'Intertextuality, collaboration and gender', in Silvia Bigliazzi and Sharon Wood (eds), *Collaboration in the Arts from the Middle Ages to the Present* (Aldershot, 2006), 139–50
Spanish Gypsy	[Thomas Middleton, William Rowley, Thomas Dekker and John Ford], *The Spanish Gipsie* (1653), Wing M1986, ed. Gary Taylor, in Middleton
Speed	John Speed, *History of Great Britaine* (1611), STC 23045
Spousals	Henry Swinburne, *A Treatise of Spousals* (1686), Wing S6260
Spring's Glory	Thomas Nabbes, *The Springs Glorie* (1638), STC 18343
Stafford-Clark	Max Stafford-Clark, *A Jovial Crew: Theatre Programme* (1992), unpaginated
STC	*A Short-Title Catalogue of Books Printed in England, Scotland, & Ireland, and of English Books Printed Abroad, 1475–1640*, 2nd edn, begun by W. A. Jackson and F. S. Ferguson, completed by Katherine F. Panzer, 3 vols (London, 1976)
Steggle, *Brome*	Matthew Steggle, *Richard Brome: Place and Politics on the Caroline Stage* (Manchester, 2004)
Steggle, 'Redating'	Matthew Steggle, 'Redating *A Jovial Crew*', *RES* (2002), 365–72
Steggle, *Wars*	Matthew Steggle, *Wars of the Theatres: The Poetics of Personation in the Age of Jonson* (Victoria, BC, 1998)

Stephens, *Essays*   John Stephens, *Essayes and Characters* (1615), STC 23250

Stephens, *Satirical*   John Stephens, *Satyrical Essayes* (1615), STC 23249

Stern   Tiffany Stern, *Documents of Performance* (Cambridge, 2009)

Stow   John Stow, *A Survey of London* (1633), STC 23345.5

Sullivan   Garrett A. Sullivan, *The Drama of Landscape* (Stanford, Calif., 1998)

Swearing   Geoffrey Hughes, *An Encyclopedia of Swearing* (New York and London, 2006)

Swinburne   A. C. Swinburne, 'Richard Brome', *Fortnightly Review*, 57 (1892), 499–507

Symonds   J. A. Symonds, 'Review of the dramatic works of Richard Brome', *Academy*, 5 (21 March 1874), 304–5

Taylor, *Travels*   John Taylor, *Tailors travels from London to the Isle of Wight* (1648), Wing T520

Taylor, *Works*   John Taylor, *All the Workes* (1630), STC 23725

Teague   Francis Teague, 'The Phoenix and the Cockpit-in-Court playhouses', in Richard Dutton (ed.), *The Oxford Handbook of Early Modern Theatre* (Oxford, 2009)

Thomas   Thomas Thomas, *Dictionarium Linguae Latinae et Anglicanae* (1587), STC 24008

Thomas More   [Anthony Munday, Thomas Dekker, Henry Chettle, Thomas Heywood and William Shakespeare,] *The Book of Sir Thomas More*, ed. W. W. Greg (Oxford, 1911)

Tilley   M. P. Tilley, *The Proverbs in England in the Six-teenth and Seventeenth Centuries* (Ann Arbor, Mich., 1950)

Trial of Treasure   *A New and Mery Enterlude, called The Triall of Treasure* (1567), STC 24271

Two Wise Men   *Two Wise Men & All the Rest Fooles* (1619), STC 4991

Venner, *Baths*   Tobias Venner, *The Baths of Bathe* (1628), STC 24641

Venner, *Via Recta*   Tobias Venner, *Via Recta ad Vitam Longam* (1620), STC 24643

Vines   Richard Vines, *A Treatise of the Right Institution, Administration, and Receiving of the Sacrament of the Lords-Supper* (1657), Wing V575

Walbancke   Matthew Walbancke, *Annalia Dubrensia: Upon the yeerely celebration of Mr Robert Dover's Olympick Games upon Cotswold-Hills* (1636), STC 24954

Walton   Isaac Walton, *The Compleat Angler* (1653), Wing W661

Ward   A. W. Ward, *A History of English Dramatic Literature to the Death of Queen Anne*, 3 vols (1899)

Westward Ho   Thomas Dekker and John Webster, *West-ward Hoe* (1607), STC 6540, ed. Fredson Bowers, in Dekker, *Dramatic Works*, vol. 2

Wheatly   Charles Wheatly, *A Rational Illustration of the Book of Common Prayer* (1720)

Whincop   Thomas Whincop, *Scanderbeg . . . To which are Added a List of All the Dramatic Authors* (1747)

White   Martin White, *Renaissance Drama in Action* (London and New York, 1998)

Whitlock   Keith Whitlock, 'John Playford's *The English Dancing Master*', *Folk Music Journal*, 7 (1999), 548–78

Wilkins, *Discourse*   John Wilkins, *A Discourse Concerning a New World & Another Planet in 2 bookes* (1640), STC 25641

Wilkins, *Essay*   John Wilkins, *An Essay towards a Real Character, and a Philosophical Language* (1668), Wing W2196

Wilson, *Rhetoric*   Thomas Wilson, *The Arte of Rhetorique* (1553), STC 25799

Wilson, *Select Airs*   John Wilson, *Select Ayres and Dialogues for One, Two, and Three voyces . . . composed by John Wilson, Charles Colman, Doctors in musick, Henry Lawes, William Lawes, Nicholas Laneare, William Webb, Gentlemen and Servants to his Late Majesty in his Publick and Private Musick; and Other Excellent Masters of Musick* (1659), Wing W2909

Wing   *A Short-Title Catalogue of Books Printed in England, Scotland, Ireland, Wales and British America, and of English Books Printed in Other Countries, 1641–1700*, 2nd edn, rev. and enl., compiled by Donald Wing *et al.*, 4 vols (New York, 1972–98)

Wise Woman   Thomas Heywood, *The Wise-woman of Hogsdon* (1638), STC 13370

Wit   *A Pleasant Comoedie, wherein is Merily Shewen: The Wit of a Woman* (1604), STC 25868

Witch of Edmonton   [William Rowley, John Ford and Thomas Dekker,] *The Witch of Edmonton* (1658), Wing R2097

Withals   John Withals, *Dictionarie in English and Latine* (1616), STC 25886

Witty Fair One   James Shirley, *The Wittie Faire One* (1633), STC 22462

Womack   Peter Womack, 'Richard Brome, *A Jovial Crew*', in *English Renaissance Drama* (Oxford, 2006), 256–60

Woodbridge, 'Jest books'   Linda Woodbridge, 'Jest books, the literature of roguery, and the vagrant poor in Renaissance England', *English Literary Renaissance*, 33.2 (2003), 201–10

Woodbridge, *Vagrancy*   Linda Woodbridge, *Vagrancy, Homelessness, and English Renaissance Literature* (Urbana and Chicago, Ill., 2001)

INDEX

309